World History in Parallel

PART ONE: THE WORLD 1500 TO 1800

PHOEBE BANKART, M.A.

World History in Parallel

Part One ◇ The World 1500 to 1800

LONDON ◇ GEORGE PHILIP AND SON LIMITED

World History in Parallel
is published in two volumes:

Part One: The World 1500 to 1800
Part Two: The World since 1815

PRINTED IN GREAT BRITAIN   S B N 540 00000 0

In recent years historians have been giving a great deal of thought to the question of what kind of history ought to be taught in our schools. The subject is vast and ever-growing, while the portion of the weekly timetable allotted to it is usually small. The teacher is therefore forced to be selective and must often reject fields of study which, however valuable in themselves, are nonetheless pushed out of the syllabus by others deemed to be even more important. The old assumption that the student's prime historical need is to know the story of his own country is being challenged. Even to extend the boundaries of his knowledge to embrace the continent of Europe may not seem to be enough in an age when the television screen brings him visual information each evening of events occurring in every quarter of the globe. A number of teachers believe that they have a duty to give many, though not necessarily all, their students an opportunity to acquire some basic knowledge of the history of the world in modern times.

However, even those who are convinced on this point do not find it easy to incorporate world history into their syllabus. One difficulty is that many teachers have themselves never studied this branch of the subject, either at school or at college. Consequently they do not feel competent to select the salient facts and trends. Furthermore they complain of a lack of suitable textbooks. This book has been planned and written with the intention of doing something to fill that gap.

In teaching, as in studying, history on such a wide canvas we come up against the difficulty of perceiving the concurrency of world events. It is relatively easy to grasp, separately, the succession of events in different areas, but it is hard to realise their reaction to one another. For example, we do not readily think of the French Revolution as having a direct effect on political events in Indonesia; nor do we expect the preparations for the launching of the Spanish Armada to have hampered the efforts of English merchants to gain a commercial foothold in India. I have tried in this book to bring home to the reader the complex and fascinating relationships between events in different parts of the world.

P. B.

On page 8 there is a photographic reproduction of a late
sixteenth-century map of the world by Hondius.

Photograph acknowledgements

Acknowledgement is made to the following for permission to reproduce
copyright photographs: The British Museum, *page 122*; British Railways,
page 163 (*top*); The High Commissioner for India, *page 127*; Koninklijk
Instituut voor de Tropen, Amsterdam, *page 201*; Paul Popper Limited, *page 55*;
The Radio Times Hulton Picture Library, *pages 8, 13, 18, 21, 25, 38, 41, 60,
80, 89, 92, 99, 107, 119, 139* (*right*), *145* (*foot*), *148, 165, 173, 180, 196, 204*;
The Royal Institution of Great Britain, *page 142*; The Science Museum, *pages
152, 155, 163* (*foot*); The United States Information Service, *page 110*.

CONTENTS

World History in Parallel is a selective study of the world from 1500 to the present. Each chapter deals with important aspects of the development of a country, region or continent, and at intervals there is an overall review of the world situation at a specific date. Thus this first part opens with a review of the world in 1500.

The world in 1500

There are two principal land-masses in the world, one being Europe-Asia-Africa and the other the double continent of America. It was in the first of these that the early civilisations grew up from which our present way of life has developed. Consequently it is from the viewpoint of this land-mass that geographers look at the world. On the west of it lies Europe, which has therefore come to be known as 'the West'. Of course the bulge of Africa is just as far west as Europe; but it is not counted as part of 'the West' because—for reasons which will be explained later—most of Africa remained cut off from the rest of the world until about a century ago. The Americas were also cut off from the other continents until nearly five centuries ago. In fact the reason why the year 1500 has been chosen as our starting-point is that it was just about then that European explorers first discovered America. Obviously the explorers sailed westward, and that is why the American half of the world is known as the Western Hemisphere. The other land-mass is therefore of course the Eastern Hemisphere, and its Pacific coastline is called the Far East. The region that lies more or less midway between the Far East and the West is called the Middle East, and it is at this centrally situated region that we shall take our first close look.

THE MIDDLE EAST

The Middle East lies partly in north Africa and partly in western Asia. If you look at a modern political map, you will see that the countries into which it is divided today are Egypt, the Sudan, Israel, Jordan, Lebanon, Syria, Iraq, Saudi Arabia and Persia. Most of the region consists of sandy deserts, though the Nile valley, the Mediterranean coast and the land between the Tigris and Euphrates are all very fertile. This chain of rich land, which forms roughly the shape of a horse-shoe, is often called 'the Fertile Crescent'. Naturally life lived in the cities and farms of the Crescent differs greatly from that of the nomads in the desert. But there is one important link binding the people of the whole region—they nearly all belong to the Muslim religion.

The Prophet Mohammed, founder of Islam (which is another name for the Muslim faith), was an Arab and he lived from about 572 to 632 of the Christian era. In the centuries following his death his Arab followers poured out of their native peninsula and conquered almost the whole of the Middle East, as well as the northern fringe of Africa. Wherever they went they imposed their new religion; and as all Muslims have a special legal, social and political system based on the Koran—the Holy Book of the Prophet—the whole region has always tended to be closely knit together.

In the year 1500 most of the Middle East, apart from Persia, was under the rule of the Turks, who were also Muslims. At this time the Turks were still expanding their power. The capital of their empire was Constantinople (now called Istanbul), and although this city lies in Europe and was on the very edge of their dominions, this did not prevent them from exercising a firm and often harsh rule over their Middle Eastern subjects. Unfortunately the Turkish sultans thought more about exacting taxes than about caring for the welfare of their people, and much necessary work was neglected. Even the irrigation system, so vital in such an area, was not properly maintained, with the result that the whole economic life of the Middle East was in decline, and the output of food was far smaller than it had been in the days of the Roman Empire.

However, though agriculture declined, commerce flourished, for the great spice trade between Asia and Europe passed right through the region. Caravans of camels, loaded not only with pepper but also with silk and other luxuries, passed regularly across the desert, coming either from the Persian Gulf or the Red Sea and converging upon the Mediterranean ports. This trade brought huge profits to the Arab merchants, but unfortunately for them some Europeans, only two years before, had discovered an alternative route to the spice-lands round the south of Africa. Great changes were therefore already impending, but the Arabs did not realise this as yet, assuming that the century opening before them would be much the same as its predecessors.

INDIA

India was an important source of the spices which found their way to Europe, and it was in India that a Portuguese explorer called Vasco da Gama had arrived in 1498. He landed in Calicut, the capital city of a small but powerful state on the south-west coast. The Zamorin, or ruler, was extremely interested to see these strange-looking men in his capital, and gave them a warm welcome. He had no notion that they intended to upset the trade on which his little kingdom depended, and readily sold them a cargo of pepper. When the European ships, with their holds full, sailed home *via* the Cape of Good Hope, they were ushering in a new era in the history of Europe and Asia.

Calicut was one of the many states into which India was divided at that time. The two most important were a Muslim Sultanate based on Delhi in the north, and the Hindu Empire of Vijayanagar in the south. The sultans of Delhi had once been extremely powerful, but a century earlier their territory had been invaded by the savage Mongol conqueror, Timur the Lame. Timur's followers had wrought such havoc that northern India was still weak, and was indeed to continue in a state of unrest until the rise of the great Mogul Empire about thirty years later.

THE REST OF SOUTHERN ASIA

The remainder of southern Asia was in a condition somewhat similar to that of India. There were a number of Muslim sultans scattered over the region, especially on the coasts, while the rulers of the hinterland were often Hindus or Buddhists. Trade was brisk, and many of the exports from the region were carried in Arab ships. But among the vessels which plied busily around these waters, there were also many from China.

CHINA

China was in 1500 the most powerful empire in the world. The country itself was huge, and in addition the Emperor, whose subjects regarded him as almost divine, had established his overlordship over most of the sultanates of south Asia. Korea and Japan also acknowledged his suzerainty. Their rulers, along with those of Siam, Java, Sumatra and Malaya, sent rich tributes every year to Peking.

China was a very ancient country, and had been ruled by a long succession of dynasties. The present Emperor belonged to the Ming Dynasty. His power was immense, but he could not of course attend personally to all the business of administration. His vast domain was therefore parcelled into districts, each under the control of a Viceroy. The Viceroys were efficient and loyal, and China was enjoying a wonderful period of peace and prosperity. Art and culture flourished, but the Chinese were curiously self-sufficient. They were so obviously superior to all their neighbours, as far as political power was concerned, that they had become convinced that they had no equals in any sphere. They distrusted and despised foreigners of every kind; and all they wanted was to continue their present way of life undisturbed.

JAPAN

Japan at this time presented a strong contrast to China, although on the surface the two countries had a lot in common. Japan was of course much smaller, but each state had an emperor and each emperor was regarded as being godlike. The Japanese, however, took their idea of their ruler's divinity so far that they did not even think it suitable that he should rule. He was too important for that; and so all the day-to-day work of a king was carried out by a high official called the Shogun, whose office like that of the Emperor was hereditary.

This curious arrangement made for divided responsibility, and in 1500 Japan was suffering under a weak Shogun. Moreover the country was riddled with rebellion. The Japanese social and economic system was feudal, which means that a man's importance was determined by the amount of land he held. The great landowners, if they quarrelled with the Shogun, could order all their tenants to fight for them. Rebellion is always easy under the Feudal System, and the task of the central government of Japan was made all the harder because the country consists of a number of islands. In the west particularly the feudal lords were extremely unruly. So that whereas China stood immovable in the face of all foreign attacks, Japan was ripe for invasion and conquest, should a determined enemy come along.

SIBERIA

Siberia, the vast tract of land stretching across northern Asia, had no political importance at this time. The people living in the region were nomads, wandering from one district to another and without any kind of state organisation.

RUSSIA

There was no state of Russia in the year 1500, though there were a group of people known as Russians, who lived in a principality which was called Muscovy because it was centred on the city of Moscow. This relatively small territory was geographically in Europe, but so far on the eastern fringe of that continent that the people had no contact with western Europe at all. It is true that there was no physical barrier separating them from their nearest neighbours the Poles, but there was a barrier of tradition, for the Russians belonged to the Greek Orthodox Christian Church, while the rest of Europe was Roman Catholic. This meant that throughout the centuries Russian priests attending church councils had travelled not to the west but always southward to Constantinople, which was for centuries an important Christian centre until

4

its capture by the Turks in 1453. Few Europeans at the beginning of the sixteenth century knew anything about Russia. There was however among the rulers of Muscovy a faint stirring of interest in the lands lying to the west, which they felt to be more civilised than their own.

EUROPE

By 1500 Europe was emerging from the Feudal Ages,* a period which is usually reckoned to have started about A.D. 800. During that time Europe, like Japan, had been organised according to the Feudal System, so that ownership of land was the key to social position. The majority of the people were peasants working small holdings of land. In each village the peasants were all bound to obey their local lord, who in turn would probably owe obedience to a still greater landowner. At the top of the political pyramid was the king of the country; but kings had often found it extremely difficult to rule because the great lords might at any time call on their tenants to rebel. Since they owed obedience to the lord rather than to the king, his men would respond to his call without any feeling that they were breaking the law. Consequently the Feudal Ages had seen a great deal of civil war.

On the other hand Europe was in some ways very closely knit. The people were all Christian and they all belonged to the Roman Church, which was organised under the supreme authority of the Pope, or Bishop of Rome. Every man, from the lowest peasants to the kings themselves, acknowledged the supremacy of the Pope. All church services and prayers were in Latin, and not only the Bible but practically every other book written was in Latin. Consequently the small minority of people who could read and write, all spoke and read a common language. They could wander from one part of Europe to another and feel equally at home wherever they went. The same was of course true of the priests. Nor were the educated classes the only section of society to enjoy this feeling of European unity. Each class of men tended to have a great deal in common with their counterparts in other parts of the continent.

By 1500, however, this social fabric had deteriorated and nations were now beginning to emerge. People were falling into the habit of thinking of themselves first as Englishmen or Frenchmen or Spaniards, and only afterwards as Europeans. But the habit had not yet got a grip of the whole continent. Much of central Europe was still divided into tiny feudal states, loosely bound together in the Holy Roman Empire, and the connecting link uniting the scholars of every country was still

* Very often called the Middle Ages.

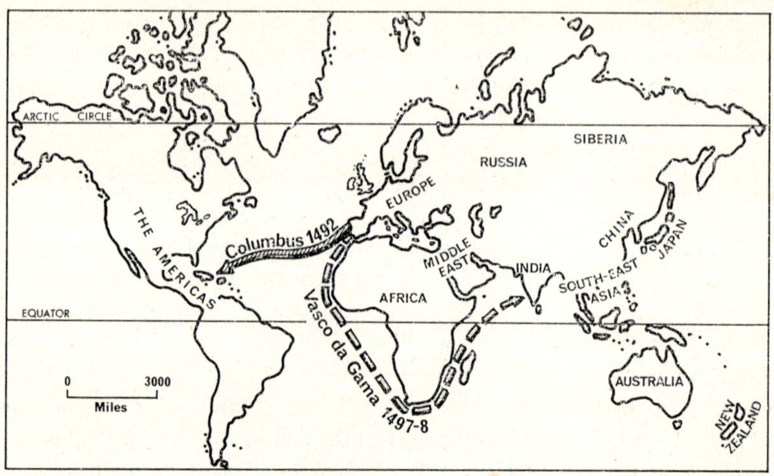

Map 1—The world showing the routes of Columbus and Vasco da Gama

unbroken. This was indeed the hey-day of culture and education. The great Renaissance of learning was at its height in 1500. Great works of art were being produced, new knowledge was being gained and the energies of Europeans were being poured out in a burst of activity. The general thirst for knowledge had lured sailors to explore uncharted seas. Eight years earlier Columbus had crossed the Atlantic, while it was only two years since Vasco da Gama had reached India *via* the Cape of Good Hope.

AFRICA

To understand the situation of Africa in 1500 you must look at a physical map. Then you will see that the great Sahara Desert cuts off the main part of the continent from the Mediterranean coastlands. This northern fringe has always had a close contact with both Europe and Asia, but the vast region south of the Sahara was for thousands of years impenetrable, since waterfalls and dangerous shoals made it impossible for ships to sail up the rivers into the interior. Nevertheless Portuguese explorers had lately become familiar with the outline of the continent, for they had sailed round it in order to get to India. And since Europeans put a very high value on the spice trade, they now began to take a considerable interest in Africa. They managed to carry on a little trade at certain points on the coast where ships could sail close to the land. The great majority of the inhabitants of that vast continent, however, pursued a primitive way of life, knowing nothing at all of the outside world, and even ignorant that there was such a thing as the sea.

THE AMERICAS

The peoples living in the Americas were equally ignorant of any continent outside their own. Columbus had reached one of the outlying islands off Central America eight years before, but though the native Americans with whom he had had dealings were much impressed with his appearance and that of his men, the inhabitants of the mainland knew nothing of these events. The vast double continent housed hundreds of different tribes. Among them there were two important empires, one in Mexico and the other in Peru; but generally speaking the land was divided up into numerous small and unimportant communities. Most of the people lived a primitive life, and even the most civilised had no written records.

THE REST OF THE WORLD

Australia, New Zealand and the islands of Oceania were at this time entirely cut off from any communication with either of the two great land-masses of the world. The next four centuries were to see a great work of exploration which would finally embrace every part of the world. This expansion was the work of Europeans, which explains why the people of this one continent were able to secure such a dominating position in the world for the greater part of the period we are to study.

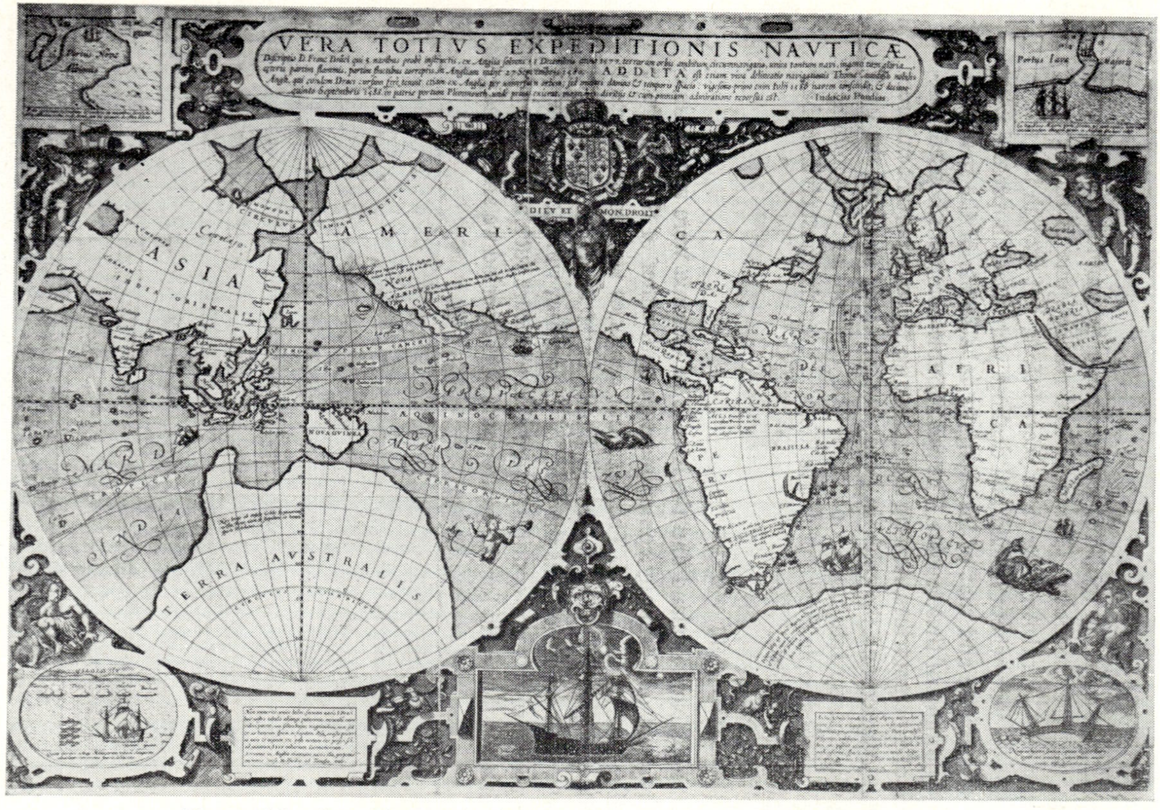

The world as it was known in the late sixteenth century. This map by Hondius
showed the voyages of Drake and Cavendish.

1 The expanding life of Europe in the sixteenth century

The voyages of discovery

The sixteenth century was an intensely exciting time in the history of Europe. Men's imaginations were actively at work, their curiosity was endless, and the horizons of their knowledge were expanding day by day. Perhaps the most exciting of all the developments of this fascinating period were the voyages of exploration, which took European sailors right round the world.

Causes of the voyages of discovery

We are today so used to living in a 'small world' which can be encircled by aeroplanes almost in a matter of hours, that it is hard for us to think ourselves back into the minds of the forward-looking Europeans of the fifteenth century. They knew that the earth was round and that if they sailed to the west they would eventually arrive in the east, but they greatly under-estimated the size of the world. Naturally they knew of the existence of Asia and Africa, since these continents have a land-connection with Europe; but they had never heard of any other continent, and therefore supposed that the Atlantic Ocean, which washed the western shores of Europe on one side, washed the eastern shores of Asia on the other. They appreciated that the Atlantic is a very large piece of water, but had no idea how large, for it was only during the fifteenth century that ocean-sailing on a large scale became practicable.

In earlier times ships had been obliged to keep fairly close to land, as the mariners depended on the sun and the stars to tell them their direction, and would have been lost in cloudy weather unless they had some landmarks to help them. In the thirteenth century, however, the magnetic compass, which had been discovered (but not very usefully employed) by the Chinese, was in regular use in Europe, having been brought there in all probability by the Arabs. Indeed the Arabs played a vitally important part in the development of European civilisation. From the eighth century onwards they ruled a large empire in the Middle East, which extended into North Africa, and also far into Asia. They were great traders, and travelled widely, picking up ideas and items of knowledge which they transmitted—sometimes as a result of the Crusades—to Europe.

For a time the compass remained a rarity, but by the fifteenth century it had become a fairly common piece of equipment on European ships. It was this which made it possible for long voyages to be undertaken, should anyone feel a strong enough impulse to venture out into the unknown. But to cross the ocean in the fifteenth century required as much courage as is needed to venture into outer space today: in fact it needed more, because there was no radio communication. The explorer of those days had to cut adrift from all contact with his own kind.

Nevertheless, despite the difficulties, enough men were found who were eager to embark on these great adventures. The causes of their readiness are partly to be found in man's innate curiosity; to find the other causes we have to look far both in time and space. One contributing factor was that back in the thirteenth century Jenghis Khan, the great Mongol warrior, conducted a brilliant military campaign which led to the establishment of a vast Mongol empire, stretching from east to west across Asia and penetrating right into Europe. It did not last long, but while the Mongols were in power it became possible for the first time for travellers to go unimpeded from Europe right to the Far East.

Not many people took advantage of this opportunity, but the famous Italian explorers, Marco Polo and his father and uncle, went to China and stayed there for many years. The book which Marco wrote when he returned made an enormous sensation. Only a small minority of people could read and write, but the story of the Polo journey was eagerly passed from mouth to mouth, and inspired not only curiosity but greed. For Marco described Japan and China, which he called Zipango and Cathay, as immensely rich lands. Obviously the man who could reach them would not only feast his eyes on great beauty but would also have a wonderful opportunity to line his pockets. After the Mongol power broke up, the journey could no longer be made by land; but when the magnetic compass made it possible to sail from one continent to another, the stories of old Cathay were again remembered.

Nearer home, though still very far from Europe, were the spice lands of southern Asia. Europeans had known a great deal about these ever since the soldiers who visited the Middle East on Crusade had tasted the spices of the east and brought samples home with them. Food in the Feudal Ages was inclined to be insipid at the best of times, and was often actually bad. The difficulty was that the farmers of those days—and indeed for several centuries to come—had no knowledge of sowing root crops to provide winter fodder for cattle. There was therefore no way of keeping the beasts alive during the cold months, and apart from a few saved for breeding purposes, all the farm animals were killed off in the autumn, and the carcasses salted. This method of preserving them rarely proved adequate, and by the early spring most of the meat supply was exceedingly unpalatable. Nor was there much to eat as an alternative. Flour milled from the previous harvests was made into bread, and vegetables were grown, but the slaughter of the cattle meant a severe winter shortage of milk and butter as well as of meat. The gardens of Europe produced mild herbs, but nothing sharp enough to make this kind of food tasty.

Until the return of the first Crusaders it was assumed that nothing could be done to solve this problem; but once the Europeans had tasted spice, once they knew what it could do in the way of disguising what was bad and improving what was dull, all but the poorest resolved never to relapse again into their former monotonous diet. They were determined to buy spice and pepper, no matter what they cost—and they were extremely expensive. The merchants of Genoa and Venice, who were fine sailors, used to go across the Mediterranean to the Levant, where they bought spices from Arab merchants and returned with them to Europe. It happened that during the thirteenth century a Shah of Persia broke the usual rule of forbidding foreigners to pass through Persia to India, one of the principal spice-growing areas. This permission was not continued for long, but it enabled the Europeans to discover that pepper could be bought cheaply at source, and that it was the profiteering of the Arabs which made it so expensive. Here was another motive for finding an alternative route from Europe to Asia.

Exploring to the East

The introduction of the magnetic compass was of vital importance, but there were still other practical problems to be solved. The first nation to settle down seriously to the task was Portugal, under the leadership of a member of the royal family, Prince Henry, who earned for himself the title of Henry the Navigator.*

The Portuguese have such a long coastline that they are naturally a seafaring people, and Prince Henry determined that they should equip themselves to open up for the first time an all-sea route to Asia. Hitherto spices and other goods bound for Europe had been taken by ship either

* Henry the Navigator (1394-1460) was the great-grandson of one of the Kings of England, Edward III. Edward's fourth son, John of Gaunt, had a daughter Philippa who was married to the King of Portugal and became the mother of Prince Henry.

up the Persian Gulf or up the Red Sea; but whichever of these routes was followed, it was always necessary for part of the journey to be made overland by camel caravan across the desert to the Mediterranean Sea. If it was possible at all to find an alternative way of carrying spices, then that way must lie round the continent of Africa, the shape of which was at that time completely unknown to the people of Europe. If the Portuguese were to explore it, they would need to have at their command all the knowledge of sailing available at that time.

Prince Henry therefore established a School of Navigation in one of his castles by the sea. He persuaded certain Arab seamen to join him, and to disclose many secrets of navigation which had hitherto been unknown to Europeans. He also bought up all the maps and charts he could get hold of, as well as making a collection of mathematical and other instruments. Since he was anxious that no other nation should share the advantages which Portugal was accruing in this way, the doings of the School were cloaked in great secrecy.

Practice had to be developed along with theory, and a series of exploratory voyages were launched with the object of sailing round Africa. This was a gargantuan task, for the west coast of that continent, from north to south, measures some five thousand miles. Moreover the early part of the journey was particularly discouraging, since the ships had to sail past the great Sahara Desert which extends for nearly two thousand miles. Added to the natural and reasonable fears of the sailors, there were terrifying legends. It was even believed by some of them that anyone who sailed past the Sahara would become black-skinned. However, the captains who persisted were better educated, and their patient attempts continued even after Prince Henry was dead. At last their efforts were crowned with success. In 1487 a captain called Bartholomew Diaz achieved the supreme feat of rounding the Cape of Good Hope. He first called it the Cape of Storms, but the Portuguese King of the time, recognising that this voyage would be a landmark in his country's history, altered the name. After this the final step was relatively easy. In 1498 another captain, Vasco da Gama, not only rounded the cape, but crossed the Indian Ocean and landed on the west coast of India, at Calicut, an important centre of the spice trade.

Portugal had now fulfilled her main task of exploration, and could begin the work of exploiting her new discoveries.

Exploring to the West

The next European country to achieve a great success in the field of

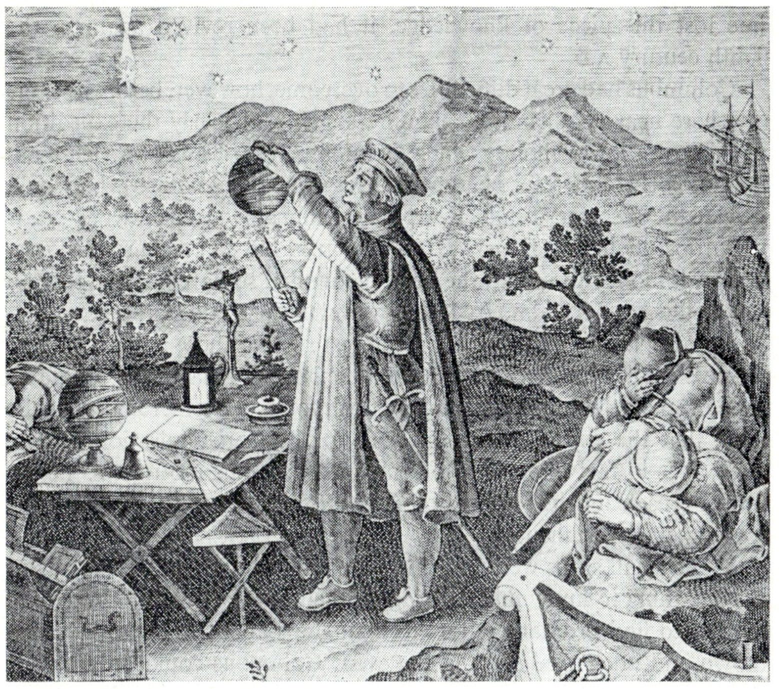

A Renaissance explorer taking readings with an astrolabe,
an instrument used in astronomy

exploration was Spain. Infact the Spaniards' most successful voyage was undertaken some five or six years before Vasco da Gama's. On the other hand they did not pursue the painstaking preparation that Prince Henry had embarked upon. Instead they had the good fortune to reap the benefit of a courageous idea conceived by a single sea-captain, who was not even Spanish. This was Christopher Columbus, or Cristofero Colombo, a native of Genoa (1451-1506).

Like most Genoese, Columbus was passionately interested in the sea and also interested in trade, and he devoted much thought to planning a sea-route to the spice-lands of Asia. By the latter part of the fifteenth century it was of course known that Portugal was developing the south-east route round Africa, and it was clear that they would permit no poaching by their neighbours. But since the world was round, there was no reason—in theory—why ships should not sail westward across the Atlantic and arrive in India. The roundness of the earth had been known to the ancient Greeks, and though Europeans had for a

13

time lost this piece of knowledge, it had been revived again in the eighth century A.D.

Columbus had great difficulties to overcome, however, before he came anywhere near acquiring or manning his ships. Clearly the expedition would cost a lot of money which Columbus, who was not a rich man, had not got. He therefore had to interest some royal patron who would provide the necessary funds. He approached many of the crowned heads of Europe, including Henry VII of England; but to ordinary business-men with money to invest, the project sounded so hare-brained that no one would support him. At last however he persuaded the King and Queen of Spain to back him. It is interesting that these monarchs were not particularly impressed by Columbus' hopes of starting a profitable trade in spices. What finally induced them to hand over £15,000 was the belief that the expedition would lead to the Christianisation of new lands. It is in fact important to remember that this motive was nearly always present in the voyages of discovery. It certainly influenced the Portuguese government.

Three small ships were bought and equipped without difficulty. But it is one thing to know that a voyage is theoretically possible, and quite another to find ordinary sailors to man ships about to set sail for un-known and uncharted seas. In the event Columbus could only get his crews together by emptying the prisons; men condemned to death or to long sentences had so little to lose that they were prepared to risk almost anything. Even so their nerve failed and they became mutinous when, after toiling westwards for over nine weeks, there was no sight of land. It was only by the strength of his own personality that Columbus was able to control them. He had believed that it would take only a month or so to cross the Atlantic, but he remained convinced that they would reach land eventually, and sure enough, after two months and nine days they arrived at one of the islands in the Caribbean Sea. Columbus never doubted for a moment that they had reached India, and he returned to Spain in triumph, taking with him not only samples of gold and cotton, but also some captured 'Indians'. This mistake was to have long-lasting results, for the original inhabitants of the American continent are known to this day as Indians (in the north Red Indians), and the Caribbean Islands are called the West Indies.

Columbus made further voyages of discovery to other islands of the region and also to Central America. This he took to be another bit of India, and wherever he landed, he claimed the land for his sovereigns. Later King Ferdinand appointed him Viceroy of the new territories. At

14

one time he fell foul of a Spanish grandee who came out to the new colonies, and he was disgraced; but Ferdinand and Isabella pardoned him and restored him to favour. Nevertheless it soon became clear that, even if the Spanish had reached India, they had not arrived at the coveted spice-growing region. In 1502 Columbus set out on what was to be his last voyage of exploration, an attempt to penetrate further westward along what was thought to be the coast of Asia. He sailed into the Gulf of Mexico, but of course he failed in his purpose, since there is no way through to the west from that gulf. In fact the double continent of America is shaped in such a way that the Spanish sailors were always being deluded. If you look at a map, you will see how many possibilities there were of an expedition apparently rounding what seemed to be an island lying athwart the route to India, only to come up once more against a coast stretching obstinately northward or southward for hundreds of miles.

The first man to realise the truth—that here was a vast continent and beyond it yet another ocean to be traversed before Asia would be reached—was Ferdinand Magellan (1470-1521), a Portuguese. Magellan took an active part in his country's opening-up of da Gama's new route to India, and served for several years with the fleet in the Indian Ocean. But despite his distinguished services he was accused of theft, and went home without permission to appeal to the King of Portugal. Having obtained no satisfaction, he renounced his nationality and entered the employment of the King of Spain, taking with him a friend of his who was a geographer.

Magellan was full of a plan for reaching the spice-lands from the west, and in September 1519 he set out with a fleet of five ships. They sailed right down the coast of South America, and in November 1520 they successfully rounded Cape Horn, passing through the straits which are called after Magellan. They were the first Europeans ever to sail upon the Pacific Ocean, to which they gave this name because at first they encountered very calm weather there. Then they set out on their long and lonely voyage right across the greatest ocean in the world. Not unnaturally the men mutinied, but Magellan crushed the movement with complete ruthlessness, and eventually achieved his purpose by landing on the Philippine Islands in eastern Asia. Here the little fleet rested for some months, and Magellan's life came to an untimely end in a war being fought between rival Filipinos in which he took part. However, his second-in-command carried on. Defying the Portuguese ban, he pursued his way across the Indian Ocean, rounded the Cape of Good

Hope, and arrived back in Spain in September 1522. Thus for the first time the world was circumnavigated.

The search for a north-west and for a north-east passage

Spain and Portugal reaped enormous advantages from being the first in the exploring field. The Portuguese were able to secure a monopoly of the spice trade, and made huge fortunes as a result. The Spanish did not at first succeed in breaking this monopoly, but on the other hand they soon discovered that South America and Mexico were both unbelievably rich in gold, silver and other precious stones, as well as in less spectacular products which also brought in a fat profit. Delighted with their new-found wealth, both nations were determined to keep out all rivals. Portugal announced that no ships of any other nation would be allowed to use the south-east route to Asia *via* Africa, while Spain took the same exclusive attitude about the south-west passage round Cape Horn. They were for the greater part of the sixteenth century the two strongest naval powers in the world, so they were able to enforce their prohibitions.

Nevertheless, these enthralling discoveries gave a great impetus to seafaring all over western Europe, and those countries with plenty of coast began to develop their shipping apace. The most successful were Holland, England and France. These nations were none of them powerful enough as yet to challenge the two giants, Portugal and Spain, but they determined to search for alternative routes that had not yet been claimed. Since there existed both a south-east and a south-west passage, it was logical to suppose that similar passages to India could be found *via* the north of America or the north of Europe and Asia. Unfortunately for the many explorers who devoted their lives to the search, the facts of geography make the north-east and north-west passages almost impassable to ships. For in the northern hemisphere the land masses of the continents extend so far towards the Pole that the seas beyond them are frozen for the greater part of the year.

Two English captains, Chancellor and Willoughby, set out in 1553 to find the north-east passage; but two of the ships became trapped in the ice of the White Sea, and all the men on board were frozen to death, including Willoughby. The more fortunate Chancellor survived and became the first Englishman of modern times to land in Russia. As a result of his visit the Russian Czar, Ivan IV, sent letters and presents to Queen Elizabeth I. Another famous English expedition, which was looking for the north-west passage, set sail in 1610 under Henry Hudson.

16

They failed in their main purpose, but they discovered the vast bay in North America, which is named after Hudson. Refusing to give up, Hudson decided to winter in this bay with a view to continuing the exploration the next summer. This decision was however unwise; the supply of food was inadequate and the sailors suffered terribly. At last they mutinied, cast Hudson with eight other sailors into a small boat, and set them adrift. Nobody knows what happened to them after that but the mutineers eventually reached England, which is why we know as much as we do of Hudson's fate.*

The French also attempted to find this elusive passage, and their efforts bore useful fruit, for they discovered, incidentally, the St Lawrence River, which provided them with a means of penetrating far into Canada. The forests were full of animals with attractive fur, and a trapping industry was established. The French also sailed into the Great Lakes, and one of their explorers, La Salle, even paddled down the Mississippi.

Francis Drake, the great English sea captain, who commanded the second voyage to circumnavigate the world (1577-1580) once prayed that when it fell to his lot 'to endeavour any great matter', God would help him to remember that it was 'not the beginning but the continuing of the same until the end, until it be thoroughly finished, which yieldeth the true glory'. This would have been a fitting prayer for any of the great European explorers of the sixteenth century. Their motives were mixed; they were often cruel and sometimes they were inspired almost entirely by greed; but they were also possessed of splendid courage and a fresh enthusiastic curiosity that has put all succeeding generations in their debt. For they showed the rest of mankind the true size of the world we live in, and made possible the modern study of geography. A further and unforeseen result of the activities of the explorers was that they ushered in the beginnings of modern capitalism. We have seen that Columbus had difficulty in finding a king to finance his first voyage. Later explorers found an easier way of raising money. As the prospects of any expedition bringing back a rich cargo became more definite, merchants and business-men became willing to invest sums in voyages of this kind. No one merchant had enough money to do this on his own,

* During the twentieth century, ships specially equipped as ice-breakers have succeeded in opening a route along the north coast of Asia for a few weeks each summer. But the most dramatic voyage in the Arctic was that undertaken by the *Nautilus*, an atomic submarine of the United States Navy, which in 1958 passed through the region of the North Pole under the ice. This achievement was reminiscent of the great exploring feats of the sixteenth century.

Printing in the sixteenth century

but a number of them would combine, and the profits of the enterprise would be shared among them in proportion to what they had contributed. This was the beginning of modern investment and the buying and selling of shares.

The Renaissance or Intellectual Revival

The strong impulse to explore which seized upon Europeans in the fifteenth century, was but part of a great outburst of activity known as the Renaissance—or rebirth of learning. One cannot say precisely why in certain periods men suddenly take a great leap forward in their understanding of the world around them; but we can detect certain events and inventions which set the stage for the Renaissance.

We have seen how the Crusades introduced pepper to Europe, so that a strong vested interest in spice-lands was aroused. We have also seen how Marco Polo fired the curiosity of Europeans, while the wandering Arabs, by spreading the knowledge of the magnetic compass, provided the wherewithal for that curiosity to be satisfied. Another invaluable gift which the Arabs gave to Europe was paper. This commodity was unknown during the Feudal Ages, with the result that all books had to be written on pieces of goat-skin or sheep-skin, carefully cleaned,

18

bleached and scraped. The material thus processed, known as parchment, was in short supply and therefore extremely expensive. Moreover every book had to be copied out by hand. This was usually done by monks; it was a laborious process, and meant that books were immensely precious and very rare. So even if everyone could have been taught to read, no useful purpose would have been served, since there simply were not enough books to supply more than the small class of scholars already in existence. Practically all these scholars were monks or priests, and they came from every country in Europe. They could, however, read each other's books without difficulty as they all spoke and wrote in Latin.

All this was dramatically changed when paper came into use in Europe. The secret of making this cheap but invaluable commodity came originally from China. In the eighth century a Chinese military expedition travelled westward across Asia and eventually fought a battle against an Arab army at Samarkand, near Afghanistan. A number of prisoners were taken, including some paper-makers, who taught their skill to their captors. Over the next few centuries this knowledge was passed from one Arab to another until it was taken right across the north coast of Africa and over to Spain. Some important parts of the process had by then been forgotten, and the first Spanish paper made was of poor quality. But enterprising craftsmen set about improving it, and by the fifteenth century good paper was available all over western Europe. The invention of printing then followed quickly and naturally. Consequently the production of books increased a thousandfold. Anyone who was rich enough to enjoy a little leisure found it worth his while to learn to read, and also to have his children educated. But not all those who now knew how to read, knew Latin; and so scholars gradually began to write books in their native languages. They also undertook the translation of any book that seemed important enough to justify the effort involved.

It happened that the developing of printing coincided more or less with the conquest by the Turks of Constantinople, which had always been a great centre of learning and contained many libraries. When it became clear that nothing was going to prevent a Turkish victory, most of the scholars in the city fled to western Europe, taking with them collections of priceless books including copies of the most important books written by the great thinkers of ancient Greece. The ever-growing class of scholars in Europe seized on this new source of knowledge and eagerly devoured the scientific and philosophical writings of the Greeks.

It was perhaps this fact more than any other which has caused this period of European history to be described as one of rebirth, since many old truths, formerly lost, were now rediscovered. But it would be wrong to imagine that the thinkers of the time were solely or even mainly concerned with the past. On the contrary they were forging ahead and making fascinating discoveries of their own.

Geography

Naturally one branch of study in which they were making enormous strides was geography, since the great explorers were continually adding to man's knowledge of what the world is like. It will be remembered that Magellan had a close friend who was a geographer, and that they used to go on their voyages together. Between them these two broke entirely new ground by establishing the position of the southern tip of South America, and finding that there is a strait separating the mainland from the island of Tierra del Fuego.

The greatest geographer of the Renaissance was Gerardus Mercator (1512-1594), who began his career as a land-surveyor and maker of instruments at Louvain in what is now called Belgium. He was intensely interested in maps and globes, and as this study was growing more and more popular, Mercator was in due course appointed a lecturer at Duisberg University in Germany. His greatest claim to fame is his invention of what is called the Mercator Projection, a map lay-out which makes it possible for the lines of latitude and longitude to be drawn at right angles to each other. There are drawbacks to this projection, as it distorts the size of land-masses, those near the Equator appearing smaller, and those near the Poles larger, than they really are. Nevertheless charts of this kind are extremely useful to the navigators of ships, and about two centuries after Mercator invented them they began to be widely used in various types of atlas. Mercator was a most industrious worker and produced a large number of maps, making his first map of the world as early as 1538. Of course it was not accurate, because at that time a good portion of the earth had still to be discovered. But if you try to imagine what it would be like to have no idea of the shape of your own country, or of the continent you live in, or even of the world, you will realise the immense value of the work of the sixteenth-century geographers, who were the 'founding fathers' of map-making.

Science and mathematics

The achievements of the geographers depended not only on the discoveries of the great seamen, but also on the new developments being made in mathematics and astronomy, both of which sciences made great strides at this time. Indeed the exciting discoveries being made about the surface of the earth were equalled by those being made about

GERARDUS
MERCATOR

the universe. The three men who contributed most to this new understanding of the heavens were Copernicus, a Pole (1473-1543), Tycho de Brahe, a Dane (1546-1642) and Johannes Kepler, a German (1571-1630).

In order to appreciate the work of these men it is necessary to take a brief look at the kind of scientist who preceded them. We already know that the sixteenth century, though it was so wonderfully rich in clever and original thinkers, did not see the beginning of the Renaissance. On the contrary, there had been a partial rebirth of learning as far back as the thirteenth century. Before that Europe had been in the grip of violence for so long that the old Roman civilisation had been destroyed, and education had become a privilege for a tiny minority. The best that this minority could do was to preserve and cherish for the future a little of the knowledge that had been rescued from the past. They did little thinking of their own. In fact those who passed for scientists were mainly alchemists, who pottered about in laboratories trying vainly to discover the 'philosopher's stone', a legendary commodity which was supposed to be able to turn base metal into gold. There were also astrologers who claimed to foretell the future by reading the stars. For this purpose they used the recorded observations of the planets which had been made by Ptolemy, a Greek astronomer of the second century B.C., and had been handed down through the ages. But neither the alchemists nor the astrologers could be called scientists in the true sense of the word. They were not seekers after knowledge; they merely accepted without question the traditions of their day.

In the thirteenth century, however, there was a small burst of curiosity and fresh thinking. The greatest scholar of the period was an Englishman called Roger Bacon (1214-1292). He was a brilliant university lecturer, but gave up this work in order to devote himself to scientific experiments. He had an extraordinary grasp of what was possible for man, and made some remarkable prophecies. He wrote:

> Machines are possible for navigating without rowers, so that great ships, suited to river or ocean, guided by one man, may be borne with greater speed than if they were full of men. Likewise cars may be made so that without a draught animal they may be moved with unimaginable speed. And flying machines are possible, so that a man may sit in the middle turning some device by which artificial wings may beat the air in the manner of a flying bird.

We know that his conception of an aeroplane was slightly off the mark, but his prophetic vision of steamships and motor cars takes one's breath away. Bacon's work, however, was not immediately followed up. The stream of genius dried up for a couple of centuries.

The real name of Copernicus was Nicolas Koppernigk, but like many scholars of that time he liked to Latinise his name. He studied astronomy, though he made few attempts to observe the planets for himself. He was content, as other astronomers had been for a thousand years, to use Ptolemy's tables. He did however differ from his predecessors in one respect. He found himself unable to believe that the earth remained still and fixed while the sun, the moon and all the planets revolved around it. He did not get quite as far as realising that the sun is the centre of our part of the universe, but he wrote a book stating that the earth is rushing through space.

Copernicus was not happy about his new idea; in fact it worried him because he felt that if it became known everybody would laugh at him. There was even a danger that they might be angry and afraid. For several centuries men had believed unquestioningly that the earth was fixed and the centre of the universe, and this was a safe and comforting belief that they might not wish to have disturbed. But Copernicus seems to have feared ridicule more than anything else. He therefore kept his book unpublished for thirty years, and it was only shortly before his death that he was persuaded by a younger and more enterprising friend to have it printed. It did not make an immediate sensation, but later proved to be a source of inspiration to Johannes Kepler, who was a man of much greater genius than Copernicus.

Three years after the death of Copernicus, which occurred in 1543, Tycho de Brahe was born in Denmark. He was a man of a very different stamp. There was nothing timid about him; on the contrary he was overbearing and tyrannical. He was not an original thinker and discovered no new scientific laws, but he made one invaluable contribution to science. He was the first scientist of modern times to appreciate the necessity for constant and precise observations of the stars. Although his family had never intended him to be an astronomer, he became interested in the subject when he was only fourteen, and from then onwards he kept tables of the movements of the planets always to hand, and spent every minute that he could gazing at the heavens. Three years later he had proof that the accepted tables of the day were inaccurate, and he then embarked upon his life-long task of taking accurate observations.

Tycho was a rich man, and spent fabulous sums on astronomical instruments, which he had specially made for him. Some of them were nearly forty feet in diameter. He became famous throughout Europe, and Denmark was very proud of him. The Danish King actually gave him an island, where he ruled supreme and constructed a number of observatories, which were in constant use by himself and his assistants. He was however a jealous man and refused to publish the invaluable tables that he was steadily compiling. He hoped one day to devise a theory which would supersede that of Copernicus, but in this he never succeeded.

Meanwhile all the important astronomers in Europe were yearning to get a look at Tycho's precious tables. The most anxious of all was Kepler, who in contrast to the prosperous Tycho was always as poor as a church mouse, and could afford no instruments of his own. He secured the appointment of Imperial Mathematician at the court of the Holy Roman Empire; but as the salary was small and always in arrears, this did not do him much good. He was a tremendous worker, and during his lifetime of just on sixty years his output was enormous. He founded the science of optics, and fathered a succession of theories about the universe. Some of his early ideas were very wide of the truth, but before his life was over he had discovered three great astronomical laws and had set the science of astronomy upon its modern path.

When he was in his late twenties Kepler (in order to prove a theory which eventually turned out to be wrong) became frantic to meet Tycho and study his observations. Fortunately for him Tycho eventually visited the Holy Roman Empire, and the two great men met—but they did not meet as equals. Tycho was very much the nobleman, while Kepler was as shabby as he was poor. However, Tycho gave him a job, and he eagerly looked forward to poring at last over the astronomical tables. To his great disappointment he was still not given free access to them, but he happened to be on the premises at the time of Tycho's death and promptly stole all the papers. This was fortunate for science, as Kepler made excellent use of them. In due course he published them, and as a result of the help they gave him in his studies he eventually discovered his three great laws of astronomy. The first of these was that the planets travel round the sun not in circles but in ellipses. His second and third laws explained why the planets proceed at different speeds in different parts of their revolutionary journey.

To the end of his life Kepler was dogged by poverty. For example he could not afford a good telescope. This was particularly tantalising for him when Galileo, an Italian scientist, succeeded in 1610 in making an instrument that magnified several hundred times. Thus armed, Galileo observed for the first time that there are satellites revolving round the planet Jupiter. This discovery caused an enormous sensation all over Europe, and inspired Kepler with a prophetic vision of space travel. Greatly excited, he wrote:

> There will certainly be no lack of human pioneers once we have mastered the art of flight . . . Let us create vessels and sails adjusted to the heavenly ether, and there will be plenty of people unafraid of the empty wastes. Meanwhile we shall prepare for the brave sky-travellers maps of the celestial bodies. I shall do it for the moon; you, Galileo, for Jupiter.

Galileo meanly refused to lend Kepler any of his telescopes, for he was extremely jealous of his own unique fame. His arrogance even led him to state in one of his pamphlets 'You cannot help it that it was granted to me alone to discover all the new phenomena in the sky and nothing to anybody else.' His attitude to his fellow men did not make him popular; in fact he had a genius for making enemies, and in this way got himself into trouble with the Roman Catholic Church.

All the Christians in Europe had been obliged during the sixteenth century to make frequent adjustments to old beliefs which the new discoveries were challenging. In particular the recent astronomical discoveries contradicted certain statements in the Bible, such as Psalm 19 which speaks of the sun rejoicing 'as a strong man to run a race'; or Psalm 93 which praises God because 'he hath made the round world so sure that it cannot be moved'. It is difficult for us today to appreciate how serious these difficulties appeared in the sixteenth and seventeenth

GALILEO

centuries; but we must remember that the idea of the earth moving round the sun is quite contrary to what we *appear* to see, and Copernicus never proved his point—he merely stated his belief. It could not be proved until more recorded observations were available than had been made in his day. Luther and his followers condemned Copernicus' book when it first came out, and the Roman Church declined to admit that new thinking on the Bible was required on this point until such time as the astronomers had produced actual proof of the earth's motion. Galileo was not content with this, however, and insisted that the Church was under an obligation to *disprove* the new theory. He was so uncompromising in his demand that he was hauled before the Inquisition, the Church court responsible for judging heretics, and was forced by the threat of imprisonment and even of torture, to disown a book that he had written on the subject.

It was this episode in Galileo's life that, so to speak, hit the headlines of history more than any other; but despite his development of the telescope, he did little for astronomy—far less than Kepler did. On the other hand he founded the modern science of dynamics, and actually wrote an important book on the subject when he was in his seventies. He went blind before he had finished it and the final chapters had to be dictated.

It is only possible here to mention a few of the outstanding giants among the scientists of the Renaissance; but all over Europe scholars were thinking, writing books, lecturing in the universities and corresponding freely with one another on a rich variety of subjects. Men of letters specialised far less in the sixteenth century than they do today. Kepler, for example, wrote important books on two or three different branches of science. Nor did he confine himself to science; he also wrote on the subject of music; furthermore he regarded science and religion as two parts of a single whole. The scholars of the Renaissance were essentially all-round men.

History

Moreover, the scholars were as keenly interested in the past as in the living world around them. The books rescued from Constantinople, just before that city fell to the Turks, brought the Europeans of the day into close touch with the culture that had flourished in their continent before and during the rule of the Roman Empire. A very limited knowledge of the great thinkers of ancient Greece had always been preserved and handed down from one generation to the next; but in the course of time errors had crept into the copies of the manuscripts, which gave rise to misunderstandings. During the Renaissance historians had their ideas rudely shaken and the horizons of their knowledge vastly widened.

Art and architecture

The men of the Renaissance began to take a fresh interest in the remains of ancient buildings which had survived since Greek and Roman times but had long been neglected. The architecture of that earlier period became very popular, and many new buildings were designed in the classical manner. It was a prosperous period for the upper classes, and patrons and employers were usually to be found for the painters, sculptors, goldsmiths, silversmiths and architects who were thick on the ground in the sixteenth century. In Italy the influence of ancient Greece and Rome on art was particularly strong, and among the many great artists of the period the names of Leonardo da Vinci (1452-1519),

26

Michelangelo (1475-1564) and Raphael (1483-1519) are outstanding. In northern Europe the Dutch school of painting was especially fine, but the artistic revival made its appearance in every part of the continent.

Literature

This wonderful richness of talent was just as remarkable in the field of literature. As early as the fourteenth century Dante had broken with the traditions of the Feudal Ages by writing his great poem, *The Divine Comedy*, not in Latin but in his native Italian. Later in the same century Geoffrey Chaucer wrote the *Canterbury Tales* in English. During the next hundred years or so literature declined, but in the sixteenth century there was a rich outcrop of writers all over Europe. By that time the invention of printing had made publication easy, and the reading public had expanded enormously. There was a rush to translate from Latin or Greek the works of ancient authors, while a spate of original books in all the European languages flowed from the printing presses. This burgeoning of literary genius was particularly remarkable in England, where Shakespeare was only the greatest of a generation of great writers.

Religion, philosophy and politics

The interest of the men of the Renaissance in religion was intense. This subject will be discussed separately in the next section, but it may be mentioned here that some of the greatest thinkers of the early sixteenth century were happy to apply their new knowledge to a greater understanding of God. For example a number of early manuscripts of the New Testament had come to light, and these were used to correct mistakes in the official Latin version. The Bible was also translated into most European languages.

Yet in some ways the Renaissance weakened the authority of the Church. Impressed as they naturally were by the fine human achievements which they saw multiplying around them, men began to value themselves more highly as human beings, and to feel less convinced than their forefathers had been that man's success is dependent on God's help. This way of thinking, which is called humanism, was further encouraged by the new appreciation of the greatness of ancient civilisations which had flourished before the establishment of Christianity.

Many of the humanists were however not only men of the finest moral stamp, but also loyal supporters of the Church. Outstanding was a Dutch scholar called Erasmus (1467-1536). He was a man of wide learning, who travelled all over Europe, had friendships with most of the sovereigns of his day, and spent some years in England, where he lectured at Cambridge University. He was an example of the movement at its most generous and liberal. In some of his writings he showered sarcasm on the stupidities of his fellow-men; but basically he loved mankind, and steadily refused to be drawn into the violent quarrels that broke out between different groups of Christians in 1517.

The breadth of the Renaissance

Finally we must take a brief glance at the career of Leonardo da Vinci, because his many-sided genius is so typical of the Renaissance. He was a superb painter and also a sculptor. Early in his life, in order to further his skill in these arts, he made a careful study of anatomy. His interests were boundless. Although he never actually practised as an architect, he left behind him a number of ideal plans for churches and other buildings. Furthermore, he made valuable contributions to the sciences of astronomy, botany, zoology, physics, geography, meteorology, hydrodynamics, aeronautics and others. He was also a mathematician, and he earned his living at one time as a military engineer. Leonardo stands alone, but many of his contemporaries, though lesser geniuses, showed an immense interest in a vast range of subjects, and not infrequently distinguished themselves in several.

The Reformation and the break-up of Christian unity

To understand the tremendous impact which the new learning had upon the Christian Church in Europe, it is necessary to look back and consider what the situation had been in the centuries before the Renaissance.

During the Feudal Ages Europeans valued unity above all things. They were thankful to have emerged from the turmoil of the Dark Ages, when the whole continent had been splintered with perpetual wars; and as soon as some kind of order had been restored, round about the ninth century, they had instinctively made their new political system as much like the old, lost Roman Empire as possible; for traditions which had been handed down by word of mouth informed them that, under the rule of Rome, law and order had been everywhere maintained.

Thus the chief ruler in the Feudal Ages, who was elected, had the title of Holy Roman Emperor, though the centre of his domain was actually in Germany. In theory all the lesser kings had to obey him. In the same way there was a supreme bishop among the rulers of the Church. This was the Bishop of Rome, known as the Pope. Practically the whole of Europe had become Christian, and west of Russia there
28

was only one Church—the Church of Rome. The priests of every nation not only read the mass in Latin, they also spoke this language and wrote books in it. It was in fact the language of every educated person, and if it had not been for the Church, there would have been no education at all. Throughout the Dark Ages the monasteries had managed somehow to keep intact a small residue of books and knowledge, and when life became more peaceful the monks and priests founded schools, taught in the universities and also carried out the work that is now performed by civil servants. Kings selected their chief ministers from among the bishops, but the secular work of the clergy was certainly not more important than their spiritual functions. The mass of the people in Europe were illiterate. They had no means of finding out about God or of knowing what was in the Bible, except by hearing it read and explained by the priests. Moreover the sacraments of the Church—baptism, penance, communion and so on—were part and parcel of their lives; and for these they had to depend entirely on the priesthood.

The most terrible thing that could happen to a man was to be excommunicated—that is, expelled from the Church. In 1077 the Holy Roman Emperor Henry IV, who had engaged in a dispute with Pope Gregory VII, was excommunicated. He found it so impossible to continue ruling under this ban that he went to the Pope at Canossa to beg forgiveness. He got his pardon, but was obliged to wait three days in the snow before he was admitted to the castle.

This episode gives us a striking example of the power of the Church, but it also shows that in actual practice Feudal Europe did not always achieve the unity for which it craved. Indeed it was hardly ever achieved; for human beings find it extremely difficult to live up to their own ideals. The various kings frequently defied the Emperor and, as we have seen, the Emperors and Popes fought each other for supreme power. But amid all the disputes there was a general point of agreement, namely that new and unconventional ideas were a danger to all. Heretics who tried to preach beliefs that were not approved by the Church were invariably punished, with the full consent of public opinion. But now the Renaissance was breeding a completely different attitude to new ideas—on the part of the clergy as well as of the people. The popes of the time were enthusiastic patrons of the new learning and the new arts. Nevertheless it was inevitable that sooner or later the combined effect of the invention of printing, the spread of education, and the translation of the Bible into the languages of the people, should bring about a challenge to the authority of the Church.

There were also other causes working towards a clash. In the first place kings were becoming much more powerful. This was due in part to the invention of gunpowder. In the Feudal Ages the greatest threat to kingly power had been the feudal lords, who could shut themselves up in their walled castles and defy their sovereigns. But now that guns made short work of demolishing castle battlements, the kings were able to control their nobles and so to increase their own authority. This being so, it is not surprising that they began to resent the right of the Pope to interfere in affairs of state. Their subjects often shared this resentment, for the beginnings of nationalist feeling were becoming apparent. The humanist scholars were also disposed to question the position of the Church, though their motives were different. As they came to think more and more highly of the individual, they felt that each human being should be free to approach God directly and without the intervention of a priest. This idea was slow to grow, but even in the early years of the sixteenth century it was present in Europe.

All these tendencies to criticise the existing order were sharpened by the fact that the Church at that time was undoubtedly passing through a period of slackness and was much in need of reform. Such periods have occurred at intervals throughout the life of the Church, as they are bound to do in any institution made up of human beings. In the days of Erasmus the popes were worldly; many monks and nuns were deplorably lax; a large proportion of the parish clergy were ignorant; and a number of religious customs, which had once been good and reasonable, had become sadly corrupted.

Erasmus was very conscious of all these evils. He knew also that the some kind of thing had happened before, and that in the past energetic reform movements had put matters right. He therefore wrote books advocating just such a reform movement. But before his words, and those of men like him, had achieved their effect, another set of events occurred which diverted the development of Christianity in Europe along completely different lines.

Martin Luther (1483-1546)

In the University of Wittenburg in Germany one of the lecturers was a monk called Martin Luther. His father had been a miner, but he was obviously a clever lad and was therefore given a good education. He entered the University of Erfurt at the age of eighteen and studied law. At the last moment, however, he decided against being a lawyer and entered a monastery. He was described by his superiors as a model monk and later was ordained a priest. But it was not in him to accept easily all that he was taught. For years he wrestled mentally with the question of how a man may attain salvation, and finally he came to the conclusion that it is by faith. Compared with faith, the actions or 'works' of a man seemed to Luther unimportant; and he therefore attached little importance to the many 'good works'—such as the repeating of prayers or the performance of some other penance—by which men and women, under the guidance of their priests, strove to make amends for their sins in the sight of God.

In 1511 Luther visited Rome and was shocked by the abuses which he saw in the Papal Court. Six years later he suffered an even greater shock. By then a new Pope, Leo X, had been elected, who was anxious to rebuild St Peter's Cathedral in Rome. The work he started was carried on by his successors, and St Peter's is in fact one of the outstanding architectural achievements of the Renaissance. Of course a church designed on such a magnificent scale cost a lot of money, and in order to raise funds, Leo sent a man called Tetzel round Europe to sell indulgences. He was unfortunate in his choice of an agent. Tetzel was so anxious to make money that he cared little for any other aspect of his mission, and in offering the public his indulgences he made claims on their behalf which shocked many people and drove Luther to take drastic action.

The practice of granting indulgences, which had once been a reasonable one, had grown corrupt with the passage of time. It was of course recognised that a sinner's guilt could be wiped away only by God's grace and his own sincere repentance. But even when guilt had by these means been removed, punishment still remained, both here and hereafter. It was believed, however, that by good works a man might hope to win a reprieve from some of the punishment which he admittedly deserved. It was also believed possible for a man or woman who had an indulgence to transfer it by prayer to some loved person who was already dead. Among the range of good works that might possibly gain indulgence, one was of course the giving of alms to some worthy object, and this was the aspect of the matter which Tetzel was stressing in 1517.

Luther had already come to the conclusion that salvation must be by faith not by good works, and he determined to expose what he regarded as a scandal. He therefore wrote out ninety-five statements (or theses) giving his views, and pinned them on the door of a church at Wittenburg. His action caused a sensation, and scholars all over Germany began debating these matters. Luther, who was an extremely able speaker, defended his views and in the process began to discover fresh points on which he could not agree with the Church. He had no idea at first of a complete breach with Rome; he merely called for reforms; but he developed his idea of salvation by faith, and finally wrote of the 'priesthood of all believers'. This amounted to an attack on the very foundations of the Roman Church, since it meant that every individual was in a sense a priest, in that he was entitled to stand before God without any intermediary in the shape of an ordained cleric. This was

MARTIN
LUTHER

a cardinal belief of the majority of the Protestants (as Luther's followers were later to be called, on account of their protest against the existing order).

Luther was excommunicated and his books were burnt. But the movement which he had started, which is known as the Reformation, could not be stifled. Men like Erasmus, who had wanted reform but were horrified to see the disruption which had begun in the Church, refused to have anything to do with Luther. The Pope naturally tried to suppress the movement, and hoped that the excommunication of the rebel monk would achieve this purpose. But Luther, so far from submitting to Rome, publicly burned the papal bull containing the denunciation against him. Charles V, whose Empire was split by the controversy, then intervened and summoned the Diet (a sort of parliament) to meet in the town of Worms in 1521, and ordered Luther to appear before it to answer the charges against him. That the Diet would condemn him was a foregone conclusion, but Luther was determined to

32

take this opportunity of proclaiming his case. He boldly defended his opinions, ending with the ringing words, 'Here stand I. I can do no other. So help me God.' He was outlawed but was allowed to leave Worms safely, and as he enjoyed the protection of one of the German princes, he was able to continue his work of translating the Bible and spreading his revolutionary religious ideas. Before long it became clear that he had started a flood which no one could hold back. All over Germany, which formed a large part of the Empire, the numerous princes all took sides either with the Pope or with Luther, and it looked at one time as if there would be a large-scale war to settle the matter. In 1555 however the princes met and made what was called the Peace of Augsburg, by which it was settled that each prince should decide for himself whether he would remain a Roman Catholic or become a Protestant. His subjects would have to follow his lead. There was however a measure of liberty left to them, for if they disagreed with their Prince, they were free to go and live in another state whose ruler favoured their own religious views. If they insisted on remaining, they were liable to persecution.

Calvin and Zwingli

Luther was the first leader to launch his protest against Rome, but many others followed his example. Consequently the Christian Church in Europe was split not merely into two, but into a large number of splinters, some of them very small indeed. Once it had been admitted that an individual could set himself up against accepted authority, there was no logical way of stopping the process, although persecution as a method was freely adopted by all parties.

Among the numerous imitators of Luther, two stand out. One of them, Ulrich Zwingli (1484-1531), played the same part in Switzerland that Luther had played in Germany. The religious beliefs of the two men were similar, but neither of them would accept completely the viewpoint of the other. Zwingli wielded considerable influence, but was no more able than Luther had been in Germany, to win over all his fellow-Swiss; so each canton became either Protestant or Roman Catholic, and the citizens had to conform or go.

Also closely connected with Switzerland was John Calvin (1509-1564), although he was by birth a Frenchman. He was of course brought up in the old faith, but in 1530 he was converted to Protestantism. As the King of France had remained loyal to the Roman Church, Calvin was faced with the risk of persecution. He fled to Switzerland so that he might have liberty to worship as he thought right. He settled in Geneva, where he carved out for himself an extraordinary position. From 1536 until his death in 1564 he was the unquestioned ruler, both spiritual and secular, of the city state. As far as power was concerned, he was, on a small scale, both Pope and Holy Roman Emperor at once. Moreover, although he had himself defied the authority of his native state, he had no intention of allowing any of his Swiss subjects to defy him, and his rule was entirely autocratic. His case is only one example of the intolerance that the Protestants felt for each other as well as for Rome. The latter half of the sixteenth century was an age of intolerance all round.

The results of the Reformation

What had been the one Christian Church in Europe was now broken into fragments. Every sect believed that it had the secret of divine truth, and they all burned and tortured one another. The liberty of thought which might have resulted from the Reformation was destroyed because everybody denied to others the freedom he claimed for himself. A most unhappy result of this was a series of religious wars, which distracted Europe for nearly a century, and caused endless suffering to the common people. The kings on the other hand derived considerable advantages from the Reformation, since their power was enormously increased by it. For the rulers of Protestant countries now had the right to determine what religion their subjects should follow. Even the Roman Catholic sovereigns gained extra authority, because the Popes, realising that these kings would never be content with less power than their Protestant neighbours, made a series of treaties, or concordats, with them, entrusting to them privileges that had formerly lain with the Pope himself.

An outstanding example of the power of the sixteenth-century kings is to be seen in the course of the Reformation in England, where a number of contradictory changes followed one another with bewildering speed. Henry VIII, who died in 1547, had refused to continue obeying the Pope, but in other respects remained a Roman Catholic. During the next reign, which lasted six years, the people were forced to become extreme Protestants. Then there was a fresh turnabout. Mary I reunited the country with Rome, and for the next five years Protestants were persecuted. Finally Elizabeth I (1558-1603), anxious to avoid the religious wars that were raging elsewhere in Europe, decided on compromise. The result was the foundation of the Church of England, which while certainly not Roman in its allegiance, is not strongly Protestant. Throughout these years of change there were many Englishmen who were prepared to be burned alive for what they believed to be right: but it remains true that the English Reformation depended on royal decisions rather than on popular leaders.

An interesting though indirect result of the Reformation was the establishment of European colonies in North America. Most of these were founded by Protestants who were not allowed to worship as they pleased in Europe, and so went to seek a home elsewhere.

The Counter-Reformation

In the early days of the Reformation the Roman Church had tried to suppress the movement by force. When it became clear that this was impossible, the Popes and bishops—though still using force when they thought necessary—concentrated mainly on putting their own house in order. Many of the abuses that Erasmus and Luther had condemned, were rooted out, and an effort was made to close the Roman ranks so that no more members should be lost. From 1545 to 1563 a great Council of the Church was held at Trent in north Italy. New rules were drawn up, and efforts were made to limit the freedom which had been a feature of the Renaissance and which seemed from the Roman point of view to have done so much harm. Thus a list of dangerous books, known as the *Index*, was compiled, and members of the Church were forbidden to read any of them, in case their faith should be disturbed. Moreover greater powers were given to the Inquisition. This was the Church Court of Justice dealing with cases of heresy; the methods it employed, both to extract confessions from suspects, and to punish those it condemned, were often barbarously cruel.

Important as the Council was, however, the most effective work in arming the Roman Church against further undermining by the Protestants was undertaken by the Jesuit Order. This was founded by a Spaniard called Ignatius Loyola, who began his career as a soldier but underwent a remarkable conversion in 1521 at the age of thirty. He decided that in future he would become a soldier of Christ, but he needed many years of stern preparation before he felt equal to the task to which he believed himself called by God. In 1534 he was joined by a few like-minded men and founded his Society of Jesus, the members of which are vowed not only to the usual monastic ideal of poverty, chastity and obedience, but also to a lifetime of missionary work. In the early days of the Order much of the missionary work was directed to winning back Protestant Europe; but the Jesuits also opened up new trails. Led first by Francis Xavier, one of the founder-members, they went to preach the Gospel to the peoples of Asia and the natives of the

35

newly found continent of America. The Jesuits were also fine scholars, and carried much of Europe's new knowledge as far away as to Japan.

Finally it may be noted here that the disunity of the Christian Church which the Reformation had precipitated, continued unhealed until the twentieth century. At last in 1948, after much thought and discussion, the World Council of Churches came into being, and held its first Assembly at Amsterdam. Nearly all the non-Roman Churches—including the Orthodox Churches of the Middle East—became members. This movement did not confine its activities to the discussion of doctrine. On the contrary it was felt that an important step would be taken towards unity if members of different Churches were to work side by side in the struggle being waged against hunger and disease in the many poverty-stricken regions of the world; so a joint organisation for social service was set up, known as Christian Aid.

The World Council of Churches had not been in existence for more than a dozen years before efforts were begun by both sides to bridge the gap that separated its members from the Church of Rome. In December 1961 the Council's third Assembly, which was held in New Delhi, was attended by Roman Catholic observers. In the following October Pope John XXIII (pope 1958-63) presided over the first session of a General Council which he had summoned to Rome, and to which he in his turn had invited observers from other Christian denominations. A few months later he died, but his successor Paul VI continued his work of *rapprochement* with the other Churches.

2 The European infiltration into Asia and America

Vasco da Gama's feat in crossing the Arabian Sea and landing in India was one of the turning-points in history, for it marked the first instalment of the great overspill of Europe into the rest of the world. For centuries Europeans had travelled very little. Even the traders tended for the most part to hug the coasts, while the Venetians and Genoese, who carried on a thriving trade with Asia, usually bought their goods in a southern Mediterranean port, relying on Arab merchants to look after the transport from the unknown lands of Asia to that point. Once da Gama had blazed the trail in 1498, however, Europe began to exert a steady pressure on Asia which led eventually to the founding of huge empires that ruled—directly or indirectly—the greater part of the continent. In fact the four and a half centuries from 1498 to 1948 have been described as the 'da Gama Epoch'—the period of western domination over Asia.

The pioneering work of the Portuguese

You must not however think that the Portuguese had any such plans in their minds when they first arrived at Calicut on the south-western coast of India. They were not interested in land empires, but were inspired by the desire to make money. There are many types of foodstuffs which Europeans like to eat but which cannot be grown in Europe. We have seen that in the fifteenth century, people's diet was far less varied than it is today, and that since the beginning of the Crusades there had been a steady and insistent demand for pepper and other spices, which grow in great abundance in India and the Indonesian islands. The Portuguese made up their minds to establish their own trading connections with the spice-lands in order to break the monopoly of the Arabs who had hitherto carried these goods through the Middle East to the Mediterranean. The Arab merchants made enormous profits on the trade, with the result that the people of Europe had to pay absurdly high prices for their pepper. The Portuguese, however, were not opening up the new route with the kind intention of selling pepper cheaply. On the contrary they were determined to sell just as dearly as the Arabs and to divert the profits to their own pockets.

Mixed with this desire for money there was a religious motive, for the Arabs were Muslims. Eight successive Crusades, or holy wars, had

Vasco da Gama being received at the Court of the Zamorin at Calicut

been waged by the Christians of Europe against the Muslims, and the Portuguese regarded their trading enterprises as being in a sense a fresh crusade. It must always be remembered that throughout the late fifteenth and the whole of the sixteenth century Europe was conscious of the terrible threat of Turkey. Here on the south-east tip of the continent was a militaristic Muslim power, with a recent history of successful conquest, which seemed likely at any moment to overwhelm Christendom. Fear breeds hatred, and most Europeans snatched gladly at any chance of harming Muslims. Like the Spanish, the Portuguese had particular reasons for hating them, because parts of their land had for centuries been under the rule of the Muslim Moors.

It was therefore with the triple intention of lining their pockets, harming the infidels, and winning prestige that the Portuguese embarked on their project of penetrating into Asia. Their first task was to ensure that no one else should reap the benefits of their explorations. They therefore announced that they would not permit the sailors of any other nation to use the Cape route. Since at the time they had the most powerful fleet in Europe, they were able to enforce this prohibition; and they then set about driving the Arab traders from the Arabian Sea. In 1506 a man called Affonzo Albuquerque was put in command of the operation and proceeded to build up Portuguese power according to a careful and logical plan.

To understand what Albuquerque achieved, you must look at the map on page 44. He was not trying to conquer a lot of territory, but to establish little pockets of power at vital points around the sea. He began by sending embassies to the more important of the rulers on the east coast of Africa, including the Emperor of Ethiopia. Then, bearing in mind that the Red Sea had been one of the two main sea-routes along which the Arabs carried the spice-trade, he gained control of Socotra. The other Arab route had been up the Persian Gulf, and Albuquerque therefore made friendly overtures to the ruler of Ormuz. He also tried to secure the friendship of the ruler of Calicut, who was known as the Zamorin.

It was at the Zamorin's court that Vasco da Gama had landed in 1498, and he had been given a most friendly reception. But when it became clear that the Portuguese were hostile to all the Arab merchants, the attitude of Calicut changed. The city was an important port, and the Zamorin was naturally annoyed when he realised that the newcomers were driving away his other customers. He, in his turn, grew hostile to the newcomers, but neither he nor Albuquerque was strong enough to destroy the other. The Zamorin made more than one attempt to drive the Europeans out of the Arabian Sea, but he was hampered by the fact that he could get no help from his ally, the Sultan of Turkey. The Sultan, whose empire was suffering terribly from the loss of the spice-trade, was only too anxious to fight the Portuguese; but obviously they had to be fought at sea, and the Turkish fleet was based on the Mediterranean and unable to reach the theatre of war. Nevertheless the Zamorin continued to put a brake upon Portuguese alliances in India. He could not keep them out of the country completely, because India was at that time much divided between rival rulers. In particular there was bitter hostility between the Muslim Grand Moguls in the north and the Hindu empire of Vijayanagar in the south. Trading on these differences, and playing off one party against the other, the Portuguese managed to acquire Bombay, Goa, Cochin and one or two other points on the Indian coast.

By 1510 Albuquerque had built up such an effective chain of power-points round the Arabian Sea that he was in effective control of that piece of water. He then decided to go further afield and to make his ships masters of the Indian Ocean as well. Looking again at the map, you will see that the key to the east was the Straits of Malacca. These narrow waters were the scene of busy and prosperous trade, and though fairly easy to defend, would obviously be a most valuable conquest. In 1511 Albuquerque launched a successful attack on Malacca, aftewhich the way lay open not only to the East Indies but also to China. Flushed with continuous success, the Portuguese proceeded to explore both these new openings. In China they met their first serious rebuff, but in the East Indies (or Indonesia as these islands are now called) they did better, for the region was weakened by local wars between Muslims and Hindus. The Portuguese captured Amboina, and then succeeded in establishing various strong points similar to those gained round the Arabian Sea. The damage they had inflicted on the commerce of the Middle East was now so severe that the Sultan of Turkey made a final effort to expel them. In 1538 he sent the Egyptian navy down the Red Sea to fight them; but the Portuguese won the battle that ensued. For the time being they seemed to be invincible.

The arrival of the Dutch

The further Portugal extended her power to the east, however, the harder it became for her to spare all the shipping required to patrol the Cape route. Such patrol work was essential, for the other countries of Europe were becoming resentful of the fact that they were paying just as much for their spices as they had done in the days of the Arab monopoly. Any European nation would have liked to challenge the Portuguese, and it was natural that the country that eventually succeeded in doing so was one with a long coastline, and therefore a long seafaring tradition. Holland had as yet hardly become an independent nation, but her merchants and sailors were extremely enterprising. In 1595 a Dutch fleet sailed round the Cape of Good Hope, mainly to see if it could be done. Finding that it could, a group of Dutch merchants then formed an East India Company in 1602, and set about driving the Portuguese away from their conquests in the Arabian Sea.

This however did not prove as easy as the Dutch had hoped, despite the fact that they received help from Calicut. Forced to admit that for the present Albuquerque's system of control was still too strong for them, they then went further east and concentrated on some of Portugal's outlying conquests. In 1605 they captured Amboina, and from there gradually worked back in a westerly direction, capturing Portuguese positions as they came. In 1619 they took Djakarta; in 1641 Malacca and Colombo; and in 1660 Cochin. By this time the power of Portugal in Asia was completely broken. All that remained of the grand imperial structure of the sixteenth century were a few little pockets of power, or enclaves, along the western coast of India.* The later colonial empires were destined to last much longer.

The unsuccessful attempt of the English to challenge the Dutch

Just at the time when the Dutch were making up their mind to challenge the Portuguese monopoly of the spice trade, the same idea was entering the minds of a number of English merchants and seamen. An English

ALBUQUERQUE

East India Company was therefore founded, similar in many ways to the Dutch company, and English ships, having successfully passed round the Cape, prepared to join with Holland in seizing the Portuguese commercial empire in the East Indies.

Two unpleasant surprises, however, awaited them. One of these was the unwillingness of the Indonesian people to take any English goods in exchange for their own products. This was a serious blow, for though the English merchants were not particularly short of gold (which was

* One of these, the valuable island port of Bombay, was ceded to England in 1662 as part of the dowry of a Portuguese princess, Catherine of Braganza, when she married Charles II. Goa and the other enclaves remained under Portuguese rule even after India became independent in 1947, and were finally taken by the Indian Government by force in 1961.

acceptable) they were reluctant to pay it out. The enormous expansion of trade that had taken place in Europe since the voyages of discovery, had forced men to think a great deal about economics, though this word had not yet come into use. An economic theory had been developed which is known as mercantilism. The basis of this theory was the belief (now known to be false) that gold is wealth. Those countries who could, hastily took possession of gold or silver mines, while those who had no minerals of this type, regarded it as a matter of the utmost importance to sell abroad each year more goods than they bought, so that they would build up a store of gold.

The merchants of the English East India Company were thus extremely anxious to discover something other than gold which they could exchange for the spices of Indonesia. In due course they learned that the Indonesians wanted cotton and also that cotton grew plentifully in India. They therefore looked for a trade opening in India, and in 1612 they were allowed to establish a trading station (called in those days a factory) in Surat. Here they could buy plenty of cotton; but they still could not exchange it for spices in the East Indies—this time because of the hostility of the Dutch in the area. Holland was determined to maintain exclusive control of the spice trade she had stolen from Portugal, and the English, defeated in their original aim, had no alternative but to concentrate all their Asian commercial enterprises in India. Most of that vast country belonged during the seventeenth century to the great Mogul Empire, which was a power to be reckoned with. The foreign merchants were obliged to behave themselves or run the risk of losing their concessions. They soon recognised this fact and treated the Indian government with great respect. In return they were given permission to establish new factories at Madras and Masulipatnam in 1641, and in 1690 they founded a further station in Calcutta.

The arrival of the French

Although France has a considerable coastline, and therefore has always been a seafaring nation, the French were very late in securing a share of the Asian trade that had been snatched from the Arabs. This was partly because during the latter half of the sixteenth century the country was using up all its energies in a civil war fought between the Roman Catholics and the Protestants. Early in the seventeenth century an attempt had been made to copy the example of Holland and England by founding an East India Company, but it came to nothing. In 1664, however, France made a more determined effort to keep up with her neighbours. A government-sponsored company was formed with the intention of ousting the Dutch from their monopoly position. They began with an attack on Ceylon, but found, as the English had found before them, that the Dutch in the seventeenth century were a hard nut to crack. They too were obliged to give up the project and to confine their activities to founding trading stations on the mainland of India. Their principal factory was set up at Pondicherry in south India.

The reaction of Asia to the European infiltration

The first Asian reaction to the arrival of the Europeans was one of pleasure and interest. The strangers were not seeking to conquer any Asian ruler—they merely sought permission to trade. Indeed when Vasco da Gama first visited the court of the Zamorin, he behaved with the greatest courtesy and respect. It is true that relations between Calicut and Portugal soon worsened as Albuquerque tightened his control of the Indian Ocean, and the various sultans of Malaya were likewise bitterly resentful of his attack on the Straits of Malacca. But this on-slaught was not followed up in the way that they had at first feared. The Europeans merely took control of strategic points on the coast, and used their possession of fire-arms, which were at that time unknown in Asia, to grab the lion's share of the trade. Their task was made easy in the Indonesian islands by the fact that most of the coastal lands were ruled by Muslims, while the interior regions were inhabited by Hindus. With these two religious groups constantly hostile to each other, it was easy for a determined foreigner to establish himself. So the sea-empire of the Portuguese was built up. As far as the land was concerned, they were interested in it only as providing useful bases and producing the kind of goods that could be sold at a profit in Europe. In India the British and French bases were never conquered: the merchants were merely permitted by the government to come and trade—as long as they behaved themselves. For Mogul India was a great power.

The Europeans in China

Greater still was China, which at the beginning of the sixteenth century was the most powerful empire in the world. This truth was learned by the Portuguese the hard way. Shortly after gaining control of the Straits of Malacca, they decided to open up trade with China, and an expedition was sent in 1517 under the leadership of a man called Pirez, who took with him a cargo of pepper to be exchanged for Chinese goods. Marco Polo had written a tantalising account of the silks, porcelain and other

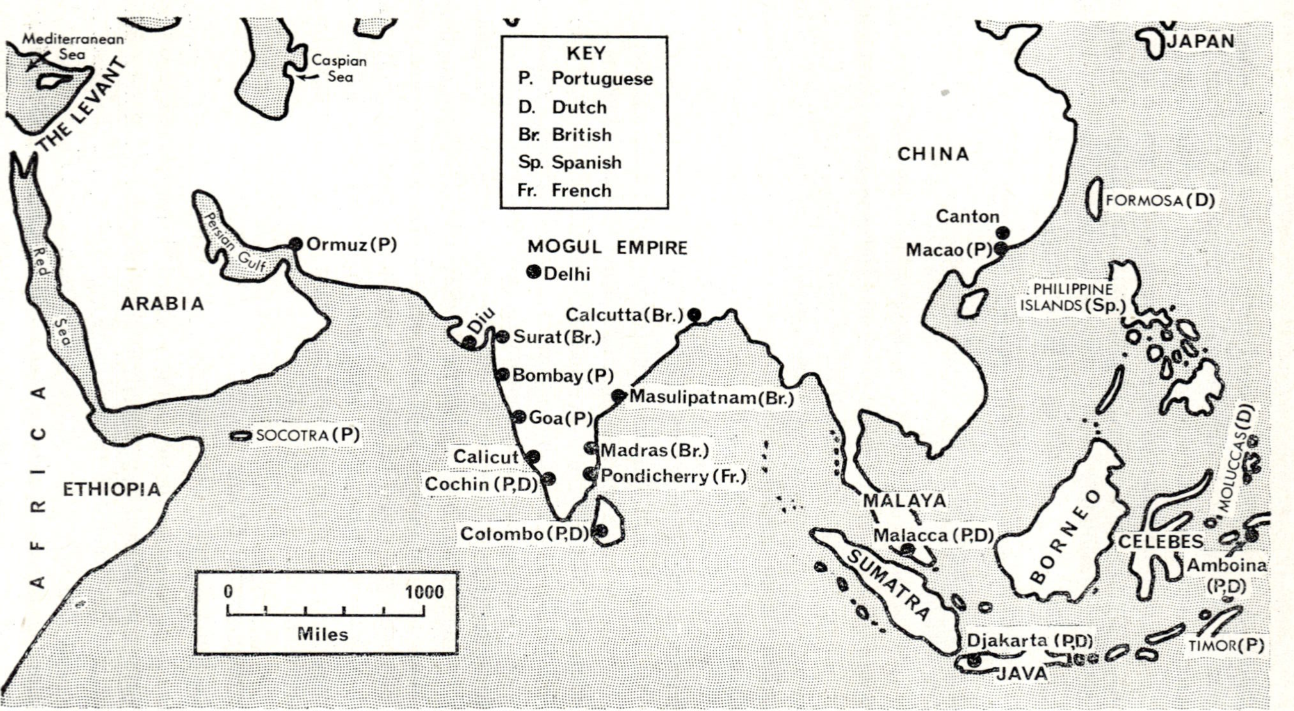

Map 2—European penetration of South-east Asia

beautiful materials which abounded in China, and it was obvious that there were great opportunities here for an extremely profitable luxury trade.

Pirez landed at Canton and asked permission to travel to Peking, the capital, for an interview with the Chinese Emperor for whom he had brought a letter from his own King. Things moved slowly in China, but eventually permission was received and Pirez started on his way, leaving a Portuguese admiral in charge of his ships. This admiral was apparently an impatient man, or else he underrated the strength of China. Without waiting for Pirez to return he landed a party of soldiers and began to build a fort on the Chinese coast. He was immediately stopped, and a report of the outrage was forwarded to the Emperor on whom it had a strong effect. Even before this he had begun to have second thoughts about Pirez, for he was the Overlord of most of the sultans of Indonesia, and had now heard from them that the Portuguese were not to be trusted. Consequently when Pirez arrived in Peking he was thrown into prison, where he stayed until his death six years later. The admiral had meanwhile been expelled, and the whole embassy was a complete failure.

The Portuguese, however, did not give up quickly. Numerous attempts were made to placate the Chinese, and at last in 1557, as a reward for having helped to suppress some pirates who had been terrorising the Chinese coast, they were given permission to land on the peninsula of Macao. There they established a permanent trading station, but they were only allowed to remain on sufferance and were never able to found anything that could be called a colony.

In 1571 some sailors arrived from Spain, and tried to open diplomatic relations between Peking and Madrid. They were no more successful than the Portuguese had been, but they were allowed—subject to very strict conditions—to do a certain amount of trading in Canton.

Even when they had been driven out of Indonesia by the Dutch, the Portuguese managed to retain their station in Macao. The Dutch attempted to dislodge them, but having failed, established instead a base on the island of Formosa which was not at that time a part of China.

China in the seventeenth century

Thus the great Chinese Empire remained quite unshaken by the first impact of Europeans upon it. But by the beginning of the seventeenth century China had become far less strong in fact than she appeared to be. For thousands of years the country's history had followed a repeating pattern. Some strong warrior would seize the throne and establish

45

a dynasty, or family of rulers. So long as his descendants continued to be strong men, the dynasty would remain in power; but if the family declined and produced a series of weak rulers, some other claimant would depose the ruling house and establish a new dynasty. The Emperor who imprisoned Pirez belonged to the Ming Dynasty. He was strong enough, but during the next hundred years the Mings became weak and degenerate. At length their power was challenged from an unexpected quarter.

To the extreme north-east of the Empire was Manchuria. The inhabitants of this region, the Manchus, were not Chinese at all, but had been conquered and incorporated into the Empire. The Chinese despised all foreigners, including the Manchus, who certainly were decidedly less civilised than the other inhabitants of the Empire. But the Manchus were a warlike people, and early in the seventeenth century a great national leader called Nurhachi came to the fore. Nurhachi hated the Chinese because they had murdered his father, and although his chances of ever inflicting any real harm on the Empire must have seemed remote, he determined to try what he could do. With great cunning he began by attacking Mongolia, which was a vassal state of China but not easy to defend. Having conquered this province, Nurhachi in 1618 actually made war on the Emperor. But he had bitten off more than he could chew. The Ming dynasty was not yet too weak to defend itself against a rebel, and when Nurhachi died in 1626 he had not come anywhere near conquering China. On the other hand his forces had not been crushed, and the struggle was carried on by another warrior called Tien Tsung.

Tien Tsung realised that it was useless to renew the attack on China unless or until he saw some really advantageous opening. So he bided his time. Meanwhile the Ming Emperors had become steadily less efficient, and at last a rebellion broke out inside China under the leadership of one Li Tzu-cheng. The rebels gained many adherents and the Emperor felt that his throne was threatened. In desperation he actually appealed to Tien Tsung for help. Delighted at the opportunity, Tien and his Manchu warriors moved in. They suppressed the revolt and then, inevitably, refused to go away. The last of the Mings was dethroned in 1645, and the Manchu dynasty was established.

For nearly two hundred years the new dynasty continued strong and successful, and the Empire grew in size. Mongolia, which had been wrested from China by Nurhachi, was now brought back to the Empire; and before he invaded China Tien Tsung had succeeded in annexing Korea. This policy of expansion was continued. In due time Sinkiang was conquered and Tibet made a dependency. China also conquered Formosa, which though geographically separate, was of strategic importance to the country. When the Ming dynasty fell, a certain Koxinga remained loyal to the old order and resisted the Manchus as long as he could. When forced to leave China, he withdrew to Formosa, driving out the Dutch traders. His nuisance-value on the island was immense, and he carried out so many raids on the mainland that the Chinese government could not afford to ignore him. They never succeeded in defeating him, but after his death they won back Formosa from his son.

Meanwhile, despite internal weakness followed by rebellion and civil war, China had not been obliged to make any concession to the Europeans. The Portuguese continued to trade in Macao; and the Spanish in Canton were later joined by a limited number of traders from some other nations. But the Chinese government openly despised traders of any sort, and the foreign merchants were forced to suffer many indignities. They made such profits, however, that there were always enough of them to find it worth while and to keep the trade going. Apart from these limited concessions, the Emperors of China continued to follow a rigid policy of excluding all foreigners from their land. This at least is true of foreigners who approached China by way of a sea-port. The land frontiers were not so easy to guard, and during the seventeenth century the Russians began a steady expansion across the northern part of Asia.

Thus it was inevitable that the Russians would sooner or later come into conflict with the Chinese. When this happened China was forced to abandon her usual attitude of aloof superiority and face the task of reaching agreement with Russia. In 1689 the Treaty of Nerchinsk was signed between the two powers, which defined the frontier between them; it also provided for Russia to send representatives to Peking, which gave her a decided advantage in China over any other European nation.

Japan and the Europeans

Once a dynasty was established in China, the Emperor enjoyed absolute power and was treated with the greatest deference by his subjects. The Emperors of Japan, however, enjoyed an even more exalted position. They were considered to be so god-like that they were not even expected to carry out the work of government, which was entrusted to another hereditary official called the Shogun. The Shoguns were all-powerful rulers and directed policy; but they were supposed, in theory at least, to consult the Emperors on all matters of importance.

This extraordinary system of government worked better than might be expected, but it was not working at all well at the time when the Europeans first arrived in the Far East. At that time the feudal lords in the western part of Japan were in open rebellion against both the Shogun and the Emperor. After the Pirez fiasco the Portuguese sent an embassy to see if they could establish trade relations with the Japanese. Had the rebellious lords made common cause with the Europeans, nothing could have saved Japan from foreign conquest, but fortunately a patriot called Nobunga managed to make himself Shogun. He sternly repressed the rebellion and presented a strong front to the Portuguese. He permitted them to enter the country for trading purposes, and also allowed Christian missionaries to come and preach. Those who came were mostly Jesuits, and included the most famous of all the Jesuit missionaries, Francis Xavier.

This friendly state of affairs continued until the succession in 1582 of a new Shogun, Hideyoshi, who became uneasy at the growing power of the Portuguese. Their weapons of war were much more effective than the swords and spears of the Japanese, and it was clear that if any fresh feudal rebellion broke out, they would be able to sway the issue. Moreover they claimed the right to defend the areas in which their Christian converts lived, and for this purpose actually landed heavy artillery in the country. Deeply worried, Hideyoshi forbade any further missionary activity, but allowed the Portuguese traders to remain. He was perpetually on the look-out for any foreign threat, however, and on one occasion suddenly ordered the execution of all the Spanish traders who had been previously allowed into the country. These unfortunate men were crucified because Hideyoshi had learned of Spain's imperial conquests in other parts of Asia.

In 1603 another change took place in the Shogunate and a new dynasty was founded by Ieyasu Tokugawa. The Tokugawa family remained in power until 1868, and proved themselves to be strong and able rulers. By the seventeenth century the full danger of European aggression in Asia had become apparent, and in 1637 the Tokugawa began a strict policy of excluding foreigners. Missionaries had already been expelled; now most of the traders were sent after them. However, as in China, a few exceptions were made: the Portuguese were al owed to continue trading in Nagasaki, and the Dutch and English in Deshima close by.

There was one important difference between the Japanese and the Chinese policy of exclusion. The Emperors in Peking considered all

A Dutch trading station in Japan in the early seventeenth century

matters of trade to be beneath their notice; and it was only the eagerness of the Chinese merchants to trade with the West that kept the commerce going in Canton and Macao. In Japan on the other hand the government was not quite so detached. The Shoguns realised that some of the products of Europe could be very useful, and when permitting the Europeans to carry on a limited trade, they made it a condition that a certain number of cannon should be sold to Japan each year. They also felt some interest in European science, and a few Japanese were encouraged to learn Dutch in order to study the sciences. The Japanese exclusion policy was therefore never complete, but the exceptions made were carefully devised and very much in favour of the Japanese, who thus showed that they did not really regard everything European as undesirable. The Chinese on the other hand were genuinely convinced that foreign customs, foreign knowledge and foreigners themselves were immensely inferior.

The Spanish in Asia

We have seen how the Portuguese, who were followed later by the

49

Dutch and the English, gradually penetrated further into Asia, starting from the west. First they controlled the Arabian Sea; later they pushed through the Straits of Malacca and began to take over certain ports in Indonesia; finally they sailed on to China and Japan.

Spain meanwhile was sending her ships across the Atlantic and exploring the Americas. Then between 1519 and 1522 a small Spanish fleet won immortal fame by sailing right round the world. After crossing the Atlantic, rounding Cape Horn and traversing the Pacific, this fleet, under the leadership of Magellan, reached Asia from an easterly direction. They landed on the Philippine Islands (so called by the Spanish in honour of their King), where they remained for a few months. Later in the century they returned and conquered the islands. They already had a vast empire in America, which was yielding them a rich profit in gold, silver and other precious stones, but the Spanish were drunk with success. They had now superseded the Chinese as owners of the biggest empire in the world, and felt that there was no limit to what they might do. Moreover they were influenced by the sixteenth-century passion for dabbling in the spice trade, and the Philippines produced spice. So in 1571 the Spanish occupied the islands. Their tenure was not easy, for both Hideyoshi and Koxinga tried to wrest their conquest from them, while the Dutch, the Portuguese and the British were also anxious to drive away these new rivals in the Far East. Nevertheless the Spanish held on, and succeeded to a remarkable degree in imposing their own ideas upon the Filipinos. They regarded it as one of their prime duties to christianise the people, and sent out a large number of friars who converted the majority of the population.

Meanwhile in 1581 Spain had even absorbed Portugal, thus acquiring yet another empire to add to her already immense possessions. But this arrangement came to an end in 1640 when the Portuguese regained their independence.

The new type of imperialism introduced by the Dutch

When the Spanish conquered the Philippines in 1581, they were introducing a new trend into European relations with Asia, for they were acquiring a land-empire. Previously the Europeans had established beach-heads on land, merely as a means of controlling the sea. But having decided to act as imperial rulers, the Spanish did the job thoroughly. Before long their language, their customs and culture, as well as their religion, had spread over the islands. On the whole their rule was reasonably popular, for the first two hundred years at least.

50

In the second half of the seventeenth century the Dutch also began to impose their control over the interior of some of the Indonesian islands, but their motives and methods were markedly different from those of the Spanish. They were not seeking to spread their own civilisation over new lands, but still merely pursuing economic advantage. They were already buying large quantities of spices and selling them very profitably in Europe, and they realised that there were other tropical products which would find a ready sale at home. But while the Indonesian peasants grew plenty of spices and were willing to sell any quantity, they were not in the habit of producing surplus supplies of the goods that the merchants from Holland now demanded. Consequently the Dutch decided to force them to change their farming methods. The Indonesians put up a fierce resistance, but in Amboina, the Moluccas and the Banda Islands they were defeated and conquered. They were then subjected to a disastrous type of imperialism, which had nothing to do with the government of Holland but was organised by the East India Company—a group not of statesmen but of traders. Unfortunately for the Indonesians these traders were well backed by military force, and the unfortunate peasants were compelled to grow not the foodstuffs they needed for themselves and their families, but the kind of crops which would sell well in Europe. A Dutch historian, describing the terrible effect this had on the people, has said that as a result of this interference 'the small mountainous islands could not produce food enough, and the inhabitants were obliged to buy a supplement of rice from the Company. It sold this commodity to them at too high a price, which made the situation still more desperate. Thus the economic system of the Moluccas was ruined, and the population reduced to poverty.'

Fortunately for the peoples of Asia this type of imperialism was not imitated by the other foreign traders: generally speaking the European empires were still sea-based. The larger Asian countries, such as India, remained in control of their own affairs, while China and Japan were following a policy of exclusion. Nevertheless the commerce between Asia and Europe was firmly established, and was steadily growing. Moreover, whatever the governments in Peking and Tokyo might think about it, plenty of Asian merchants were doing well out of the new development and had a strong vested interest in its continuation. The Filipinos had, it is true, lost their political independence, but were fairly well contented. Some of the smaller sultans who had been overthrown were less resigned; but the victims most to be pitied were the peasants who were forced to serve the economic needs of customers they had never seen and knew nothing about.

The infiltration into America

Just as da Gama's voyage of 1498 started Europeans upon the penetration of Asia, so did Columbus' famous voyage of six years before usher in the conquest of large portions of the great double continent of America. At first, as you will remember, the European explorers regarded this double continent as a nuisance—a vast obstacle lying between them and their real goal, the spice islands. But before very long they found that America could yield them lavish wealth of another kind. Both Mexico and Peru are exceptionally rich in gold and silver. Since the main motive of their explorations was the desire to get rich, the Spanish now happily abandoned the search for spice and set about taking possession of these valuable mines.

Thus a completely different type of imperialism was practised in America from that which was shaping Asia. Mere control of ports was no good: whole territories must be conquered, and a start was of course made with Mexico and Peru. The existing governments in these areas were overthrown and the European conquerors set about the task of sending loaded treasure-ships back to Spain. But they had no intention of doing any rough work themselves, and they compelled the native inhabitants, whom they called 'Indians', to labour in the mines and to work for them on their farms.

The American Indians, however, proved to be lacking in stamina. They could not face the rigours to which they were subjected, and they died like flies. This presented the Spanish with a problem. Even if they had been willing themselves to undertake manual labour, the climate was too hot for them. They therefore looked round for an alternative source of labour. It was at this point that an English seaman, John Hawkins, hit upon the revolting idea of bringing African slaves to America. He established a regular trading connection, going first from England to West Africa, where he either captured, or more often bought, numbers of Negro men and women. These unfortunate victims were herded on to the ships and confined in the holds. The conditions in which they made the voyage across the Atlantic, which might last seven weeks, were unspeakable; and always many of the human cargo died from their sufferings. Those who survived were sold in the slave markets of the Spanish colonies. They never saw their native land again; they rarely saw their own families. The Spanish purchasers could buy whom they fancied, without any reference to friendship or family ties. Moreover, once they had secured their human property, they could beat them or ill-treat them according to their whim, for the slaves had no rights and no redress in law.

The Negroes are a hardy people, however, with great powers of endurance. They came to terms with their unhappy lot, served their masters well, settled down, married one another and begot children, who were of course slaves from birth. This natural increase, reinforced by the continuing slave-trade, led to the establishment of a whole race of black-skinned people living among the brown-skinned natives and the white-skinned conquerors.

The Spanish and Portuguese spread over the whole of America south of the 30th Parallel. Towns and cities were built, and in the rural areas huge agricultural estates grew up, where sugar, cotton and tobacco were produced for the markets of Europe. But throughout the sixteenth century the most highly prized of all American exports were the gold and silver. Shipload after shipload was sent across the Atlantic, and the whole economy of Europe was changed as a result. Whereas in the Feudal Ages, wages and rents had often been paid in kind, now money became the basis of exchange, and the system of capitalism developed. The economists of the day, who believed firmly in mercantilism, were delighted at the influx of gold, though later they grew puzzled when they found that the final effect of the imports was to raise prices rather than to increase wealth.

This failure to understand the true nature of wealth brought about the downfall of Spain. In the middle of the century her power and prestige were colossal, and she was the terror of Europe. But before another fifty years had passed, her authority dwindled. She now no longer counted for much in Europe, though she succeeded in retaining her hold over her American colonies for another two centuries.

3 The Middle East from 1500 to 1800

In the year 1500 the people of Europe were mainly preoccupied with their own intellectual activities. They were also thrilled by the great voyages of discovery, while a good deal of energy was going into their own internal wars and quarrels. Nevertheless, in the midst of all this activity, they were casting uneasy glances towards the Balkan Peninsula in the south-east, where the Ottoman Turks—a warlike and ambitious people—had recently entrenched themselves.

The Turks originally came from central Asia, and during the thirteenth century a group known as the Seljuk Turks had conquered most of the Middle East from the Arabs. They were irresistible on the battlefield, but in one sense it was the Arabs who had conquered them, for the Turks were converted to the religion of their defeated foes and became Muslims. The Seljuk Empire later broke up into a number of small states scattered over the Middle East, some of them Turkish and some Arab. About the year 1300 a Turk called Othman founded one such little state in the north-west corner of the peninsula lying between the Mediterranean and the Black Sea, which was then called Asia Minor but has since acquired the name of Turkey. Othman's descendants were better warriors than their neighbours, and they began to build up a new empire. Moreover, unlike their Seljuk predecessors, they began to cast predatory eyes on Europe.

Just across the Bosporus lay the Byzantine Empire, the last surviving remnant of the mighty power of ancient Rome. A thousand years earlier, in 330 A.D., the Emperor Constantine had come to the conclusion that the Roman Empire was too large and cumbersome to defend itself; so he divided it into two parts—the western half which still had Rome as its capital, and the eastern half centred on the city of Byzantium. This city he re-built and named Constantinople in honour of himself. In the succeeding centuries the Western Roman Empire was completely destroyed, but the Eastern—or Byzantine—Empire lived on. At first the emperors held sway over much of the Middle East, but after the Arab prophet Mohammed had founded the new religion of Islam in the seventh century, they lost their hold over the Middle East and even over Asia Minor. But though their political power steadily dwindled, their magnificent and impregnable capital remained—a great storehouse of culture and the principal centre of the Greek Orthodox Church.

54

By the fourteenth century the diminished empire lacked the strength to resist the Othman (or Ottoman) Turks. Constantinople itself still defied attack, but the Turks had little difficulty in bypassing the city and invading the hinterland of the Balkans. They then established themselves in Greece. At the same time they were also spreading their power all over Asia Minor. Their success was not entirely unbroken and in 1402 they suffered a severe defeat at the hands of the Mongols, but within half a century they had so far recovered that in 1453 they achieved what had hitherto been thought impossible—they stormed and captured Constantinople. Many of the city's scholars fled to Italy, and this former stronghold of Christianity was swallowed up by Islam. Even the great cathedral of Saint Sophia was turned into a Muslim mosque.

After this the tide of Turkish success swept on triumphantly. Early in the sixteenth century they added Syria and Egypt to their domains, and soon they had imposed their rule over the whole of the Middle East.

The Turkish onslaught on Europe

The Turks owed their success very largely to the fact that they were

The cathedral of St Sophia, Constantinople. This great church was turned into a Muslim mosque when the Turks captured the city in 1453.

well-disciplined and skilful soldiers. This enabled them to win victories over the Arabs whom they conquered, and over the Persians whom they defied. But in fighting Europeans they had a special incentive, for ever since the First Crusade had been fought at the end of the eleventh century, there had been open hostility between Muslims and Christians. When the Turks were converted to Islam, they eagerly embraced this ancient quarrel, and in the sixteenth and seventeenth centuries it was their aim to overrun Europe, replacing the cross of Christ by the crescent of Islam. The main onslaughts against Europe were led by the Sultan Suleiman the Magnificent, who reigned from 1520 to 1566.

Suleiman was a tireless fighter and as soon as he came to the throne, he immediately set about extending his power northward through the Balkans. He captured Belgrade in 1521, and after winning the Battle of Mohacs in 1526, he took possession of all southern and central Hungary. In 1529 Suleiman led his victorious troops into Austria itself and actually laid siege to Vienna. The siege did not last long, for the rulers of Europe, horrified at this penetration by the infidels to the foremost capital of the continent, the very seat of government of the Holy Roman Empire, rallied to its defence and relieved the city within less than a month. But though Vienna was saved, the Turks remained in Hungary, and Suleiman continued to threaten Austria until his death.

Nor were his victories won only on land. He was also extending his power steadily, from east to west, through the Mediterranean Sea. Rhodes was captured in 1522; Tripoli (now Libya) in 1556; and Tunis in 1570, a few years after Suleiman's death.

Naturally the Europeans made considerable efforts to resist this perpetual aggression. The Holy Roman Empire, which was right in the line of advance, was constantly at war with Suleiman and later with his successors; while the Venetians were roused to fierce resistance against the Turkish domination of the Mediterranean, which had for centuries been under their own commercial control. In 1537 a Holy League against the Muslims was formed between Venice, the Pope and the Emperor. The League did not achieve much and before the end of three years Venice was obliged to cede more territories to Suleiman, though it is true that he would probably have done even better if the league had never been formed. In 1571 another Holy League was formed, and even succeeded in winning a resounding naval victory at Lepanto (off western Greece) under the great Austrian commander Don John.* But despite

---

* Don John was the illegitimate son of the Emperor Charles V, and a half-brother of Philip II of Spain, of both of whom we shall hear more in Chapter 4.

Map 3—The Turkish Empire in the eighteenth century

this encouraging triumph, the war ended once again in a Turkish success, and the new sultan, Selim II, wrested the island of Cyprus from the Venetians.

After this the Turks left Europe alone for a while, though of course they continued to administer the extensive European lands that were within their empire. But for the best part of a hundred years their attention was turned mainly to the east, where they continued their long record of success. About 1640 the Ottoman Empire reached its widest extent, but a few years later Sultan Mohammed IV, who was weak and ineffective, came to the throne. Renewed squabbles broke out with Austria, and the Turks at first suffered some reverses. In 1683, however, they were back on their old form, and for the second time they besieged Vienna. This time the siege lasted for two months, and the peoples of Europe were sufficiently shaken to make another united effort against the infidels. The Pope demanded support for a last Crusade. In response to this appeal France, Venice, Russia and Poland all came to Austria's aid. By far the greatest service was rendered by the Poles—an unusual circumstance, as their peculiar governmental system of an elected monarchy usually precluded them from playing any effective part in European affairs. The system was open to much bribery, as well as foreign interference, and often brought unsuitable men to the throne. But in 1683, by a fortunate chance, the reigning king was John Sobieski. He was a brilliant general and successfully raised the siege. But though driven back from Vienna, the Turks obstinately carried on the war until

1699, when they were at last forced to yield some of their recent gains to Austria and Poland.

The greatest days of the Ottoman Empire were over, but the Sultans remained masters of the Middle East and still retained their power over the major part of the Balkan peninsula.

The commercial life of the Middle East

We have seen that from the military point of view the history of Turkey throughout the sixteenth century, and for much of the seventeenth century, was a story of unbroken success. In the economic field, however, the picture was not so rosy. For the principal event of the year 1498 was destined to have serious effects on the Middle East. You will remember that one of the main motives of the prolonged Portuguese effort to reach India was the desire to injure the Arab traders by diverting the immensely valuable spice trade from the Middle East. So after da Gama had landed in Calicut, the King of Portugal lost no time in assuming the resounding title of 'Lord of the Conquest, Navigation and Commerce of Ethiopia, Arabia, Persia and India'. He was thus declaring himself the controller of a large number of the sultan's subjects: nor was the boast an idle one, for the efficiency of Albuquerque did much to make good this claim. The Arabs put up the stiffest resistance that was in their power, but as they had no fire-arms they had no chance of success. It is interesting to note that on this point (though on no other) the Venetians were in complete agreement with the Turks. For the city of Venice was as much threatened as the port of Alexandria by the opening of the Cape Route. The Venetians therefore sold timber to the subjects of the Sultan in order that the latter might build battleships to fight the Portuguese.

When Suleiman the Magnificent came to the throne he was anxious to do all he could to ward off this Christian menace in the Arabian Sea. His troops habitually used fire-arms, and they had proved again and again that they were a match for European armies. But Suleiman was balked by the fact that there was as yet no Suez Canal. He had therefore no means of getting his Mediterranean fleet to the Red Sea. All he could do was to order his vassal, the ruler of Egypt, to engage the Portuguese, and this attempt failed.

Soon the majority of the spice trade was passing to Europe *via* the Cape of Good Hope. The cost of pepper brought to Europe this way was only one third of the cost involved in the overland route. Consequently Alexandria (once the leading port of the Middle East) dwindled

58

from a great city to a small town, and the prosperity of Egypt vanished. The surrounding farmers, having lost most of their customers, drifted away, and the region sank to the level of subsistence agriculture.

Nevertheless the flow of trade through the Middle East never dried up completely. Not even Albuquerque could exert absolute control over the whole of the Arabian Sea and the Indian Ocean, and a certain number of Arab ships slipped through his net. Silks, spices, dyes and coffee continued to pass up the Red Sea or the Persian Gulf, and thence overland to the Mediterranean. Caravans of up to six hundred camels were still fairly common; and despite the hostility between Europe and Turkey, Venice signed a treaty with the Sultan in 1521 which gave her merchants special concessions to handle the European end of this trade. Venetians residing in the Turkish Empire were even to be allowed special tax exemptions and the right to live according to their own laws instead of obeying those of the Empire. Treaties of this type were made later with other European powers as well, and were known as 'capitulations'. The word capitulation in this case carried no suggestion of yielding, but merely referred to the conditions of the agreement.

The Venetians, however, though they were still able to bargain with the sultans for privileges, and though in the intervals of such bargaining they organised leagues against the Sultan, had really had their day. The leading role in Mediterranean commerce was now being played by the French.

The foreign policy of France in the first half of the sixteenth century was in many ways extraordinary. You will recall (Chapter 1) that the Reformation began in Europe in 1517, and that though the new ideas gained many supporters in the Holy Roman Empire, both the Emperor and the King of France remained staunch members of the Roman Church. One would therefore expect to find these two monarchs close allies. But in fact the Emperor Charles V (1519-1555) and Francis I of France (1515-1547) were bitter enemies. Even so, one would still expect that Francis would have confined to Europe his search for allies against the Holy Roman Empire. On the contrary, as early as 1536, only seven years after the first siege of Vienna, he signed a treaty with the arch-infidel himself—Suleiman the Magnificent. The agreement was directed mainly against Charles, but it provided also for granting to French traders privileges equal to those enjoyed by the Venetians. Having once gained a footing in the region, the French succeeded before long in completely ousting the Venetians, whose once-glorious sun was now waning. Perhaps because both governments were in perpetual conflict

59

with the Holy Roman Empire, a very cordial friendship grew up between Constantinople and Paris.

On a lower level, however, the French merchants fared worse, for the Ottoman Turks expressed open contempt for Europeans. Indeed the French traders went in such constant danger of insult and even of violence that they habitually wore Turkish dress in order to escape notice. It was only towards the end of the eighteenth century, when

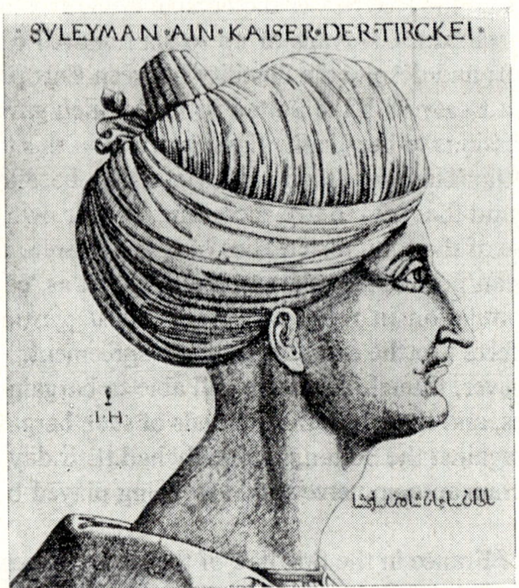

SULEIMAN
THE
MAGNIFICENT

Turkish power had definitely declined, that the foreign merchants ventured to proclaim their presence openly. Even when things were at their worst, however, they still found it worth their while to be insulted and even to be described by local officials as 'naked and hungry barbarians', for they made immense profits. In this acceptance of humiliation in the interests of money-making, they resembled the European merchants in China who doggedly endured insults in Canton.

Shortly after the French had established their commercial influence in the Middle East, the English tried to take advantage of the enterprise; but they offered for sale the good woollen cloth which had an excellent reputation in Europe but was too thick and hot to appeal to the Arabs. So the French, whose wares were more acceptable, kept what was almost a monopoly. In the late eighteenth century, however, the British returned.* By then they had control of a large part of India and were

* In 1707 England and Scotland were united into a single state.

regularly sending cargo-ships back to their own country. Warren Hastings, a British Governor in Bengal, made an arrangement with Egypt by which cargoes were sent by ship up the Red Sea and then transported overland to the Mediterranean. This more than halved the travelling-time to London, but the concession was soon withdrawn. It had only been forthcoming because Egypt had temporarily rebelled against the Sultan. As soon as the authority of Constantinople was re-established, the French monopoly was restored.

The Sultans, however, had by now lost most of their former strength. Before many years had passed, Egypt again revolted. This time it was the French, not the British, who took advantage of the occasion: under their great general, Napoleon Bonaparte, they landed an invading army —which they would never have ventured to do if their old ally had been in control. This attempt to conquer Egypt came to nothing, but the presence of the French soldiers in the country for some few years had a lasting effect. For the first time the people were given a glimpse of what good government could be; and afterwards they never again accepted quietly the misrule of the Turks.

The Turkish system of government

Although the Turks were—at their best—excellent fighters, they were rarely good administrators. Suleiman, the great sultan of the sixteenth century, was however an exception to the general rule, and the Turks themselves appreciated his unusual qualities. It was the Europeans who called him The Magnificent: his own subjects named him The Lawgiver, because he issued a whole code of laws controlling the tenure of land. He also paid attention to water-supply, always a matter of vital importance in the Middle East. He greatly improved the supply to Mecca and Jerusalem, and by digging canals in Iraq did something to control the frequent floods which had formerly been a scourge in that region. Nor were his interests limited to purely practical matters. Like many of his contemporary rulers in Europe, he was a keen patron of art and architecture. He built four magnificent mosques in Constantinople, and he was himself a poet.

Unfortunately Suleiman had few imitators. Most Turkish rulers— both the Sultans and the provincial governors—completely neglected irrigation, with the result that many formerly productive areas sank back into desert. This caused terrible hardship to the peasants, who indeed led a miserable existence under Ottoman rule. The main trouble was that the Turkish army, which won for itself such fame, had to be maintained. This need overrode all other considerations, so that the sole task of a provincial governor was to raise taxes and provide an adequate number of men for military service. If this was done no questions were asked, and no administrative skill or training was therefore required. And as numerous opportunities existed for pocketing a portion of the tax-money, there were always many candidates for office: the prize usually went to the man who offered the largest bribe. Consequently there was no continuity of rule at all, and governors often held office for only a year at a time. This deplorable system vitiated what was good in Turkish rule, for there were a few good features. Promotion, for example, was open to members of any race. It is true that this generous concession was more or less forced upon the Turks, since they were a minority in their large empire and could not fill all the posts themselves. Nevertheless rights of citizenship were open to any man—provided that he spoke the Turkish language and conformed to the Muslim faith. Although the latter condition debarred the Christians from government service, they were not treated with undue harshness.

The great fault of Turkish rule was, however, the complete absence of any sense of responsibility towards the ruled. Their welfare was never considered, and the peasants in particular were treated as mere beasts of burden. This meant that the heart of the Empire was rotten.

Turkey and Russia

Consequently the military triumphs which had added glory to the Ottoman Empire in its early days, were not maintained. In 1640 the Empire reached its peak, and even up to the first quarter of the eighteenth century the Sultans could hold their own. Peter the Great of Russia, who reigned from 1682 to 1725, and whose policy was to expand his country's trade with the West, was desperately anxious to acquire warm-water ports that would give his ships access to the Mediterranean. He thus tried hard to wrest from the Turks a portion of the land round the Black Sea, but failed to do so. Half a century later, the Russian Empress Catherine made the same attempt successfully and without much difficulty. Russia, however, was not to prove a serious enemy until after 1815.

Turkey and Persia

During the seventeenth and eighteenth centuries the Turkish sultans directed most of their military energies against Persia, despite the fact that this eastern neighbour was another Muslim power. For the Muslims, like the Christians in Europe, were divided by religious quarrels. The Turks belonged to the Sunni sect, while the Persians adhered to the Shiah branch of Islam. This difference gave rise to constant hostility between the two powers, and they were perpetually struggling for the domination of Iraq, which occupied a sort of no man's land between them and was a coveted prize because its great twin rivers, the Tigris and Euphrates, supplied excellent farming land and also functioned as a vital trade route. Both empires had reached their greatest heights at about the same time, for between 1587 and 1629 Persia was under the rule of an outstanding Shah called Abbas I. Like Suleiman, he was interested in canals and in architecture. He built some splendid palaces in his new capital of Isfahan, and he did much to encourage Persian trade and industry, especially the manufacture of carpets. He was also an able administrator, and he achieved considerable success in war. During his reign the Turks were held in check; but later the two powers waged a ding-dong struggle which weakened both without benefiting either. The Turks, who had captured Baghdad in 1638, retained that city, together with the control which it gave them over the valley of the Tigris and the Euphrates, and thus appeared to be the victors in the long struggle.

By 1800, however, the Ottoman Empire was really a hollow shell, ready to fall before any resolute attack.

The world in 1600

In the last chapter we followed events in the Turkish Empire far beyond the year 1600, but we must now go back to that year and take a glance at the situation in each region of the world at that point of time.

THE MIDDLE EAST

The sixteenth century had been a period of mingled good fortune and disaster for the Middle East. The Portuguese had dealt a terrible blow to the commercial prosperity of the Arabs by diverting the spice trade to the African route. On the other hand an unexpected ally had been found in France, and by the year 1600 the worst effects of the disaster were beginning to wear off. The trading class was therefore beginning once again to revive. But the Egyptian peasants had been ruined, and the agriculture of the whole Turkish Empire was in a decadent condition. Politically, however, the sultans were at the height of their success. Their repeated efforts to invade Europe had been beaten back, but they had extended their power right along the coast of North Africa. Further east, Persia, under Shah Abbas I, was enjoying a period of triumphant achievement, comparable with the Renaissance that had taken place earlier in Europe.

INDIA

India was in much better shape in 1600 than she had been a century before. From 1526 the Muslim empire of the north had been ruled by a strong dynasty known as the Great Moguls. Akbar, the greatest of all these rulers, was on the throne, having succeeded in 1556, and had steadily increased his political control until his dominions spread far to the south. Moreover he was a statesmanlike monarch who cherished a vision of national unity, and he took steps to weld his Muslim and his Hindu subjects into a single whole. He had friendly relations with the Portuguese, and his empire had suffered no serious ill-effects from their intrusion into the region.

THE REST OF SOUTHERN ASIA

The rest of Southern Asia, on the other hand, had suffered considerably during the sixteenth century. In 1500 the traders and sultans and others who were in touch with public events knew that Vasco da Gama had visited Calicut. The expedition had made quite a sensation, but no one in Asia realised at that time the significance of the European voyage. By 1600, however, nearly the whole spice trade of south Asia had come under Portuguese control. They had established bases on the Indian coast, in Colombo, in Malacca and in the East Indies, and they were also seeking to supervise all the commercial shipping in the Indian Ocean. It seemed that their sea-empire was securely founded and likely to last a long time, but in fact a small Dutch fleet had entered the area only five years before in 1595. The situation in 1600, therefore, already held seeds of change.

In the Philippine Islands the Spanish were firmly establishing their imperialist rule.

CHINA

China was not as strong in 1600 as she had been in 1500, for the empire was experiencing the kind of decline that recurred at intervals right through Chinese history. The Ming Dynasty, once so powerful, was no longer producing capable and effective rulers. This weakness at the centre affected the whole of the country, and there was a good deal of unrest and discontent. The empire however still presented an uncracked front to foreigners. The Portuguese had been given limited trading rights in Macao, and a few Spanish merchants had been admitted to Canton; but the Europeans knew that they were there only on sufferance and were obliged to submit to whatever conditions the Chinese authorities imposed on them.

JAPAN

For Japan the sixteenth century had been a period of revival. Nibunga and Hideyoshi had restored the Shogunate to its old strength, and the country was once again under firm government. The rebellious feudal lords had been suppressed, and a new era of national prosperity had begun.

SIBERIA

During the sixteenth century Siberia's isolation from her neighbours had been broken. By 1555 Russia had succeeded in asserting her over-lordship over part of the region, and was receiving an annual tribute in the form of 1000 sables. Then from 1580 onwards Russians began a slow but gradual process of emigrating eastward into these vast and sparsely populated lands.

RUSSIA

The passage of a hundred years had brought several important changes to Russia. In the first place the country had steadily expanded, both in Europe and in Asia. Moreover, Ivan the Terrible, who reigned from 1533 to 1584, had adopted an entirely new policy. Hitherto the Russians had shown no interest in Europe, but Ivan determined to try to forge links with the west. He even changed the name of the country and his own title. He came to the throne as Prince of Muscovy, but later styled himself Czar of Russia, choosing the title of czar because it is a form of the old Roman word Caesar. Fate played into his hands by sending to his court some English seamen who had been wrecked off the Russian coast. This led to the establishing of diplomatic relations with England. Even now Russia remained an unknown quantity to most Europeans, but a start had been made.

EUROPE

The sixteenth century had been an immensely eventful period for Europe. The eastern part of the continent had gone in constant fear of the Turks, so that for the people living in that area the century had been one of unease. On the other hand the countries on the western seaboard had followed up the discoveries made at the end of the preceding century and established new empires overseas. So far only two European states had played an important part in this development—Portugal and Spain; but the seamen of other western powers, notably England, Holland and France, had made a name for themselves during the century. Portugal derived considerable profits from her maritime empire in Asia, but the outstanding success of the sixteenth century was Spain. With the vast treasure that she was harvesting from the New World, and the prestige of her new conquests, Spain dominated Europe until the 1580's. Then there came a sudden collapse. She suffered some serious military defeats, but the real cause of the decline was that her new-found wealth did not last. As the science of economics was not understood at that time, no one in the sixteenth century realised that the great influx of gold and silver into Europe was likely to result in a rise in prices and a consequent fall in the value of money. Spain was of course the principal sufferer, but the whole of Europe was affected to some extent.

Although the economic processes were not yet understood, the mastery of knowledge in other fields of science had proceeded apace throughout the century, and was still being energetically pursued. There had also been great changes in the political organisation of the continent.

National boundaries were becoming much more definite and exclusive, and kings enjoyed far greater power than they had a hundred years earlier. Moreover the sense of European unity which had still survived in 1500 was now gone. The events of the Reformation had removed the connecting link imposed by a common obedience to the Pope, and had contributed to the rivalry between nations.

By 1600 a failure in the Portuguese dynasty had led to that country being swallowed up for a time in Spain; but even this increase of strength could not disguise the fact that Spain was on the decline. On the other hand England was established as an important state, and Holland—a newly created republic—was rising into prominence. France was distracted by civil wars, and Italy and central Europe were still parcelled into little states. The danger from Turkey was not completely over, but was not nearly so threatening as it had been at the beginning of the century.

AFRICA

The lives of the vast majority of Africans were no different in 1600 from what they had been in 1500. But in the west of the continent, along the Gulf of Guinea, a flourishing trade had been established with visiting European ships. It was now not only the Portuguese who called on their way to Asia; English seamen also made regular trips. Unfortunately the chief commodities in this commerce were human beings, who were bought by the Europeans and sold into slavery in Spanish America.

THE AMERICAS

The sixteenth century had brought extraordinary and profound changes to the American continents. The region lying to the north of the Gulf of Mexico remained more or less as it had been; but the mainland south of that point, as well as the West Indian islands, had been altered beyond belief. The Aztec and Inca empires—the only two states of any size—had both been conquered, and all the lesser tribes either defeated in battle or else won over to the Spanish cause. Everywhere the flag of Spain was flying; nor was this a symbol of remote control. Emigrants had come over in their thousands, and they had also introduced enormous numbers of African slaves. So that the political organisation, the social life, the towns and buildings, and even the racial character of the inhabitants, were all completely different from what they had been in 1500.

The only non-Spanish colony was Brazil, which belonged to Portugal.

AUSTRALIA AND NEW ZEALAND

Despite the fact that first Magellan and later Drake had sailed right round the world, neither Australia nor New Zealand had as yet been discovered by the people of any other continent. The inhabitants of these lands therefore continued to live their own life, undisturbed by outside influences.

4 Europe and the Divine Right of Kings

The theory of Divine Right

Every system of government has a theory behind it. Sometimes the men responsible for drawing up a constitution start with a particular theory, which they try to embody in the system they are devising. More often a type of government grows up first, and then interested and thoughtful people examine the system by which they live and seek to discover what it is precisely that 'makes it tick'.

In the Feudal Ages in Europe, political thinkers concentrated on the fact that all human activities can be divided into two categories—spiritual and secular. The Church was obviously the body which must control all the former activities, and the acknowledged head of the Church was the Pope. To his supreme authority every man and woman should bow in every matter relating to his religious devotions, his beliefs, his spiritual life and even his marriage. The Pope was therefore something much more than the lord of all the clergy: he exercised, through the bishops and priests of every land, a considerable influence over the ordinary man in the street and over the peasants in the fields. And the immense importance of the spiritual life was something of which the average European in those days was very conscious. Nevertheless there clearly are other facets of life, and every man owed to his king or other lord absolute obedience in secular matters. There were hundreds of such lords, but since western Europe was thought of as a single whole, the Holy Roman Emperor was deemed to be supreme over them all.

There were certain defects in this theory, the chief being an uncertainty as to the exact boundary between the authority of the Emperor and that of the Pope. Indeed a number of wars were fought on this very issue, despite the fact that such wars—or indeed any wars within Europe—were a direct contradiction of the core of the whole theory, which was the unity of Christendom. It is exceedingly difficult for any nation or community to live up to its political ideals; and the higher the ideals, the more frequent are the lapses. There was much that was fine and noble about this conception of unity and authority, and those who defied it felt obliged to make a considerable effort to justify their rebellion. Moreover, though the theory never exactly fitted existing circumstances, the facts roughly corresponded with it for a considerable period of time.

By the end of the sixteenth century, however, the political scene had fundamentally changed. The Holy Roman Emperor, whose position had never been as great in practice as it was in theory, had become merely one of several important rulers, while the Pope had been robbed by the Reformation of a large part of his authority. All the power lost by these potentates had been scooped up by the national kings, whose importance had increased immeasurably during the course of a hundred years.

During the Feudal Ages kings often had a hard time. Their authority was constantly being challenged by the great lords or barons, and unless they were gifted with outstanding talents, they found it extremely difficult to hold their own. The Feudal Ages came to an end when a number of causes combined to undermine the power of the feudal lords. One of the prime causes was the invention of gunpowder, which became known in Europe during the fourteenth century. The innovation took some time to come into general use, but once kings had cannon at their disposal, walls ceased to be an effective defence; consequently great nobles began to live in mansions rather than in castles, and rebellions became far less common and far less successful. The kings were not the only ones to benefit from the decline in the power of the barons. The common people were also immensely relieved, for they had suffered terribly from rebellions and civil wars. Consequently they were prepared to give all their support to any king who could keep the lords in order. The merchants also had a strong vested interest in the preservation of law and order. This class began to grow in importance with the great voyages of discovery, which brought new commodities into the European markets and gave a tremendous boost to trade. In every country the merchants used their wealth and influence to back the kings, who at the end of the first quarter of the sixteenth century enjoyed a degree of power that would have dazzled their predecessors of a hundred years before.

Then came the Reformation to load the kings with yet more power. When Martin Luther pinned his thesis to the church door at Wittenburg, he was taking a stand on religious principle, and not concerning himself with politics. He had however set an example of defying authority, which before long incited the German peasants to revolt. Luther was horrified by this outbreak of violence, and did all he could to help the local princes to suppress it. They succeeded in doing so, and then after many disputes between those who supported Luther and those who remained loyal to Rome, they met at Augsburg in 1555, and laid it down that in the interests of peace, every man must conform to the religious views of his sovereign. This idea was later adopted by most of the other kings of Europe. In the Feudal Ages every man, from the poorest peasant to the king himself, had been obliged to bow before the spiritual authority of the Pope; but now the kings claimed the right to dictate to their subjects what they must believe. In some countries—notably England—the king also became the Supreme Head of a national Church. Even the kings who remained Roman Catholics were given extra powers by the Pope, so that they could enjoy a prestige comparable with that of their Protestant neighbours.

By this time the old unity of Europe had been completely shattered. The invention of printing, and even the Renaissance itself, had contributed to this result. For now that books were cheap, they were written in every language of Europe and translations of old works were made. Consequently scholars were no longer bound closely together by a common use of Latin. The reading public multiplied rapidly, and each nation read in its own language, and so became more conscious of the special national character which made it different from every other country. The feeling of nationalism, which was to become such a tremendous force in the world in the nineteenth and twentieth centuries, was still in its infancy; but it was a lusty infant which already made its presence felt by crying aloud. The citizens of each nation, stirred by this emotion, found it natural to express it by an enthusiastic loyalty to their sovereign, who seemed to symbolise the nation.

These developments, which were taking place all over Europe, can be seen most clearly in England. There, during most of the fifteenth century, the whole country had been torn by the Wars of the Roses. Rival factions of nobles were struggling for power, and there was no authority strong enough to control or to protect the common people from the nuisance of perpetual disorders. At last Henry VII (1485-1509) secured the throne and proved himself strong enough to keep the feudal lords in check. In this task he had the wholehearted support of the growing middle class and of the people, and he was thus enabled to build up his power steadily throughout his reign. His son Henry VIII (1509-1547), having started at the top of the ladder, so to speak, became even more despotic, and eventually seized spiritual power. He was no Lutheran. In fact he strongly disapproved of Luther's views; but he became impatient of the authority of the Pope when the latter forbade him to divorce his wife, and so he persuaded Parliament to declare the King the Supreme Head of the Church in England. During the next two reigns the English people were subjected to a bewildering series of religious changes, all carried out in the name of the sovereign. Then under Elizabeth I (1558-1603) the English monarchy reached its peak of power. For not only did Elizabeth by her policy inaugurate the Church of England, she also inspired intense devotion among her subjects. It has been said that the emotion of nationalism was in its infancy in the sixteenth century; but it certainly found its strongest expression in England in 1588, the year in which the Spanish Armada was repulsed. And no sovereign was ever more successful in embodying national pride than Elizabeth, or Gloriana as her adoring subjects called her.

Obviously the political theory of the Feudal Ages no longer had any relation to the political facts of Europe. Some new explanation must be sought. The Europeans of the sixteenth century differed sharply about the way in which God should be worshipped; but they were unanimous in acknowledging His authority over the world. If kings now enjoyed enormous power, it must be because God permitted them to do so. It seemed likely therefore that God, the Supreme Ruler of men, had delegated a portion of His authority to certain human beings. These chosen persons were born into a royal family not by chance but by the will of God. When the death of all senior members of the family had brought them to their inheritance, they were crowned and anointed with holy oil in a church by a bishop. This solemn ceremony finally set them apart from their fellow men. It was the duty of every Christian to obey his sovereign without question, for to disobey the king was in effect to disobey God. Even a bad king must be obeyed.

By the end of the sixteenth century the theory of the Divine Right of Kings was generally accepted all over Europe.

The republican revolt in Holland

The theory of Divine Right was however no more successful than any other political theory in commanding universal acceptance. Most Europeans of the time accepted it, but by no means all. Some nations, by refusing to accept the idea, developed new and important political theories of their own. Among these were the Dutch—the first people to carry out a sustained national revolt against their king.

The name Netherlands, or Low Countries, was in those days applied to the whole of the low-lying region now occupied by both Belgium and Holland. Then, as now, the people of this region fell naturally into two distinct groups, speaking two different languages. They were also divided

72

by religion, since the seven provinces of the north were Protestant, while those in the south adhered to the Roman Church. Despite these differences, however, both regions came under the rule of King Philip II of Spain.

Of all the despots of the sixteenth century, Philip wielded the most power, owned the most wealth, and ruled by far the widest dominions. He belonged to an interesting family which had risen to extraordinary heights of prosperity in the course of three generations. Philip's father had been the famous Emperor Charles V, who was born in 1500. Before he was out of his 'teens Charles entered into an unprecedented inheritance. Each of his four grandparents had ruled a separate territory. One grandfather, Maximilian, had ruled Austria and ended his life as Holy Roman Emperor. He married Mary of Burgundy, who was the ruler of the Netherlands in her own right. Their son, Philip the Fair, was therefore heir to both these domains. Meanwhile, further west, Queen Isabella of Castile had become the wife of King Ferdinand of Aragon. Their daughter, Joanna, who was thus heir to the whole of Spain, married Philip the Fair. Since Philip died young and Joanna became insane, their child Charles became the sole monarch of all these territories. His dominions even included Sicily and southern Italy, which had for some time been under the rule of Aragon. To set the seal upon this fantastic acquisition of power, the Electors of the Holy Roman Empire actually chose this young man of nineteen to be Emperor. His great fortune proved to be too great to be enjoyable. He spent his reign in rushing distractedly from one part of his dominions to another, chasing difficulties which he was never quite able to overcome. The Spanish conquest of South America added to his responsibilities, while the Reformation caused him endless worry. Eventually it all became too much for him, and in 1555 he abdicated. Determined that his successor should not be loaded with so great a burden, he divided his inheritance. Austria and the office of Emperor went to his brother Ferdinand, while Spain, Italy and the Netherlands came under the control of his son Philip II.

Despite the loss of Austria, Philip II still ruled an enormous empire, for by this time the Spanish penetration of the Americas was almost complete. Moreover their conquest of the Philippines was to begin in 1565, while in 1580 Philip succeeded to the throne of Portugal, which brought with it control of the Portuguese Empire in Asia and in Brazil. Thus Philip eventually ruled dominions even larger than those of his father. He seemed the very embodiment of the theory of Divine Right, and his contemporaries might well think that such an accumulation

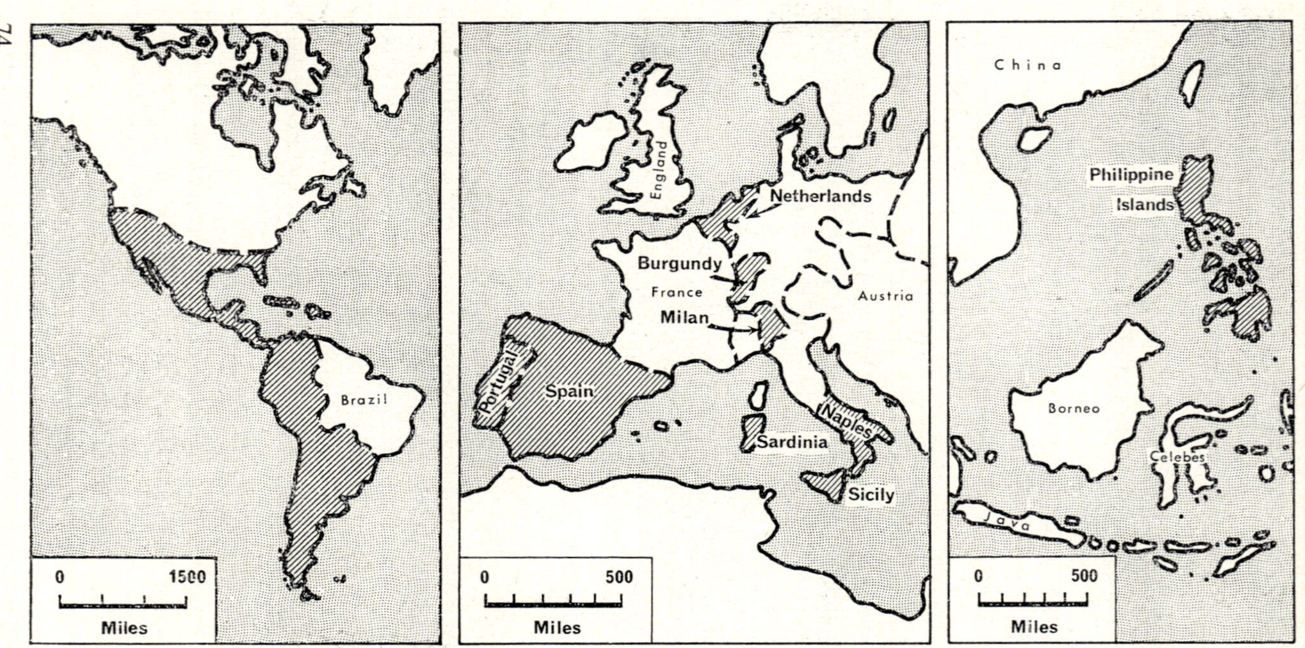

Map 4—Philip II's dominions in the Americas, Europe and Asia. The acquisition of Portugal in 1580 also gave Philip control of the Portuguese overseas empire in Brazil and in Asia.

of power in the hands of one man must represent some special purpose of God. And Philip himself believed most sincerely that he was a vice-regent of the Almighty. As a good Roman Catholic, he felt himself in duty bound to root out Protestantism from all his dominions. In Spain, Italy, Portugal and even the southern Netherlands this was an easy task; but in the northern provinces of the Netherlands he ran into serious trouble.

The Dutch, who were ardent and convinced Protestants, bitterly resented the activities of the Inquisition in their land. But their discontent was not purely religious: they were also moved by feelings of nationalism, in which they were at one with their Roman Catholic neighbours in the southern provinces. Nationalism blossomed rather earlier in the Netherlands than elsewhere, though it is possible that the opposition against Philip might have been less formidable if his government had been more efficient. In his palace near Madrid the King was completely out of touch with his subjects in northern Europe, and regarded them mainly as a source of revenue. The heavy taxes he imposed on them, taken in conjunction with religious persecution, roused them to fury, and in 1568 they rose in rebellion.

At first Philip expected that with the vast resources at his command, he would have no difficulty in subduing this small province. He soon found, however, that although he sent out to the Netherlands a succession of famous generals, including his half-brother Don John, the hero of Lepanto, he could not suppress the rebels, who were fighting on their own ground and who could often retire to islands, protected by stretches of water too shallow for the Spanish warships to enter. The Spanish soldiers hated the conditions in which they had to serve, and on occasions boredom and exasperation caused them to break out in savage onslaughts against the civilian population. This increased the hatred of the Netherlanders, and made a peaceful settlement of the dispute more and more difficult to attain.

In 1579 however Philip resorted to the astute move of trying to divide the northern provinces from those of the south. To the latter he offered actual self-government, provided only that they would recognise him as their nominal sovereign. Since the people of these provinces were Roman Catholics, their only grievances were political, and they therefore accepted the offer. But despite this defection of their allies, the Dutch refused to compromise. On the contrary they redoubled their efforts to drive out the Spanish. Their leader was Prince William of Orange, known as William the Silent, who proved to be a most able general. It was a terrible blow to them when in 1584 William was assassinated (possibly at the instigation of Spain), but still they carried on the struggle. They were desperately in need of help, however, and therefore made an appeal to Queen Elizabeth of England. Elizabeth had always carefully avoided throwing in her lot with any extreme group of Protestants. On the other hand she was certainly not a member of the Roman Church, and her seamen had for years been in a state of undeclared war against Spain. This fact might have persuaded her to answer the Dutch appeal. She was however extremely reluctant to help any rebels, as she felt that this was a dangerous thing for a sovereign to do. Eventually, on balance, she decided to help the Dutch, and an English army was sent to the Netherlands.

In the event, Elizabeth's hesitation and fears were justified, for Philip now determined to engage in one splendid naval operation which should both crush the rebellion and—by conquering England—bring back an erring member into the Roman fold. He built his great fleet, the Invincible Armada, and despatched it to the English Channel in 1588. But the expedition was badly organised and under the wrong commander. Helped by the weather, which bedevilled the Spanish from the start, the English succeeded in scattering the great Armada. Only a small and battered remnant ever got back to Spain.

This catastrophe was a turning point in Philip's reign. He had spent a vast sum of money to no purpose, and he had been humiliated in the eyes of the whole of Europe. Spanish prestige never recovered, and neither the Dutch nor the English ever felt again the fear and respect which Philip had once commanded from them.

The revolt in the Netherlands dragged on for several years, but the issue was no longer in serious doubt. As early as 1595, only seven years after the defeat of the Armada, Dutch seamen managed to sail round the Cape of Good Hope to Indonesia, despite the fact that Spain, having absorbed the Portuguese Empire, was supposed to be controlling the route in order to fend off any rival powers. The success of the Dutch merchants in forming their East India Company in 1602 shows how little they had to fear from the Spanish. Philip II, whose later years were soured by defeat and disappointment, had died in 1595, and eventually in 1609 a truce was signed between his successor and the Netherlands. No final peace was made for another fifty years, but from 1609 onwards the Dutch were recognised by their neighbours as an independent and self-governing people.

The system of government which the Dutch adopted was a curious one. They owed their independent national status to a rebellion against their king, and this fact gave them a strong distaste for monarchy. It was therefore by common consent that they formed themselves into a kind of republic. But they never seriously settled down to the task of devising a constitution: they merely borrowed the working arrangements which had been hastily adopted during the revolt to enable seven separate provinces to fight under a single banner. The system developed in this haphazard way could hardly be described as sound, but somehow it worked, and the United Netherlands enjoyed a period of great prosperity and success during the seventeenth and eighteenth centuries.

But though officially republicans, the Dutch had not quite broken with the idea of monarchy, For during the rebellion they had become so accustomed to the leadership first of William the Silent, and later of his descendants, that they were reluctant to dispense with the invaluable family of Orange. They therefore retained the office of Stadtholder, undeterred by the fact that the holders of this office had formerly been the representatives of Spain. The Stadtholders, though having very little power compared with the other kings of that age, nevertheless carried out certain important functions, and handed on their power from father to son. In 1813 the then head of the family was raised to royal status by being made King of Holland.

The Limited Monarchy in England

The extreme supporters of the theory of Divine Right might declare that it was wicked, and in fact actually blasphemous, to rebel against any king; but discontented subjects who believed their sovereign to be inefficient and untrustworthy were not likely to be persuaded of this. Thus the Dutch subjects of Philip had waged determined and obstinate war against him at the end of the sixteenth century. In the seventeenth century a long struggle began in England which fundamentally changed the system of government in that country. The final result was not a republic, as in Holland; but the English monarchy was converted from a despotism to a controlled and limited monarchy.

The triumph of the Rule of Law

The issue at stake between the English kings and their subjects was really whether or not the Rule of Law should prevail. If the king is the supreme or sovereign power in the land, it follows that he can do whatever he thinks fit, and is above the law. If on the other hand the law is held to be supreme, then everyone, including the king himself, must obey it.

The early Stuart kings, James I (1603-1625) and Charles I (1625-1649), both firmly believed that they were ordained by God to rule as they chose. Laws were man-made, but the kings had divine authority, so that it was impertinent and impious for their subjects to attempt to coerce them. Parliament, the chief function of which was to pass laws, refused to subscribe to this view. Consequently every parliament that met in either of these reigns invariably ended in bitter quarrels. The kings held one trump card, since it lay with them to summon and dissolve Parliament; on the other hand they suffered from the grievous disadvantage of being largely dependent for money on the House of Commons, without whose consent no taxes could be raised. It was a period of rising prices, and the royal income was undoubtedly inadequate, but the Commons would rarely admit this. They accused the kings of extravagance, and usually refused to vote them any money unless their own grievances were first met.

The spearhead of this attack on royal power was the new middle class. We have seen how the voyages of discovery a hundred years earlier had led to an enormous increase in trade all over Europe. The English merchants had prospered with the rest, and soon formed a very important section of the population. During the Reformation under Henry VIII the monasteries were seized by the King and put up for sale. Many of the richer merchants bought up estates in this way and turned themselves into landed gentry. This entitled them to seek election to Parliament, and they soon made their presence felt in the House of Commons. Their prosperity and importance grew steadily; so did their longing for political power.

Under the Tudor despotism Parliament had counted for relatively little, but even while Elizabeth was still alive the Commons had occasionally pressed their demands upon her. When this happened the Queen, a woman of the greatest tact and shrewdness, gracefully gave in. But when she died in 1603 she was succeeded by her cousin James, the King of Scotland. As a figurehead for the nation's loyalty, he was a sad come-down. He was ungainly in appearance, spoke with a lisp, had a morbid fear of steel, and was given to doting in an undignified way on those whom he chose to make his favourites. There was nothing in him to command the adoration which had been lavished on 'Gloriana'. His son Charles was a figure of much greater dignity, but he was totally devoid of political insight. He had firm principles, but gave the impression of being untrustworthy because he believed that his Divine Right absolved him from the duty of keeping his word to his subjects.

78

After a series of altercations with the Commons, Charles decided in 1629 that in future he would do without Parliament altogether. This meant that he would be cut off from supplies, but he proposed to levy taxes on his own account. This was illegal, but Charles considered that he was above the law. He knew of course that the Commons would be furious at being by-passed in this manner; but if he could somehow avoid ever summoning another Parliament, they would have no chance to say what they thought about it. The King therefore embarked on a programme of economy, and for eleven years did very well. Unfortunately for him, however, he felt that it was his duty to uphold the Church of England in every part of his dominion. He was a Scot by birth, but neither he nor his father had any sympathy for the Calvinist Church in Scotland. James had in his youth suffered many humiliations from the republican-minded ministers of the Scottish Kirk; he had for years looked forward to inheriting the throne of England, and warmly approved of the Anglican system of bishops and archbishops which, he felt, provided a much more comfortable and dignified background for a king. Charles shared these views, and in 1637 he announced that in future the English Prayer Book must be used in every church in Scotland. But he had completely underrated the devotion of the Scots to their Kirk. They openly defied his instructions and in 1639 embarked on an armed revolt, known as the Bishops' War because those taking part declared that they would never accept the rule of bishops. Charles was taken by surprise and his careful budgeting was upset. He had contrived to find enough money, by hook or by crook, for his normal expenses; but he had no money with which to win a war. He was obliged to treat with the Scots, and to make an agreement with them which obliged him to pay their expenses.

This rash promise forced Charles to do what he had determined never to do: he had to summon another Parliament. The Commons met in an ugly mood. They were determined that the King should never again be allowed to rule without them, and before they would even consider voting the money Charles asked for, they began to demand concessions from him. The King was so furious that he dissolved Parliament (known as the Short Parliament) after only three weeks, but this high-handed gesture did not solve his difficulties. He still had to find money for the Scots who, by way of protest, invaded England for the second time.

In these circumstances Charles had no option but to summon Parliament once again, nor could he any longer dare to dismiss the members.

THE TRIAL OF CHARLES I

He was therefore at their mercy, and they took full advantage of the situation. Law after law was passed, all designed to prevent the King from ever again attempting to rule alone. This Parliament (the Long Parliament) even passed a measure to perpetuate its own life for as long as it pleased, and its chequered career lasted for more than twenty years. In 1640, determined to isolate the King, it brought about the arrest of his two most competent ministers and faithful servants. These were Thomas Wentworth, Earl of Strafford, and William Laud, Archbishop of Canterbury.

The arrest of Laud had other motives besides the wish to annoy the King. The creation of the Church of England under Elizabeth I had been a determined attempt to avoid religious strife by bringing the whole country into one fold. The Anglican Church was broad-based and intended to include both out-and-out Protestants and also those who favoured something closer to the Roman Church. But however broad-based it might be, there were still a certain number of men and women on either fringe who found that it did not meet their needs.

Most of these malcontents were extreme Protestants known as Puritans, who many years before had begged James I to consider their grievances. James, who was still haunted by his unhappy memories of the Scottish Calvinists, curtly refused to make any concessions; and during Charles's reign Archbishop Laud, who was a High Churchman, had pursued a steady policy of suppressing Puritanism. He sought out, and deprived of their livings, any Anglican clergy who had inclinations of that kind; and he prevented Puritans from speaking in public, from publishing books, and even from meeting together. This policy had the effect of narrowing the scope of the Church of England, but it did not stamp out Puritanism. On the contrary the movement grew apace and a number of Puritans were elected to the Long Parliament. They now took their revenge.

When a man as important as the Archbishop of Canterbury could be flung into the Tower, it was clear that authority was badly under-mined and that the King himself was in some danger. He was not only endangered but publicly humiliated by the loss of Strafford, a man who believed in the Divine Right of Kings, and who was so efficient in carry-ing out the commands of his own king that he had roused the fear and hatred of all Charles's enemies. Parliament attempted to try Strafford for treason; but treason meant treachery against the King, and no one could seriously deny that Strafford had served the King with absolute fidelity. This case could not, therefore, be proved, but his enemies were determined to destroy Strafford by one means or another, so a Bill of Attainder was brought against him. This was a device which had been used fairly often in the sixteenth century, and was in fact an Act of Parliament declaring that a certain person should be executed. It required, however, not only the support of both Houses of Parliament (which was of course forthcoming) but also the signature of the King. Charles, who loved his friend, refused for as long as he dared, but a howling mob outside the palace unnerved him, and at length he gave his consent to the execution.

After this things went from bad to worse between King and Parliament until civil war broke out in 1642. Neither side could command a majority of the nation. Indeed the whole of England was sharply divided between the two opposing sides. But Parliament had two great advantages in waging a war. First, they had the support of the merchant class and could therefore get funds; secondly, they had on their side Oliver Cromwell, who was not only an excellent general on the field of battle but also a brilliant organiser. It was largely owing to his efforts that in 1645 Charles lost the war. But though the Parliamentarians had proved their own military superiority, they had proved nothing else. Charles was still the King, and at that stage no one wished to deny the fact. Consequently there was something of a political stalemate for two or three years. Charles broke it by appealing to the Scots to send an army into England. This finally alienated his subjects, for the two kingdoms, though they had one king, were entirely separate in their government, and the English regarded the Scots as foreigners.

As soon as Charles was once again in their power, the leaders of Parliament brought him to trial for treason. Charles, who faced his final ordeal with great courage, took the same line as Strafford had taken. Treason, he said, meant treachery against the king. Obviously he could not be held guilty of treachery against himself; therefore he was innocent. But Parliament held that treason was action against the state—a crime of which any king might be guilty, and of which they could with some justice accuse Charles. In January 1649 the King was publicly beheaded.

His execution was a decisive blow struck against the theory of the Divine Right of Kings; but succeeding events were to show that England was not ready to be a republic. In the course of the next ten years four or five different types of republican government were tried, and they all failed. The only man strong enough to control the general chaos was Cromwell, who was consequently made Lord Protector. But he lacked the natural prestige that attaches to a king, and found himself obliged, if he was to rule at all, to seize more power than Charles had ever ventured to exercise. After Cromwell's death in 1658 there was no adequate successor to take his place, and there seemed nothing else to do but to recall the royal family. Charles I's son, who had fled to France at the time of his father's execution, was therefore invited back to England and crowned Charles II in 1660.

THE SUCCESSION TO THE ENGLISH THRONE

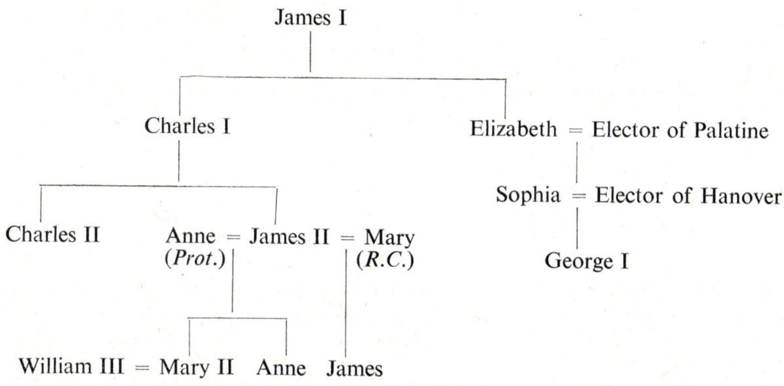

The new King was a shrewd man, and he realised that this restoration of the monarchy was not complete. If he should fall foul of Parliament, there was every probability that they would rise against him as they had against his father. He was therefore careful always to avoid any direct conflict. He kept his crown to the end, and died a king; but he never ventured to be a despot. By tact and caution he steered his way clear of any open dispute as to which was the sovereign power in the country—King or Parliament.

Charles II died in 1685, and having no legitimate son, was succeeded by his brother James, to whom tact and caution were entirely foreign. James was a Roman Catholic, and being also a believer in Divine Right, he thought it was not only his duty but his right, to try to restore the Roman Church in England. There were numerous laws on the statute book debarring Roman Catholics from holding government office or any command in the Army. James however regarded himself as above the law, and declared that all such regulations were suspended. But the Rule of Law had already triumphed over Divine Right, and James was soon to discover that he could not put the clock back. The Restoration of 1660 had shown that England could not do without a king altogether:

now the Revolution of 1688 showed that England would nevertheless only tolerate a king of her own choice.

This 'Glorious' or 'Bloodless' Revolution was carried out very quietly. For nearly four years Parliament had endured James's unpopular policy, because he was nearing sixty and when he died would be succeeded by his daughter Mary, who was married to the impeccably Protestant William of Orange, a member of the famous Dutch family. But James had married a young wife who was, like himself, a Roman Catholic; and when a son was born to him, the patience of Parliament broke. A group of members sent an invitation to William asking him to come over and take the throne of England for his wife and himself. After a little hesitation, William arrived with an army. James immediately fled abroad, and William and Mary were installed as joint sovereigns.

The absence of violence was a remarkable triumph for the Rule of Law. A king who broke the laws of England had been quietly deposed, and replaced by the choice of the law-making body, Parliament.

It was obvious to the new king that sovereignty had passed to Parliament, and this truth was immediately underlined in the Bill of Rights of 1689, an Act of Parliament which laid down certain clearly defined limitations to the authority of the monarch. William had no choice but to accept the measure, for his tenure of the throne depended entirely on the favour of Parliament.

The Party System

Meanwhile an important change had come over Parliament itself. There had always been from time to time a tendency for members to form small groups of like-minded men. But during the reign of Charles II this tendency had crystallised into the development of the Party System which is such an important feature of Parliament today.

The controversy which led to the formation of parties centred round the future James II, who was already deeply unpopular. It was known that he was a member of the Roman Church, and there were a number of people who wished an Act to be passed which would pass him over and transfer the succession to Charles's illegitimate son, the Duke of Monmouth. Charles was however opposed to the scheme. He had accepted a greatly reduced version of the theory of Divine Right, but he retained enough of the idea to believe that it was wrong to meddle with the natural succession. Since God had denied him any children by his legal wife, he assumed that it was God's will that James should be king. Those members of Parliament who wanted him to change his mind,

84

felt so strongly that they formed the habit of sitting together in one part of the House of Commons or the House of Lords, and voting in the same way on every bill. They were called by their opponents the Whigs, a name which really belonged to a very extreme group of Protestants in Ireland. They retorted by calling the supporters of Divine Right, Tories. Both names were intended in the first place to be insulting, but were later to be claimed with great pride.

Charles II was much too prudent to oppose the Whigs openly; but by playing his cards carefully, he was able to prevent them from passing the measure they wanted. But it was of course the Whigs who in 1688 sent the invitation to William. Consequently the new king (Mary was nominally his equal but in fact played little part in politics) felt obliged to choose all his ministers from that one party. This was a distinct limitation of royal power, for previously the kings had chosen their ministers where they pleased. Further limitations followed; for if the cabinet ministers were to be all of one party, it soon became clear that they must be selected from whichever party had just won an election, for no government that lacked a majority could hope to govern. So the electors were now indirectly controlling the king's choice.

The growth of the power of Parliament

William III only reigned for fourteen years, and long before his death Parliament had again become anxious about the succession. Shortly after the Revolution of 1688, an Act of Succession had laid it down that William and Mary should be succeeded by their own children. If neither of them had children, either by their present or by any later marriage, then Mary's sister Anne should succeed, and her children after her. This seemed to provide against accidents, but in the event there was a serious dearth of heirs. Mary, who died before her husband, had no children, and William did not remarry. Anne had a quantity of children but none of them grew up, so that when she succeeded in 1702, already middle-aged, there was no one to come after her other than the hated Stuarts, who were of course only too anxious to regain the crown.

Rather than allow another Roman Catholic to occupy the throne, Parliament were prepared to fix the succession on any relative of the English royal family, however remote, provided that he or she were a Protestant. They therefore selected Sophia, Electress of Hanover, who was a granddaughter of James I. Sophia died before Anne, but her son came to the throne as George I. He was completely foreign to the country, and neither he nor his son George II ever learned to speak

English. Nevertheless they were the choice of Parliament and were accepted by the people.

The motive of Parliament in settling the crown upon them had been purely to exclude the Stuarts. Nevertheless it was inevitable that the rule of a foreigner should increase parliamentary powers. For example the ministers carried out the most important part of their work when they met together at frequent intervals in a small room, or cabinet, as it was then called. George I could not, as his predecessors had done, preside over the meetings of the Cabinet. He began by attending, but as he could not understand a word of the proceedings he was forced to let one of his ministers take the chair; and in time he grew so bored that he stopped attending altogether. After two reigns (lasting forty-six years in all), the right of the king to attend Cabinet meetings lapsed, as George III found when he came to the throne in 1760 and tried to revive the custom.

Meanwhile the minister who was given the honour of presiding, naturally acquired a prestige which his colleagues did not share. He became known as the first or 'prime' minister. And from this right to preside over the Cabinet flowed all the considerable power that a Prime Minister enjoys today. Before the eighteenth century was over, he was choosing most of the ministers, and instead of receiving orders from the king, he was tendering advice.

The first man to develop the office was Robert Walpole, who held it from 1721 to 1742. The future character of the position was influenced to some extent by Walpole's personal temperament. He was a jealous man, and deliberately surrounded himself with colleagues less able than himself; this gave him a more dominating position than he might otherwise have had. But when he fell from power there was no one of equal determination to succeed him, and it was not until 1783 that another really strong personality came to the fore. This was William Pitt, who was asked to form a government at the incredibly early age of twenty-four. His talents were equal to the occasion, however, and he held office for eighteen years. Although not a jealous man in the way Walpole had been, he was intensely reserved, and this fact again tended to draw a dividing line between the Prime Minister and all the other members of the Cabinet. When Pitt died in 1806 during his second term of office, there was no question of the premiership lapsing. It had become a permanent feature of the British constitution.

Thus during the one hundred and eighty years that had passed since the accession of Charles I, sovereignty in Britain had passed from the

ROBERT WALPOLE

WILLIAM PITT

king to Parliament. King George III was of course the Head of the State; he was held in honour, and the monarch in those days enjoyed many more powers than are wielded by the Crown today. Nevertheless the Revolution of 1688 had made it absolutely clear that, while Parliament could in a crisis insist on choosing the king, the king had no longer any hope of doing what Henry VIII had often done—which was in effect to choose the members of Parliament. That right belonged to the electors. This did not mean that Britain was as yet a democracy, for the electorate was still very small. But a great advance had been made towards democracy by the substitution of a limited monarchy for the despotism that had prevailed under the Tudors.

Louis XIV of France

So far we have been concentrating on the exceptions to the general acceptance in Europe of the Divine Right of Kings. But we must not lose sight of the fact that absolute monarchy was the normal form of government in the greater part of the continent from the sixteenth century at least until 1789, and in many countries far into the nineteenth century. And the supreme example of a European despot of modern times was Louis XIV of France. He reigned for no less than seventy-two years, so that before his death even old men of eighty could scarcely remember a time when he had not been on the throne. He built himself the most splendid royal palace in Europe; and the general air of magnificence that surrounded him was so impressive that he was called the 'Sun King'. His arrogance was such that he proclaimed roundly '*L'état, c'est moi*'—'The state and I are one.'

Louis's home policy

Absolutism developed rather later in France than in other European countries, because during the late sixteenth century when Philip II was at the peak of his power and the Tudor despotism was at its height, France had been torn by religious wars. It was not until the turn of the century that order was restored, after which the monarchs began building up their power.

Louis XIII (1610-1643) had an extremely capable minister in the person of Cardinal Richelieu, who was a firm believer in Divine Right, and did all he could to establish his royal master's power. Conditions in France favoured him, for the Feudal system still survived. The peasants were obliged to live where they were born, and to work for the local *seigneur*. This meant that the majority of the population were static and inclined to be conservative, while the middle classes—in France as elsewhere—were prepared to support any government strong enough to keep order. Consequently the only threat to royal supremacy came from the nobles. Richelieu systematically set about weakening them. He destroyed their castles, and undermined their power over their poorer neighbours by introducing a new form of local government. The nobles were no longer to be appointed governors of provinces. Instead responsibility for local affairs was to be put into the hands of officials called *intendants*, who were appointed by the central government. The great lords naturally were not prepared to watch without a struggle, while their former powers were taken from them. Between 1648 and 1653 they were in armed revolt, but Richelieu's successor, Cardinal Mazarin, who was chief minister to the young Louis XIV, succeeded in suppressing the movement. It left however a strong impression on Louis, who became even more determined to make himself absolute.

Early impressions were in fact hardly required to reinforce his determination. He was by temperament a despot, and his famous words, '*L'état, c'est moi*' were actually pronounced when he was only seventeen. When Mazarin died, Louis considered himself quite old enough at twenty-three to take full responsibility for France, and he gave orders to his ministers that in future nothing was to be done without his personal permission.

In making this decision Louis was of course laying a terrible burden of work upon his own shoulders; and to his credit it must be said that he was extraordinarily painstaking and industrious. Although he encouraged his courtiers to spend most of their time in idle pleasure, he

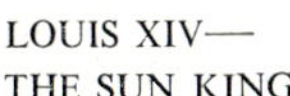

LOUIS XIV—
THE SUN KING

never adopted that way of life himself. While claiming the privileges of Divine Right, he willingly accepted its duties. Of course he was obliged to delegate a great deal of work to his ministers, but he was most careful never to select a noble for this office. He preferred men of the middle class who would feel no temptation to rebel. In the first half of his reign he was very shrewd in selecting these men, the most outstanding of whom was Jean-Baptiste Colbert (1619-1683).

Colbert

Colbert was a business-man, and believed that the prosperity of France depended on the development of her trade and industries. He was of course a mercantilist, and was therefore anxious to ensure that the country's exports should exceed the imports—in value if not in bulk. He did all he could to encourage luxury industries, such as the manufacture of silk, carpets or porcelain. Standards of workmanship were set by the government, which the manufacturers had to attain; and rewards were offered to inventors. At the same time attractive conditions were offered to any foreign craftsman who might be persuaded to immigrate. In order that merchandise might move more freely about the country, Colbert saw to it that the roads were improved, and he constructed a great canal linking the Atlantic with the Mediterranean. Water-transport was in those days by far the best and cheapest way to move loads, and one need only glance at a map to see the importance of this operation.

Colbert was also seeking fresh markets abroad, as well as new sources of raw materials. It was largely because of his influence that France at last began to take part in the European trade with Asia. She also became keenly interested in the New World. Trading stations were established in India, and French colonies were founded in North America. As part of the same policy, a great ship-building programme was instituted. Large numbers of merchant ships were built and the French Navy was developed into a formidable force.

Colbert's death in 1683 marks a turning-point in Louis's reign. No other minister served France so ably; and the loss of his influence led the King into some fatal blunders.

Louis was however an intelligent man, and was interested in literature and the arts. The life of his court was enriched by the patronage he gave to poets and playwrights. The seventeenth century was a splendid period in French literature, and dramatists such as Corneille, Racine and Molière, the painter Le Brun, and La Fontaine the writer of fables, all owed a great deal to the King's favour, while his passion for building kept the leading architects of the day in lucrative employment.

Louis's foreign policy

Even during Colbert's lifetime Louis was unconsciously undermining his minister's work. For he thought that it was due to him as the most powerful king in Europe to pursue a foreign policy of perpetual wars. He had a brilliant war minister called Louvois, who carried out an admirable job of reorganising the army. Indeed he not only reorganised it, he nearly quadrupled its size. By 1678, when he had been in charge for only six years, he had increased the strength from 70,000 to 170,000.

But all this cost a mint of money, and as fast as Colbert created wealth, Louis poured it out on his battlefields.

His main policy was to ensure that France should extend to what he called her 'natural frontiers'—the Pyrenees, the Alps and the Rhine. The advance to the mountain boundaries had been achieved in previous reigns; but Louis spent vast sums of money and many thousands of lives in trying to conquer that part of the Netherlands which lay between France and the Rhine. In all these efforts he was steadily resisted by William of Orange, who accepted the throne of England in 1688 largely because it would enable him to pursue more effectively his determination to keep Louis within bounds.

The Sun King also made it a cardinal point of his policy to seize every opportunity to add to the grandeur of his own relatives. In 1700 he saw a unique chance to add to the family heritage, and though the risks were obvious, he was unable to resist the temptation. The outcome was disastrous.

In 1700 King Charles II of Spain died, leaving no heirs. The Spanish royal family, like every royal family of the period, had connections all over Europe; and both the Emperor of Austria and Louis himself had a claim to the throne of Spain. This was a dazzling prize because of the immensely rich colonies in America. But it was obvious that the other European sovereigns—already perturbed by Louis's power—would never permit France and Spain to be joined together. Such an arrangement would clearly upset completely the balance of power. In his more sensible moments Louis had admitted this, but when Charles died it was found that he had left his kingdom in his will to Louis's younger grandson Philip. Philip was not the heir to the French throne, but the other powers would never willingly submit to any close relation of Louis being King of Spain. Instead of refusing the legacy, Louis insisted on accepting it. Thereupon there followed the War of the Spanish Succession, which lasted from 1701 to 1713.

Louis was already nearly sixty when the war began; before it ended he had had his seventieth birthday. Long before it was over France was exhausted physically and financially, for the endless expense was bleeding the country white. Moreover the powers allied against Louis had a brilliant general in the English Duke of Marlborough, who won a series of resounding victories. The end of it was that Philip retained the throne of Spain, though guarantees were given that France and Spain should never unite; but meanwhile Louis had been obliged to give up some of the territory won in his earlier wars, and some of the colonies in North

THE PALACE AT VERSAILLES

America were also surrendered. Moreover he had brought his subjects to misery and ruin; and at the end of his reign they cursed him, and even spat when he passed in the street. The gulf which he had dug between his people and himself was very deep, but something of their bitter resentment penetrated the mind of the disappointed old man. He gave his heir this piece of advice: 'Do not imitate my love for building and for war, but assuage the misery of my people.'

The Court at Versailles

Despite the failure and humiliation which his militarism brought at the end of his life, the impression made by Louis's achievements in his own country lived on. During the greater part of his reign nearly every ruler in Europe envied him, and even after his death they tried to imitate him. Above all they envied and tried to copy the superb palace he built himself at Versailles.

This vast edifice, measuring no less than a quarter of a mile from north to south, contained literally hundreds of rooms and suites, and of course the most magnificent public rooms. The most famous of all is the Hall of Mirrors, which has often been chosen since Louis's time to be the scene of historic meetings. At numerous points Louis had sun-disks erected to illustrate his own proud title of *le Roi Soleil*, the Sun King. His own apartments contained studies and offices in which a great deal of hard work was done, both by the King himself and also by his ministers. But the hundreds of nobles who flocked to court, and feared nothing so much as banishment from Versailles, spent their time in hunting and banquets, and their money on the elaborate clothes, the fine food, and the carriages and servants, which life at court demanded.

Louis was a past master in the art of building up his own importance. A complicated ritual was erected around his daily life. When he was ready to get up in the morning, a considerable group of great nobles assembled in his bedroom, each ready to perform his allotted duty. One would hand the King his shirt, another his wig, and so on. When he washed, a member of the court was specially entrusted with the duty of handing him a towel. So great was Louis's prestige that there was keen competition for the honour of carrying out such tasks. The same kind of procedure went on all day. The life of the nobility was invested with a great and artificial solemnity but was in essence empty and trivial, for Louis entrusted none of them with important affairs of state. Duties of that nature were reserved for Colbert and other men of middle-class origin.

The weaknesses of Louis's rule

In seeking to establish his own power Louis had realised that the nobles must be kept in check, but he had gone too far in sapping their vitality and robbing their lives of any useful or sensible purpose. All these men were the owners of landed estates, which they ought to have been administering, and on which the peasants were in need of help and care. But the false lure of Versailles was so powerful that a *seigneur* never dared absent himself from court voluntarily, and dreaded the thought of being sent away by the King. Staying there was terribly expensive, and all they thought of was getting more and more money out of their lands at home. The agents they employed were taught that this was their first duty. So farms were allowed to lapse into a state of decay, the houses of the peasants went unmended, and barns and gates were left to rot. Worst of all, the peasants, whose lot at the best was bound to be a hard one, were robbed of their natural masters and protectors. The Feudal System rested on the assumption that the landed gentry would take a personal interest in their estates and look after their tenants. If they failed in this, the system became intolerable for the poor.

For this state of affairs Louis must be held personally responsible. The Versailles system was his careful and deliberate creation. Moreover his refusal to give the nobles any share in the work of government had a bad effect on himself, as well as upon them and upon France. It has been said that 'all power tends to corrupt, and absolute power corrupts absolutely'. Louis was an exceedingly clever man, but as he grew older his judgement became less reliable, especially after the death of Colbert. In 1685 he made a fatal decision—one which Colbert would certainly have advised against.

It has already been mentioned that during the sixteenth century France had been torn by religious wars. When peace was finally restored, King Henry IV had wisely healed the breach in French society by issuing in 1595 the Edict of Nantes, which granted the French Protestants, known as the Huguenots, freedom of worship and full civil rights. The Huguenots belonged mainly to the artisan class and they were industrious and skilful craftsmen. It was in fact they who gave the chief support to Colbert's scheme for raising the standard of French workmanship. Louis, however, had come under the influence of his second wife, Madame de Maintenon,* who believed that it was his duty

---

* Madame de Maintenon was Louis's morganatic wife, which meant that she was never Queen of France.

94

as a good Roman Catholic to stamp out Protestantism from his kingdom. He therefore revoked the Edict. Henceforth the Huguenots were forbidden to worship as they pleased, and were denied many of the privileges of citizenship. Consequently more than a quarter of a million of them left France, taking themselves and their skills mainly to England or Holland. Both these countries benefited from the immigration, and France suffered a corresponding loss.

Louis, however, did not seem to be particularly perturbed by this unfortunate result of his action. His confidence in himself was not to be shaken until the very end of his life, nor does he ever seem to have realised the danger of concentrating so much power into one pair of hands. This is of course a peril inherent in all monarchies. The man who wears the crown wears it because of his birth, and there is no guarantee that his abilities will be equal to his task. The more absolute the monarchy, the greater is this danger. Louis XV, who succeeded his great-grandfather in 1715, was a man of average competence who managed somehow to carry the burden of his power; but the next king, Louis XVI, was quite incapable of wielding the vast authority which he inherited, and during his reign the French monarchy was overthrown.

5 The European colonisation of North America

When Queen Elizabeth died and James VI of Scotland set out for London to take up his additional duties as James I of England, he was embarking on a period of his life for which he had waited a very long time. His childhood and early manhood had been most unhappy, and he had ever in his mind the knowledge that his mother, Mary Queen of Scots, had been deposed and driven away from her kingdom by the leaders of the Scottish Kirk, who resented—among many causes of grievance—her adherence to the Roman Church. James had suffered a good deal at the hands of the Scottish Calvinists, who were really republican at heart; and he was therefore somewhat dismayed when shortly after reaching England he was presented with a petition from the Puritans, who were discontented with the Church of England.

The Puritans did not desire to leave that Church, nor did they want it to be disbanded; all they asked was that the rigid regulations might be eased a little to allow more variety in the forms of worship. But James immediately detected here a flavour of the Kirk. Firmly stating his motto, 'No bishops, no king', he refused to make any concessions. He had of course no means of knowing that in acting in this way he was contributing one of the factors to the great rebellion which his son would have to face nearly forty years later. But in fact he left the Puritans with the conviction that life in England would hold little for them until drastic changes had been brought about. That was why so many of them were ready in 1642 to take up arms against their king in order to hasten the process of change.

Not all of them, however, had been willing to wait so long. Some had sought escape by leaving England. At first they went to live in Leyden in Holland, which was—apart from Scotland—the nearest Protestant country. At Leyden they were free to worship as they wished, but they felt the unhappiness that all exiles feel in a strange land. So the most enterprising among them decided that they would prefer to uproot themselves from Europe altogether and seek a home in the New World.

The English colonies in North America

For over a hundred years the Spanish had been pouring across the Atlantic and establishing prosperous colonies in the most attractive areas of the American continents. Both the King of Spain and the individual

96

colonists made fortunes out of these enterprises, and the English, inspired by Sir Walter Raleigh, decided to follow suit. They knew of course that the Spanish would never permit any encroachment on the lands to which they had staked a claim; but there were still large tracts of North America which, though bleaker than the lands of the south, were there for the taking.

It was in the reign of Elizabeth that the first attempt was made to found an English colony, which was called Virginia in honour of the virgin queen. The project was a disastrous failure because most of the would-be colonists, having heard tales of the gold of Mexico and Peru, went out in the hope of getting rich very quickly. But the coast of North America proved terribly inhospitable, and the unfortunate emigrants either died or gave up and came home. Later however in 1606 another attempt was made, and after some initial calamities Virginia was successfully established.

It now occurred to some members of the Leyden Congregation that the colony might give them the religious liberty which they desired, so in 1620 they set sail from Plymouth in a ship called the *Mayflower*. Though the passengers have since been given the name of the Pilgrim Fathers, there were on board quite a number of people who were not Puritans at all and had no religious motive for emigrating. Owing to errors of navigation, the *Mayflower* landed not at Virginia but at Cape Cod some hundreds of miles to the north. The captain refused to go any further, so perforce the emigrants had to undertake the task of founding an entirely new colony, which they called Plymouth. In the early months they suffered terrible hardships, even worse than those endured by the first Virginians, but the native Red Indians were friendly and eventually the colony was securely established.

The success of the *Mayflower* passengers encouraged other Puritans to follow their lead, and in the ensuing years they founded four colonies along that coast, which were known collectively as New England. The Puritans made excellent colonists because they had nothing to lose. As one of the Pilgrim Fathers put it, 'It is not with us as with other men whom small things can discourage, or small discontents cause to wish themselves home again'. They had already decided that home was insupportable. Moreover they disapproved of idleness and luxury, and considered even mild pleasures wicked. Consequently they were indifferent to riches, and were prepared to work extremely hard and endure every privation. They were not however democrats inspired with a love of liberty for its own sake. The seventeenth century was an intolerant age when everybody felt sure that his own opinions were the only truth. The Puritans left their mother country because they wanted liberty of worship, but they were no sooner settled in America than they proceeded to deny that very liberty to any later arrivals whose views differed from their own.

Meanwhile English colonies of another type were being established further to the south. In 1632 Charles I gave permission to a Roman Catholic nobleman, Lord Baltimore, to found a settlement for members of his own Church on land which was cut away from Virginia for the purpose. This new foundation was called Maryland, and was remarkable in that genuine religious toleration was practised there—at least in the early days.

During the republican period in England no new colonies were founded, but Charles II's reign saw a very rapid expansion of the settlements. In 1663 Charles gave a group of interested men the right to develop the region lying to the south of Virginia, which was called Carolina in his honour, and was afterwards divided into two separate colonies, North and South Carolina. Nearly twenty years later in 1681 the King gave another large grant of land to William Penn, to whom he owed money. Penn was a Quaker and a man of peace. He gave the capital city the name of Philadelphia, which means 'brotherly love'; and this was the only colony which consistently treated the Red Indians fairly and kindly. It was called Pennsylvania after its founder.

Meanwhile the English claim to the Atlantic seaboard of North America did not go unchallenged. The Dutch, now at the height of their power, had established three small colonies in the region of the Hudson River. But when in 1664 war broke out between Holland and England, the Dutch colonies were quickly conquered. The largest of them, New Amsterdam, became New York in honour of the future James II, who was then the Duke of York. The other two were called New Jersey and Delaware.

These three acquisitions, together with Pennsylvania, Maryland, Virginia, the Carolinas and the four New England settlements, brought the total number of the English colonies to twelve. They remained at that figure until well into the eighteenth century. Then a General Oglethorpe, who wished to improve the lot of certain classes of English convicts, founded the thirteenth colony, south of Carolina; this was called Georgia after King George II. Here men were to be sent who would otherwise be in a debtors' prison, and they were to be given the chance to work and earn money in order to pay off their debts. Georgia

The Pilgrim Fathers landing at Plymouth Rock

had many teething troubles, but early in the nineteenth century the colonists began to grow cotton on a large scale. As there was a huge demand for this commodity in Europe, they soon became extremely prosperous.

The attitude of the mother country to the colonies

You will have noticed that Charles II, like James I before him, gave generous grants of North American land to prospective colonists, and you may wonder by what right he gave away territory which could not be said to belong to him at all. In fact Charles had no doubts about the rightness of his action. Provided that Englishmen did not attempt to colonise any land already claimed by another *European* power, they were, according to the standards of the time, entitled to go where they liked. The feelings and rights of the original inhabitants of the continent —the Red Indians—were simply not considered.

James and Charles were particularly happy to encourage colonisation because they were perpetually short of funds, and one of the few sources of revenue which came to them independently of Parliament was tunnage and poundage, the name given in those days to customs duties. Any new colony founded was under obligation to send all its products to England, and the kings hoped that this developing trade would bring some sorely needed cash into the royal coffers.

Moreover, not only the kings but everyone else responsible for the government of England during the seventeenth century regarded the colonies as a valuable potential source of timber and other naval stores. British shipping was developing rapidly, and hitherto goods of this kind had been purchased from Scandinavia. But a glance at the map of Europe will show how easily England could be cut off from Scandinavia in time of war—especially if the war was being fought against Holland, which was all too likely in the middle of the century. The northern colonies were well wooded, which made them a useful source of naval supplies, while those in the south had a hotter climate suited to the production of a number of luxury goods in great demand at home.

Finally the colonies could be used as a factor in foreign policy. The seizure of the three Dutch settlements in America was one incident in a long commercial struggle which was waged between England and Holland; while an important reason for the foundation of Georgia was the British desire to stake a claim to the region between Florida and Carolina before Spain had a chance to do so.

As for the motive which inspired the actual emigrants to leave their homes and cross the sea, facing certain hardships in the hope of finding happiness, this was usually a bitter discontent with the mother country. We have seen that the rigid rules of the Church of England sent the first Puritans overseas; and the strict enforcement of those rules carried out by Archbishop Laud in Charles I's reign added greatly to the number of emigrants. Some of them went to the West Indies, but the majority found the bleaker climate of New England more suited to their temperament. The Roman Catholics were equally discontented, hence Lord Baltimore's scheme for founding Maryland. Then the Anglicans themselves began to find life hard, and during the rule of Cromwell many of them (including the ancestors of George Washington) crossed to one or other of the colonies. The restoration of the monarchy in 1660 brought yet a fresh influx, composed this time of the former supporters of the republican régime. Thus the colonies were founded and peopled by men and women who had a grievance against the land of their birth.

Emigration to America offered them a genuine opportunity to secure independence from the English government, for each colony had a charter permitting it to manage its own affairs to a very large extent. Every charter provided that a legislative assembly should be elected to determine taxes and to pass laws relating to almost any subject except trade, which was under the control of England as the mother country of all the colonies. The voting system was not democratic; but then neither was the voting system in Britain at that time. Each colony also had a Council, the members of which were in some cases elected by the Assembly, in others chosen by the Governor. The Governors themselves were always appointed by the mother country, normally by the King, though both Penn and Baltimore owned their colonies as personal possessions, which they passed on to their heirs. For as long as this arrangement lasted, Pennsylvania and Maryland had their governors appointed by their owners.

Since the journey across the Atlantic took several weeks, it would have been hard for Britain to supervise the internal affairs of the colonies and indeed she had no desire to do so. Her interest in them was mainly commercial. In accordance with the mercantilist views of the period, she valued the colonies primarily as a subsidiary source of raw materials which would assist her in her unremitting efforts to export more than she imported. On no account must the colonial products be allowed to be sold to any other country, for the latter would then reap the benefit that should belong to the mother country alone.

Thus an Act of Parliament of 1660 drew up a list of goods, called the 'enumerated articles', which could be sent only to Britain. This list covered all the important colonial products. As time went on constant additions were made to the original list. Moreover the colonies were expected to stick strictly to their role of producers of raw materials. The mother country was to be responsible for manufacturing their requirements as well as her own, and a whole series of regulations forbade the colonists to make for themselves any articles which Britain preferred to make for them.

All these regulations were known as the Colonial System, and for the most part the English colonists accepted them as a matter of course, while rightly congratulating themselves on the remarkable degree of liberty that they enjoyed in comparison with the Spanish or French colonists.

The character of the colonies

The Atlantic coastline along which the thirteen colonies were ranged measures a thousand miles from north to south, even if the numerous indentations are ignored. From east to west, however, the land they covered was less than two hundred miles wide, for the Appalachian

Mountains lie parallel to the coast, and in the days when men had to depend on horses for transport, these hills presented an obstacle which, while not impassable, still did not seem worth the trouble of passing. From the Appalachians a number of rivers flow eastward to the sea. These rivers were extremely useful to the colonists, since they supplied

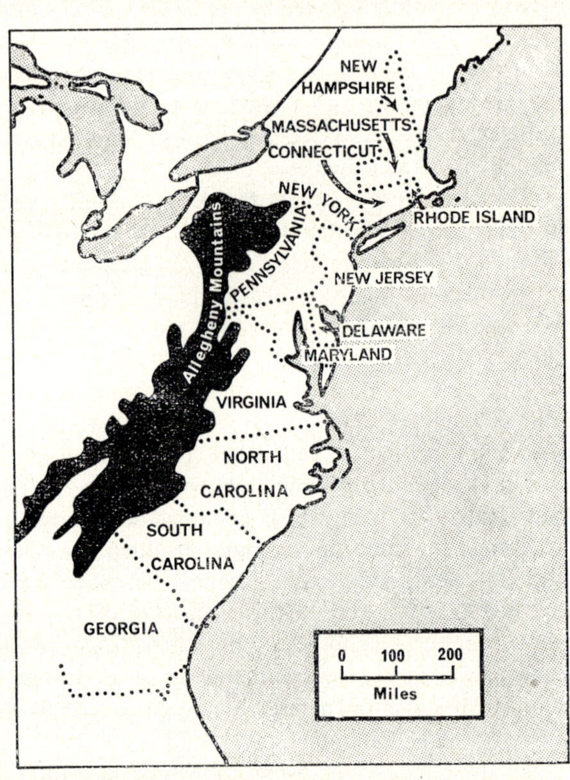

MAP 5
THE THIRTEEN
COLONIES IN
NORTH AMERICA

them with means of communication inland, and also served as boundaries between one colony and the next. Each settlement was preoccupied with its own affairs and took little interest in its neighbours. Nevertheless they fell naturally into three groups.

First, in the north, there was New England, comprising Massachusetts, New Hampshire, Connecticut and Rhode Island. Plymouth, the earliest colony of all, had been absorbed into Massachusetts. The people here were of Puritan origin and ready to work hard; but the soil was so poor that with the best will in the world they could not make a great success of farming. They therefore tended to be traders. They used

102

their abundant timber to establish a ship-building industry, and they also developed their fisheries.

Further south were the middle group of colonies—Pennsylvania, New York, New Jersey and Delaware. Here the climate was milder and the soil richer, so that farming could be developed on the English pattern. The farms were small and the main part of the work was done by the farmer and his family. Cattle were raised and crops produced of a kind that filled the immediate needs of the colonists themselves. There was, however, an export trade which was largely concerned with timber and furs, both derived from the forests in the hinterland.

Then came the southern colonies—Maryland, Virginia, the Carolinas and Georgia, which had a sub-tropical climate and had developed a way of life completely different from that in Britain. Here the land was divided up not into little farms but into huge estates, which were devoted to the cultivation of tobacco, rice and indigo. From the point of view of the mother country these colonies were the most useful, since they produced what could not be grown at home. But the lush climate had its disadvantages. It was unsuited to the white men who found it almost impossible to exert themselves in the heat. They therefore imitated the Spanish colonists and adopted the habit of buying Negro slaves. Thus provided with cheap labour, they formed themselves into a landed aristocracy. Indoors the housewife supervised her household; outside, her husband planned and directed the vast estate. But neither of them would lower themselves to do any rough work with their own hands.

The other European powers in North America

Even the southerners, however, though they did not put a great deal of personal manual effort into the development of their colonies, still took a keen interest in politics, while those in the north led extremely full lives. In addition to the routine tasks necessary to keep themselves alive, they were founding new towns and cities, working out an efficient economic system, bringing new land into cultivation and exploring their hinterland. Moreover they were never free from the fear of Indian attacks. Nor was this all: there was also the constant threat from other Europeans. The Spanish were not only firmly installed in Mexico but had also occupied Florida; and whenever war broke out between Spain and Britain in Europe, they were inclined to send expeditions against the British settlements. It is true, however, that Spain's chief centre of interest lay in South America.

The French, on the other hand, were well established on the northern continent and were determined, if they could, to drive the British away. Quite early in the seventeenth century they had founded a colony on the St Lawrence River in Canada. This settlement was completely different in character from the English colonies. It was not populated by men and women who desperately wanted a new home, but by traders who went there to engage in trapping or lumbering. Very often these men did not bring their wives with them, but took Red Indian women to live with them or to be their wives, for the French had much friendlier relations with the Indians than the British were prepared to have. But this kind of life had no very wide appeal, and only a small number of Frenchmen came out to the colony.

The French government, however, took a keen interest in the whole of North America, and was always prepared to back any extension of French influence in that continent. The trappers and traders were encouraged to explore, and were very willing to do so, since they had no deep attachment to their Canadian homes. Ranging southwards from the St Lawrence and the Great Lakes, they came upon the rivers of the Mississippi system. In 1682 the great explorer La Salle actually made his way right down the Mississippi to the Gulf of Mexico. He laid claim to the region round the mouth of that river, which France now called Louisiana in honour of Louis XIV.

By this advance the French had completely outflanked the British colonies, and in the eighteenth century they proceeded to follow up this advantage by building a line of forts along the Ohio River valley. As they had always been friendly with the Red Indians, the braves were prepared to help them against their rivals, and the threat to the British colonists became serious. Oddly enough the thirteen colonies could hardly ever be persuaded to help one another in cases of attack by either the French or the Indians; but the British government gave a great deal of thought to the defence of its empire overseas.

The accession to the English throne of William III, the Stadtholder of Holland, immediately involved the English in wars against Louis XIV, and even after Louis's death the two countries remained in a constant state of hostility throughout the eighteenth century because they found themselves in commercial rivalry in Europe and India as well as in America. The perpetual wars of the eighteenth century showed up the weakness of the French colonial system, for as the colonists had never been allowed any self-government, they were not inspired with a great passion to defend their homes. Consequently when the British in 1759 made a really determined onslaught on Canada, they won a quick victory, and at the conclusion of the war in 1763 the French government lost every scrap of North American territory. Since Spain, though claiming certain parts of that continent, took very little interest in anything north of Mexico, the British were left in triumphant possession.

The revolt of the British colonies

The British triumph was short-lived, however. During the recent wars the British army and the colonists had naturally been brought into close contact, and neither found that the other improved on acquaintance. The fact was that the colonists had grown apart from the mother country. The voyage between them took at least six weeks, so that no reply could be received to any letter in less than three months. In these circumstances the tie uniting the two peoples was bound to weaken. Moreover the daily life and problems of the Americans were entirely different from those of the British. Some of their doings, which now came to light, struck the British as quite reprehensible, notably the way in which smuggling was regularly practised and universally condoned. For by the middle of the eighteenth century the mercantilist control of trade imposed by Britain was only tolerable to the colonists because they so often evaded it. There was however another consideration which made it acceptable, namely the realisation that the colonies depended on Britain for their defence against the French. But in 1763 France was finally defeated, and consequently the colonists, who no longer needed Britain, were ripe for a quarrel.

Their freedom from military attack was not quite so certain as they at first believed; for the war was no sooner over than a Red Indian chief called Pontiac—probably incited by the French—carried out a savage raid against the British settlers. Thereupon the British government decided that there must be some joint policy for the defence of all the colonies, and issued the Proclamation of 1763 which brought under government control all the land lying to the west of the colonies. Relations between the colonists and the Indians had always been bad, and the Indian attacks were all the more deadly because the different colonies had no idea of banding together to ward off the menace. But many individuals, as well as several of the colonies, found their territorial ambitions thwarted by the Proclamation, and there was a great outcry against it. The British also proposed to maintain a permanent garrison of 10,000 men to police the frontier and keep the Indians under control.

This force would clearly have to be paid for, and Britain felt that it was only reasonable to expect the colonists to bear part of the cost, especially as her own finances were in a depleted state on account of the recent war which had so largely been fought for the benefit of the colonists. The first attempt to extract a contribution from them took the form of trying to enforce the existing trade regulations and to put down smuggling. But these evasions of the law were regarded with so much sympathy by the colonists that it was almost impossible for the authorities to collect enough witnesses to convict offenders. Customs officials were therefore issued with special documents called Writs of Assistance, which empowered them to search any house where they thought they might find evidence. This was undoubtedly an infringement of the ordinary liberties of the citizen, and the Americans—especially the American lawyers—were loud in their protests.

In any case the suppression of smuggling, even if it had been successful, would not have yielded sufficient profit to pay the costs of the garrison. Some kind of direct tax would have to be imposed on the colonists, and the British Prime Minister, Grenville, consulted the London agents of the thirteen colonies about this problem. He told them the proportion of the charges which he thought they should be responsible for, and agreed to accept any proposal they liked to make as to the method of raising the money. If however they had no alternative suggestion, he had his own idea ready—namely a Stamp Tax to be imposed on the stamps that had to be affixed to certain legal documents. As the colonists failed to put forward any scheme of their own, Grenville incorporated his Stamp Tax in an Act of Parliament which became law in 1765.

The Americans promptly raised a howl of furious protest, and began to examine more carefully their relationship to the mother country. Some of them maintained that their charters had been granted by the Kings of England, and that therefore Parliament had no rights over them. This argument however would not hold water, for ever since the Revolution of 1688 it had been clear that Parliament and not the King was the sovereign power in the British constitution. Another cry raised was that there must be 'no taxation without representation', the implication being that Parliament could only tax the colonies if colonial members were allowed to go to Westminster. No one of course seriously believed that it would be practicable to send Members of Parliament across the Atlantic: this was merely a way of saying that the mother country no longer had any rights over her colonies. The British Parliament bowed to the storm to the tune of repealing the Stamp Act, but at

The Boston Tea Party

the same time passed the Declaratory Act affirming their right to tax the colonies if they chose to do so.

In 1768 another effort to raise money was made by the imposition of customs duties on a number of goods going into the colonies, including tea. The colonists' reply to this move was to do without the articles concerned. Moreover a new field of profit opened before the smugglers, who now started to buy tea from the Dutch East Indies and to bring it into the colonies illegally. Thus the motives of patriotism and profit-making became a little confused. The climax came in 1773 when the British Government made a decision that should have given no offence to the colonists at all. At that time the British East India Company was in financial difficulties because its tea trade had suffered from the American embargo. Hoping to help the Company and at the same time to oblige the colonists, the Government gave permission for Indian tea to be sent direct to America, without having to go *via* London where a tax of a shilling had to be paid on each pound. Thus the cargo would be sold much more cheaply than usual. A ship accordingly arrived direct from India at Boston, the capital of Massachusetts, much to the annoyance of the tea-smugglers. A gang of men, dressed as Red Indians, boarded the ship, overpowered the crew and threw all the tea into the harbour. This incident became known as the Boston Tea Party.

This was an outrage which Britain felt could not be overlooked; and as the Massachusetts authorities made no attempt to bring the offenders to justice, Parliament passed a series of Penal Acts against the colony. One of these decreed that the port of Boston—the very pulse of the colony's prosperity—should be closed until the tea had been paid for; while another suspended the Massachusetts Charter and appointed a military governor with dictatorial powers.

This suspension of the charter did what nothing else had ever done: it induced the thirteen colonies to act together. They at once took steps to elect representatives who met at a Congress of Philadelphia in September 1774 to discuss this development. Shortly afterwards fighting broke out between the British and the men of Massachusetts, whereupon the members of Congress decided that all the colonies must join in the struggle. George Washington was put in command of the American forces, and on July 4th, 1776 the Second Continental Congress drew up the famous Declaration of Independence, which opened with the ringing words:

> We hold these truths to be self-evident: that all men are created equal; that they are endowed by their Creator with certain inalienable rights; that among these are life, liberty and the pursuit of happiness. That to secure these rights governments are instituted among men, deriving their just powers from the consent of the governed; that whatever form of government becomes destructive of these ends, it is the right of the people to alter or abolish it and to institute new government.

The North American War of Independence

The ensuing war lasted from 1776 until 1783. Washington was an able leader, but the battles fought were few and far between. The Americans were terribly handicapped by lack of money, for Congress was only a common meeting-ground for the thirteen colonies. It had no right to impose taxation upon them, and it was left to each legislative assembly to vote a contribution towards the funds. The high command therefore had to resort to issuing paper money, which soon became quite valueless. An even more serious disadvantage was the lack of a regular army. Each colony had a militia, but a man normally expected to serve for only four months at a time. Thus there was a perpetual coming and going, and Washington never knew what forces he could count on. Even when he had something like an army behind him, the soldiers were woefully ill-equipped because of the shortage of funds.

Even the cause of independence was not wholeheartedly endorsed by all the colonists, many of whom were either indifferent or loyal to Britain.

That the Americans won the war in spite of all these weaknesses was due partly to the inefficiency of the British command, and partly to the fact that Britain had made enemies in Europe who were glad to take this chance to get their revenge on her. The first ally to make common cause with the Americans was France, who was smarting under the humiliation of her defeat in 1763. The French navy proved extremely useful to the colonists, and French participation also changed the character of the war and turned it into a European as well as an American conflict. In 1781 Britain suffered a severe reverse when a large force, trapped between the colonial army and the French navy, was obliged to surrender. She might perhaps have recovered from this disaster had she not been in military difficulties in Europe as well. In the end Britain was almost relieved to let the American colonies go in 1783, so that she could give her full attention to her enemies nearer home. A peace conference then met in Paris.

By the treaty that followed the thirteen colonies gained a good deal more than their independence, though they failed in their efforts to secure Canada. This the British insisted on retaining, and in the following years it proved a welcome refuge for American loyalists. On the other hand Britain agreed to surrender any claim to the land west of the colonies, over which the Proclamation of 1763 had given her jurisdiction. This meant that the country between the Ohio and the Mississippi was available for colonial expansion, and it was agreed among the thirteen states that this territory was to be open to emigrants from any state.

There was some difficulty in getting the Treaty of Paris signed, because there was no single American government authorised to act for all. Congress had really no further reason for existence; it had been formed solely to enable the war to be fought, and in any case it had never been a government. Nevertheless its representatives put their signature to the agreement, and all the thirteen states agreed to abide by it. The phrase the 'United States' had occasionally been used, but in fact the former colonies showed no serious inclination to be united. They had been at one in their detestation of Britain; but now that independence had been achieved their incurable separatism rose again to the surface.

The real cause of the American revolt

In the course of their quarrel with Britain, the colonists had put forward

Signing the Declaration of Independence

a number of grievances, but none of them had been really valid. They denounced the British colonial system as tyrannical, but in fact it was extraordinarily liberal when compared with the regulations imposed by France and Spain upon their colonies. They also resented the Stamp Tax, but it was perfectly reasonable to ask them to contribute to their own defence. The British government had in fact gone out of its way to be lenient, for in justice it might have demanded that a much larger proportion of the defence cost should be borne by the colonists. Similarly none of the arguments about the legal rights of Parliament would bear examination.

Nevertheless the Americans were bound to demand independence, and it was inevitable that the British should sooner or later concede it, for the colonists had attained nationhood. They had reached political maturity, and politically speaking they were demanding a latch-key. The apron-strings which bound them to the mother country had seemed quite reasonable even half a century earlier, but now they were intolerable. It was of no use for the British to reason with them. Reason had nothing to do with the matter: the need for national independence is an emotion.

Thus we see in America in the eighteenth century a situation that was to reappear in Europe in the nineteenth, and in Asia and Africa in the twentieth. The champions of independence were determined to gain their point, at whatever cost; and the ruling power, however hard it struggled, would be obliged to give way in the end.

The union of the colonies into a nation

Not many years were to pass before the force of nationalism grew strong enough to overcome the tendency to separatism. 'Hang together—or hang separately' was the advice of Benjamin Franklin to his fellow North Americans; and his advice was taken. In 1789 the thirteen colonies joined in a federation to which they gave the name of the United States of America.

6 The Mogul Empire and the British Empire in India

We have seen in Chapter 2 how successive waves of European merchants, backed by their respective governments, infiltrated into Asia during the sixteenth and seventeenth centuries. Every one of these expeditions—whether it was Portuguese, Dutch, English or Spanish—was forced to operate thousands of miles from home, knowing that even the most essential supplies and reinforcements would take months to arrive. The enemies they faced were fighting on their home ground, with their whole population in reserve. Yet the Europeans met with few defeats; and when they were obliged to yield up one of the ports they had conquered, it was always to another European—never to an Asian power.

This does not mean, however, that Asia was weak or decadent. There were three reasons for the success of the Europeans. First, they had the use of fire-arms which were unknown to Asia at that time; second, they were able to profit from the bitter disputes between Hindus and Muslims which were rife in India and the East Indies; and third, they did not attempt too much. They were not interested in conquering large territories, but in gaining control of ports. With their superior weapons they found it relatively easy to take places such as Malacca and Colombo by storm. Conquering the whole of Malaya or Ceylon would have proved far more difficult; but that they had no wish to attempt. When they did tackle a large power, they met with swift rebuff. The Emperor of China threw the Portuguese Pirez into prison, and the utmost concession he would ever make was to allow a few Europeans to trade in Canton and Macao. In the same way the Japanese, as soon as they learned to fear the Europeans, promptly expelled them from the country. The Europeans resented each of these episodes at the time, but neither made any long-term difference to their main aim of establishing favourable trade relations.

In Indonesia they made steady progress. First the Portuguese gained control of strongpoints on the coast of all the most important islands, and later the Dutch took over and extended this empire. They were enormously helped by the fact that in these islands the coast was normally in the hands of Muslims, while the interior was Hindu. Between these two groups there was almost invariably deep hostility, and so if the Muslims were under fire, their neighbours in the hinterland were unlikely to lift a finger to help them. Eventually they would awake to the fact that they were thus putting themselves in danger; but by then it was usually too late, for the Europeans had secured a foothold and could not be removed.

The Portuguese acquisition of Goa is a striking example of the way in which religious disunity smoothed the path of the foreigners. India in the sixteenth century was divided into a large number of states, but by far the most important were the Muslim Empire based on Delhi in the north, and the Hindu state of Vijayanagar in the south. Between these two opposing empires a fierce struggle was being waged, and the Muslims had one marked advantage over their enemies: they had horses, which were almost unknown in the south. The Portuguese however were prepared to ship very good horses from Europe; and it was with this in mind that the Emperor of Vijayanagar connived at, and even encouraged, the establishment of a Portuguese base at Goa.

Even with this help, however, the Portuguese never penetrated beyond the outside fringe of India. They acquired a few ports, but neither they nor the Dutch made any impact on the vast interior of the country. Indeed, as the sixteenth century proceeded, their chance of doing so— even if they had wanted to—became more and more remote; for one of the greatest epochs in Indian history had now dawned, with the establishment of the Mogul dynasty in 1526. Moreover Akbar, the greatest of all the Great Moguls, made it the main point of his policy to reconcile Muslims and Hindus and to unite all his subjects in a single loyalty.

The reign of Akbar (1556-1605)

The dangers of disunity were impressed upon Akbar at an early age, for he came to the throne when he was thirteen and was immediately obliged to fight many enemies and to suppress many revolts in order to survive. He began as a devout and loyal Muslim, but he could not help realising that the Islamic faith, as practised in the India of his day, fell far short of its early ideals. Theoretically all Muslims are brothers, and when their armies first conquered and ruled north India in the thirteenth century, they were in truth conscious of a brotherhood which kept them loyal to one another, and united them in a general contempt for the Hindus. The unfortunate Hindus had indeed little to hope for under their rule, for in a strictly Islamic state full citizenship would be given only to the Faithful. Infidels were supposed to pay a tax called the *jizya*, which was a badge of their inferiority. Moreover, if the commands of the holy book, the Koran, were obeyed completely, no infidels would even be allowed to hold office in the state. None of the Muslim rulers of India had ever carried out these regulations to the letter; but the Hindus had always been kept in a state of subjection, and at intervals they had been cruelly persecuted.

Akbar, however, refused to follow in the well-worn path of his predecessors. He found that his fellow-Muslims were often unreliable, and he was conscious that in any case four-fifths of all his subjects were Hindus. He determined to create a unified state in which all citizens should enjoy equal privileges and be given equal opportunities, regardless of their religious opinions.

In many ways Akbar resembled the European rulers of the Renaissance, who were his contemporaries. He had a questing mind and a taste for scientific discovery. For example, he was once moved with a desire to test the truth of an Islamic tradition that everyone was born with an inclination to religion which was quite independent of any training or education imparted by human agents. To prove this, Akbar ordered that about twenty small babies should be placed in a secluded house, and the nurses who looked after them were strictly forbidden to speak a single word to them. If the tradition were correct, the children would by nature speak Arabic, and would acquire without any instruction a notion of God's existence and a desire to worship him. After three or four years the children were released—and were found to be dumb. This unexpected result seems to have done something to shake Akbar's faith. But even as a young man he had been disinclined to accept without question the faith of his fathers.

Akbar was a great builder, and in fact built himself a whole new capital called Fatehpur Sikri; and in the royal palace there he had constructed a special chamber—an architectural oddity—which was designed to enable him to listen to discussion between learned men. At first he listened almost exclusively to Muslims, but he was disgusted to find that these men could often not agree about the meaning of some text in the Koran. Akbar was a firm believer in authority, and in 1579 he therefore issued a decree naming himself as the responsible person for interpreting texts. In the succeeding years he strayed even further from the Muslim fold, for he began to invite the priests of other religions to his debating chamber. On one occasion a Jesuit priest came to dispute with the Muslims, who roundly denounced Christianity and the Bible. The Jesuit then proposed a test. A fire should be lighted: he would walk through the fire holding a Bible, and the Muslims should walk through holding a Koran. God would then make the truth manifest. The Muslim holy men refused this challenge and there is no doubt that Akbar,

114

whose courage was phenomenal, thought the worse of them as a result.

In 1582 he finally abandoned the Muslim faith and set up a so-called religion of his own, which he called the Divine Monotheism.* Anybody could join, whatever his former religion had been, and the rules were not strict. The members were asked to abstain from eating meat if they could, they were supposed to practise charity, and they were required to give a feast to their fellow-members on certain days. But their chief duty was owed not to God but to Akbar himself. They were to sacrifice property, life, honour and religion to the Emperor. This final command shows that the Divine Monotheism was no religion at all, but merely a kind of club welding together like-minded men whose overriding principle was loyalty to the throne. The whole tawdry fabrication was unworthy of so great a man as Akbar, and it was such an affront to all strict Muslims that it is extraordinary that he got away with it. The fact that no serious rebellion broke out is a proof of the great magnetism which he exercised over all his people, Muslim and Hindu alike.

The Hindus did not join the new religion in any numbers, but they were undoubtedly grateful for Akbar's attitude towards them. The exclusiveness of Islam had perpetually reminded them that the government under which they lived regarded them as foreigners in their own country. The Divine Monotheism might be trivial and silly, but at least it underlined the Emperor's belief in the equality of his subjects. He gave other proofs of this, which they probably valued even more highly. Quite early in his reign he took a Hindu princess for one of his wives, and moreover he was prepared to choose for his ministers any men who had the necessary ability. Indeed a Hindu called Raja Todar Mal was one of his most successful and best-trusted servants.

From the point of view of the Hindus the most important of all Akbar's reforms—because it affected most people—was the repeal of the *jizya*, the tax on non-Muslims. This did more than anything else to establish the Emperor in their hearts and their loyalty. Strict Muslims could not approve; but even they—shocked though they were—could not but respect and admire Akbar. Later he put their loyalty to an even more severe test by reforming the legal system. This may seem a harmless thing to do, but in Islam the law is not devised by the political authorities: it is to be found either in the Koran itself, or else in the sacred traditions that have been handed down by holy Muslim men.

* Monotheism means the worship of one god. Christianity, Judaism and Islam are all monotheistic. Hinduism on the other hand includes several gods, although the great Indian leader Mahatma Gandhi (1869-1948) was both a Hindu and a monotheist.

When they conquered India the Muslims would have liked to impose the whole of their legal system on their Hindu subjects. This however proved impossible, since the Hindus outnumbered them by four to one. They never succeeded in making any change in the villages, and even in the towns they were obliged to leave the civil laws untouched. But Hindu tribesmen were forced to obey the Muslim code of criminal law. Even Akbar did not challenge this arrangement, but he made one concession. If a Hindu were accused, a Hindu could act as judge. This horrified the Muslims because it meant that infidels were being allowed to act as interpreters of the sacred Islamic law. They did not have to endure the system for very long, however, because Akbar's legal reform did not survive him. Once his guiding hand had been removed it soon fell into abeyance. But this was not true of his administrative reforms in general: he established a system of government so efficient that nearly three hundred years later it was adopted almost *en bloc* by the British.

Akbar reigned for forty-nine years, and his energy was colossal. He was continually extending his dominions, and went on fighting frequent and successful wars until within ten years of his death. He was a brilliant and resourceful general, and in the intervals of peace he would quickly turn to the work of legal and administrative reform. He extended his trust and friendship to the leading Hindu princes and was completely successful in winning their loyalty. Never before had any Muslim ruler of India built on such sure foundations, and his work carried the country successfully through the next two reigns.

The reigns of Jehangir (1605-1626) and Shah Jehan (1626-1656)

This was fortunate, for the next two Emperors were neither of them outstanding as statesmen. Jehangir, Akbar's son, was a writer of some distinction and patronised the arts, but he was extremely self-indulgent and owed his success as a ruler to the fact that he was running on his father's momentum.

One interesting feature of Jehangir's reign, however, was the establishment of trade with England. The English had for many years been envious of the Portuguese monopoly of the spice trade; and in 1585 two emissaries, Ralph Fitch and Thomas Newbery, arrived at the Mogul court, bringing with them a letter from Queen Elizabeth I to the Emperor.* Akbar, however, was not disposed to welcome these visitors,

---

* The reigns of Elizabeth and Akbar almost coincided. She ruled from 1558 to 1603; his reign started two years earlier and ended two years later than hers. He was however several years the younger of the two, as he came to the throne at the age of thirteen, she at the age of twenty-five.

116

for this was the period when he was taking a great interest in Christianity. He already had at his court some Jesuit priests, who naturally disapproved of Elizabeth because she had led the English away from Rome and had established a national Church. It was in fact at this very time that Philip II of Spain was preparing his Armada to force England back into the Roman fold. The Jesuits exercised considerable influence over Akbar, who refused to have anything to do with Newbery and Fitch. After this failure England withdrew from the scene for some twenty years. But when Jehangir had ascended the Mogul throne, and James I the throne of England, another attempt was made. A certain William Hawkins arrived with a new letter, requesting permission for James's subjects to undertake a limited amount of trading in India. Jehangir readily agreed and a 'factory' or trading-station was founded at Surat in 1612. Three years later Sir Thomas Roe was sent as official English ambassador to the Mogul court.

Ten years later Jehangir died, and, as usually happened in the Mogul royal family, there was a civil war between his sons, each of whom claimed the throne. The victor in this struggle was Shah Jehan, who blinded his defeated brother and killed all his other potential rivals.

Although Shah Jehan had not half the ability of his grandfather Akbar, it is usually reckoned that the Mogul Empire reached the peak of its greatness in his reign. The people were less well governed and the peasants less prosperous, but Mogul art and architecture reached superb heights. Shah Jehan was himself an enthusiastic builder. He built the great Red Fort at Delhi and had placed in it the fabulous Peacock Throne, on which he and the later Great Moguls used to sit on state occasions. This throne was built of gold and so encrusted with jewels that its value was reckoned at a million pounds sterling. Shah Jehan was also the hero of a famous love affair. He fell deeply in love with one of his wives, Mumtaz Mahal, and when she died he determined to build her the most beautiful tomb in the world. At immense cost he raised the wonderful Taj Mahal, in which she was buried, and where eventually his bones were laid beside hers.

Shah Jehan's closing years were miserable, for he spent them in captivity in the great fort at Agra, across the river from the Taj Mahal. When he knew that he was dying he had himself carried onto the walls of the fort where he could gaze at the tomb of his beloved.

The reign of Aurangzeb (1656-1707)

Shah Jehan's imprisonment was the more galling because his gaoler was his own son. He had four sons by one wife, and it was therefore natural that he should declare the eldest, Dara, his heir. But one of the younger sons, Aurangzeb, bitterly resented this decision, partly because he rightly felt himself to be more talented than Dara and also because Dara was not a very devout Muslim. In 1656 it became known that Shah Jehan was seriously ill, almost certainly dying; and Aurangzeb immediately embarked on a civil war against Dara, whom he captured and killed. He then disposed of his two other brothers and it seemed that nothing stood between him and the throne. At this juncture, however, news came from Agra that the old Emperor had recovered. Obviously Aurangzeb ought to have retired, for Shah Jehan was a pious Muslim and there was no good reason for deposing him. But Aurangzeb was not the man to give up a crown that was so nearly in his grasp. He had plenty of troops at his back, and he coolly made his father a state prisoner, and took the management of the Empire into his own hands.

As soon as Aurangzeb was firmly in the saddle, he began systematically to undo the work of Akbar by reducing the Hindus to a condition of civil inferiority and persecuting them in their worship. Once Aurangzeb had adopted a certain course of action, no persuasion could make him swerve from it, and certainly no failure in his own will-power would ever cause him to desist. His single-minded obstinacy was formidable. True to the commands of the Koran, he lived a life of strict austerity. His constant self-denial even took the form of abstaining from taking a prominent part in state ceremonies. It was the normal practice in India in those days for a king to show himself to his people every day at one of the palace windows designed for the purpose. Aurangzeb gave up this habit and even effaced himself on more ceremonial occasions. The Indians were very fond of pageantry, and so this caused some discontent. Much more unpopular was the Emperor's appointment of a Censor of Morals whose function it was to ferret out all who took strong drink, were loose in their morals, or were guilty of any form of heresy against Islam. He even dismissed the court musicians and prohibited the holding of fairs. He has been called—with some justice—the Puritan in the Purple.

These regulations were exceedingly irritating to all Aurangzeb's subjects—Muslim and Hindu alike. But the Emperor had not yet finished with the Hindus. He was determined to prove to them that they no longer belonged to their own state, but were only allowed within its boundaries on sufferance. He thus proclaimed that only Muslims would be employed in the Civil Service. This was a terrible blow to the Hindu clerks, for Indian society was based on the caste system. Every man automatically followed his father's occupation and was forbidden by age-long custom to choose any other. Thus Aurangzeb's prohibition faced all these men with ruin and starvation unless they agreed to become Muslims. Even when confronted by such a threat as this, however, they refused to abandon their own religion, and the Emperor was eventually obliged to climb down because the work of government could not be carried on without the clerks.

This, however, was the only point that Aurangzeb ever conceded, for he held rigidly to all his other decrees, including his successive attacks on the Hindu temples. First he forbade any new temples to be built; this was followed by a decree prohibiting the existing temples to be repaired. Then in 1669 he ordered a wholesale destruction of both the temples and the images within them. Special officials were appointed to oversee this work, and numbers of most beautiful buildings were laid in ruins. The Hindus, who formed eighty per cent of Aurangzeb's subjects, were seething with resentment, but the Emperor refused to heed any danger-signals.

Undeterred by his unpopularity, Aurangzeb then proceeded to re-impose the *jizya*, or poll-tax on infidels, which Akbar had abolished a

Aurangzeb examining the head of his brother, Dara

hundred years before. This was of course levied on all non-Muslims, and the Christian European merchants were forced to pay it in an indirect form; but it was the Hindus who really suffered from it, for the tax fell with great severity on the poorer peasants, the great majority of whom were either Hindu or Buddhist. It is a tribute to Aurangzeb's personality that though his people were enraged and embittered, they still did not rebel. But incapable of letting well alone, the Emperor took one final step which brought a hornet's nest about his ears.

There was in north-west India a very warlike and powerful group of Hindu princes known as the Rajputs. They had been a constant thorn in the side of successive Muslim rulers until the time of Akbar, who by his policy of reconciling the Hindus, won their friendship and unswerving loyalty. For many years this loyalty remained proof against even Aurangzeb's provocations; but at about the same time as the revival of the *jizya* the Emperor took the opportunity of a failure in the Rajput royal line to try and interfere in their affairs; indeed he actually proposed to take away a baby Rajput prince and have him brought up as a Muslim. This drove the Rajputs to rebel. They felt that they could endure Aurangzeb no longer, and opened negotiations with his son, Prince Akbar. The Prince willingly joined in the plot and an armed revolt broke out. But Aurangzeb was an inspired general, and clever in outwitting and dividing his enemies. The rising collapsed and Prince Akbar fled southward, out of his father's dominions into the Deccan.

The region of India known as the Deccan was at that time mainly occupied by two independent Muslim states called Golkonda and Bijapur. For many years Aurangzeb had regarded both these states with bitter hostility because the rulers were both members of the Shiah sect of Islam, which the Emperor—a good Sunni—condemned as heretical. If Akbar should be contaminated by heresy and become a Shiah, and then return and rule the Empire, all Aurangzeb's tireless efforts on behalf of pure Muslim doctrine would go for nothing. Swiftly the Emperor pursued his erring son into the Deccan—and for some extraordinary reason remained there for over a quarter of a century, until his death in 1707.

The year 1681 splits Aurangzeb's reign into two halves. It did not take him very long to defeat Golkonda and Bijapur; in fact he made the Mogul Empire larger than it had ever been before, even under the great Akbar. He should then have returned north to restore order in the main part of his dominions, which were already feeling the effects of his absence. Instead of doing this, however, he embarked on a never-ending

120

war with the Hindu tribe of the Marathas. He seemed to have achieved victory when he captured and executed the Maratha Raja, Shambuji; but the Maratha army fought on. The Moguls, who had once been fine warriors, had deteriorated sadly during their sojourn in India. Probably the enervating climate was one cause of this; another was their love of luxury. Aurangzeb himself always lived austerely, but most of his followers, even the common soldiers, expected to be very comfortable on a campaign. Enormous quantities of baggage and an army of servants and women, larger than the army proper, trailed round in pursuit of the Marathas, who were a hardy, swift-moving band of guerillas. They eluded pursuit without difficulty, and then harried the Emperor's forces.

Aurangzeb spent the last twenty years of his life chasing these will-o'-the-wisps, pouring out his country's fast-dwindling money in a war which achieved nothing. Slowly, bit by bit, he lost all his former conquests, and in 1707 he died—in his ninetieth year but vigorous to the last.

During these wasted years spent in the south, the great Mogul Empire had rotted and decayed. Corruption and misgovernment went on unchecked because the Emperor was not there to keep order. No outstanding statesmen came to the fore; and there was no faithful minister to advise Aurangzeb, for he had made it clear that he was not the sort of man to welcome advice. In his final illness he was overwhelmed by the sense of his own isolation and of the wasted years. He wrote to his son, 'Old age has arrived, and weakness has grown strong, strength has left my limbs. I came alone and am going away alone. I know not who I am or what I have been doing. . . . I have not at all done any true government of the realm or cherishing of the peasantry. Life, so valuable, has gone away for nothing.'

He might well feel remorse, for he had reduced his dominions to such a state that it would have required another Akbar to restore the situation. Unfortunately, however, so far from having a genius on the throne, India was not even to have an emperor of average competence. The dynasty was played out. For the next hundred and fifty years there would still be a Grand Mogul of a sort lolling ineffectively on the throne at Delhi; but after the death of Aurangzeb they were a succession of cyphers, totally incapable of controlling the country.

The condition of India in the eighteenth century

India suffered many terrible misfortunes during the eighteenth century. In 1739 the Persians invaded the north, sacked Delhi, and bore away

Building a Mogul citadel at Khavarnak

the fabulous Peacock Throne. Even when they had retired, there were frequent attacks from the Afghans; and all over the country there was a breakdown of government. The Empire had always consisted of a number of provinces, which were placed under the rule of local governors or *nawabs*. In normal times these appointments were made from Delhi; but now that the emperors were too weak to get their orders obeyed, the death of a nawab was usually followed by a minor war between rival claimants for the post. The peasants, who formed the vast majority of the population, suffered severely from the unsettled conditions and the endless violence.

The Europeans in India

There was, however, one class of people who benefited from the general unrest. These were the European merchants. Four nations were represented in India. The Portuguese held Goa, the Dutch were in Cochin, and the British ruled the little island of Bombay. These were all tiny pockets of foreign rule, but in addition both Britain and France had been given permission to establish a few trading stations within the Mogul dominions. Jehangir allowed the English to come to Surat, and later similar concessions were obtained in Calcutta and Madras. About a hundred miles south of Madras was Pondicherry, the chief settlement of the French who also had a post at Chandernagore, not far from Calcutta. The French had come late into the competition for Asian markets, and when they at length arrived it was under the influence of Colbert. The British merchants resented their intrusion but could do nothing about it, for in the seventeenth century their own position in India was none too secure. They were not subjected to the humiliating conditions endured by Europeans in Canton or the Ottoman Empire; but so long as the Moguls were strong, all the Europeans had to behave themselves. There had been some brushes with Delhi, and on every such occasion the foreigners had been obliged to apologise and make their peace. Aurangzeb once seized the factory at Surat and threatened to expel all the British. He relented eventually, but the merchants knew that they were plying their trade on sufferance.

By the middle of the eighteenth century, however, the situation had changed. The foreigners were not more powerful than they had been, but in the prevailing disorder their little 'factories' were islands of calm and strength. The endless political squabbles meant nothing to them, and as they had their own paid troops, they could defend themselves against any attack.

Dupleix's bid for power

What interested the British and the French, far more than Indian affairs, was the bitter hostility that they felt for one another. In Europe the eighteenth century was a period of almost unbroken wars. Most of them were fought for very trivial causes, and the powers were perpetually changing sides and forming new alliances. The only constant factor in all this was the relentless enmity of Britain and France, who pursued for a full hundred years the quarrel initiated by William III and Louis XIV. We have seen how this quarrel was fought out on the soil of North America; and in India, too, the British and the French merchants were always at the ready to resist and oppose any course of action adopted by the other.

It was while matters were in this state that in 1741 the French government appointed Joseph Dupleix (1697–1763) Governor-General of all their Indian stations. Dupleix had come out to India as a young man, and in the intervals of carrying out the duties for which the French East India Company paid him, he quietly amassed a considerable fortune by means of private trading. A year after his appointment war was declared between France and Britain, and Dupleix at once embarked on vigorous operations against Madras. The ensuing skirmishes had no lasting result but they gave Dupleix a taste both for fighting and for politics, and when peace was restored between his own country and England he resolved to intervene in Indian affairs. All around him small civil wars were going on between rival nawabs, and Dupleix hit upon a cunning plan. He determined that whenever a promising war of this sort broke out, he would wait to see which contestant appeared to be losing, and then come forward with an offer of support from his own well-trained troops. If he should succeed in turning a near-defeat into a victory, he might reasonably expect to enjoy the gratitude and the confidence of his protégé. In fact, by threatening to withdraw his support if annoyed, he could virtually hold such a nawab in the hollow of his hand. A steady pursuit of this policy would soon build up what would amount to a French empire in India.

The scheme was a clever one, but it did not take the British long to perceive what was afoot. Their officials then fell into line by offering help to any claimant to office who was opposed by the French. Thus when a certain Chanda Sahib, who aspired to the governorship of the Carnatic, secured the help of Dupleix, the British promptly put their army at the disposal of Chanda's rival, Mohammed Ali. The situation

124

was repeated in Hyderabad where the British backed Nazir Jang, and the French Muzaffar Jang.

As the two European trading companies had almost equal strength, it was difficult to foretell at first how these struggles for influence would go; but it was eventually decided by the military genius of Robert Clive, who won for the British a decisive victory over the French. Dupleix was recalled to France in disgrace, and the British merchants, whose only aim had been to prevent French imperialism, found themselves almost accidentally possessed of considerable political influence in south India.

The British East India Company in Bengal

Dupleix left India in 1745, but the system he had started did not die with his departure. In 1756 the British once again involved themselves in a local war, this time in Calcutta. They were not very successful at first, for the victory went to Suraj-ud-Daula, the candidate whom they had opposed. Suraj not unnaturally disliked the British merchants, and when shortly afterwards they began to build fortifications in Calcutta, he sent a punitive expedition which wiped out the British community. So long as the Moguls had been powerful, they had protected the foreign merchants; but it was now useless to appeal to Delhi, and the British therefore sent out a force under the command of Clive. Suraj was obliged to yield and formal permission was given to build fortifications if they wanted to. Clive however was not content with this victory, and plotted to put another nawab in power. Suraj had several enemies, including Mir Jafar, one of his own generals. Consequently when the British and the Indians met on the battlefield at Plassey in 1757, Mir Jafar deserted and Clive won a virtually bloodless victory. Suraj was then deposed and replaced by Mir Jafar, who was a mere puppet in the hands of the British. When he attempted to act independently, they deposed him in favour of one Mir Kazim; later, when Mir Kazim also proved insubordinate, Mir Jafar was recalled.

In this ludicrous train of events the only certainty was that the British East India Company now had complete political control of Bengal. In 1764 the Mogul Emperor made an effort to drive them away, but the Indians were heavily defeated at the Battle of Buxar, after which the Company was given the *Dewani* of Bengal. This privilege meant that they now had the right to raise taxes from the Bengalis and to administer public expenditure.

That a trading company—and a foreign company at that—should be given such immense political power is almost unbelievable. The

British owed their success partly to the feebleness of the Mogul and the general disorder into which the whole country had fallen; but another important factor was the superiority at this time of European amries over those of Asia. This superiority was to be maintained for over a century, and indeed went on so long that Europeans almost began to regard it as a law of nature. The battle of Plassey was really decided by treachery, but the victory at Buxar was genuine enough. On that occasion the ruling Muslim class strained every nerve to dislodge the foreigners; nevertheless the hostility against the British was never unanimous. The East India Company had been trading in Bengal for nearly seventy years, and during that time their operations had brought about changes in the Indian economy. A new type of capitalism had developed which brought considerable prosperity to the local Indian merchants, who were Hindus. These men, who owed their wealth to the foreigners, were deeply disturbed by any Indian effort to expel the Company, and they supported the foreigners by every means in their power.

Some of them may have changed their minds, however, when they saw the havoc the Company's *Dewani* wrought in Bengal. The British merchants should never have undertaken this task, for which they were in no way fitted. Their business was to trade and to send back regular sums to their employers, who passed these profits on to the shareholders. Since the accumulation of wealth was the real purpose of the Company, the Directors had for a long time forbidden their representatives to throw away good money by dabbling in Indian politics. The headlong sequence of events started by Clive had swept away their objections, but though they might condone these political excursions, they still insisted on receiving their regular remittances. In these circumstances their harassed employees in Bengal found in the right to raise revenue a splendid opportunity to make good the losses incurred in their recent military adventures. Not being themselves tax-gatherers, they entrusted the work to Indian middlemen who, provided they handed over the required sums to the Company, were given a free hand to make whatever private profit out of the transaction they could.

As always when this kind of system is permitted, the unfortunate Bengali peasants were subjected to merciless extortion. To make matters even worse, the British merchants were themselves extremely badly paid by the Company. Inevitably they were in the habit of lining their pockets by indulging in individual trading on their own account. This, though forbidden, was nothing new. Now, however, the British used the privileged position which the Dewani conferred on them to claim exemption

An East India Company trader

from paying customs duties. The dubious trading in which they indulged and the bribes which they freely accepted, added further to the crushing burden to which the Bengalis were subjected.

An account written in 1769 by one of the Company's employees gives a horrifying picture of the effect of the British Dewani. 'It must give pain to Englishmen,' he wrote, 'to have reason to think that (since 1764) the condition of the country has been worse than ever before. . . . This fine country, which flourished under the most despotic and arbitrary government, is verging towards ruin.'

The Regulating Act of 1773

Rumours of what was going on drifted to London, and the British Government realised that some sort of official action must be taken. The Parliament at Westminster had no vestige of right to legislate for India, and the only connection that the Government had so far with that country was to give its official blessing to the East India Company. But now by an extraordinary train of events a group of merchants, who were British subjects, had acquired political power over several millions of Bengalis, and were unquestionably abusing their power.

127

In the circumstances Britain had to do something about it, and in 1773 Parliament passed the Regulating Act which provided the Company with a machinery for controlling the actions of its members and agents. A Governor-General was to be appointed by the British Government, who would regulate the affairs of the Company with the help of a Council. A supreme court was appointed which could try British subjects in India for crimes against each other and for oppression of Indians. Moreover the Company was obliged to submit its accounts for inspection so that fortunes should no longer be made by extortion.

Warren Hastings (1732-1818)

The first Governor-General to be appointed was Warren Hastings, an honest man who had been in India from the age of eighteen and probably understood the Indians as well as any Englishman could hope to do. He was genuinely anxious to construct a code of laws that would be acceptable to the Hindus, and to this end he had translations made of Hindu law-books. But despite his excellent intentions, Hastings came to grief and offended almost every class of people with whom he had to deal—including the Hindus.

In 1775 Raja Nand Kumar, a member of the Brahman caste, the highest caste in Hindu society, was suspected of forgery. He was brought before one of the newly established courts and—in accordance with English law at that time—condemned to be hanged. Kumar had been a bitter enemy of Hastings and had intrigued against him. Nevertheless the Governor-General's refusal to reprieve him was doubtless due not to private vengeance but to a respect for the law as he understood it. Unfortunately the Hindus looked at law from a very different angle. They did not regard forgery as a serious crime, and they did not believe in equality before the law. To their way of thinking a Brahman ought not to be subject to penalties which might quite rightly be inflicted on men of a lower caste. They were deeply and sincerely shocked by the episode. This is a striking example of the misunderstandings that can arise between people of different race and traditions, even where there is genuine goodwill.

Hastings's enemies in the Company, who bitterly resented his reforming zeal, did all they could to ruin him; and later when he had returned to England, they had him impeached before Parliament as a traitor. He endured the ordeal of a trial which lasted for six years, but was eventually acquitted.

The India Act of 1784

Meanwhile it had become clear from the disagreements between Hastings and the other members of the East India Company that the Regulating Act was not a success. Some new system of government had to be

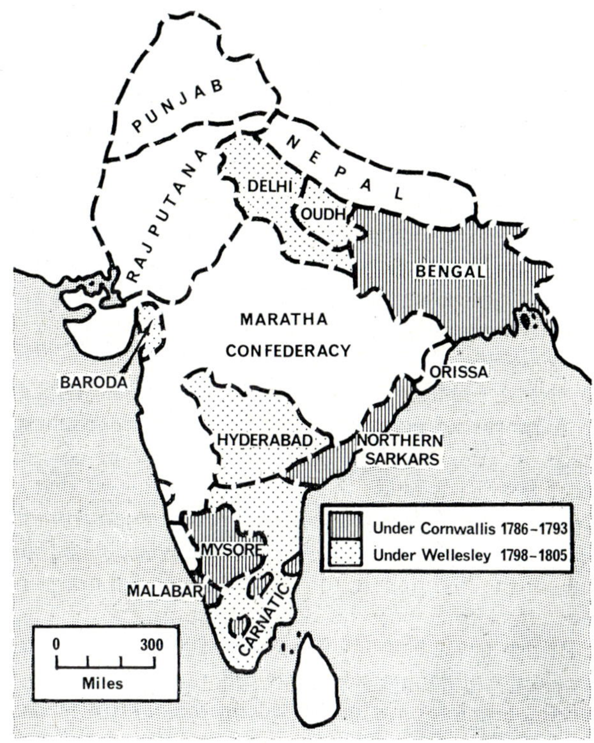

Map 6—The growth of British influence and control in India
after the passing of the India Act, 1784

devised that would keep the Company's agents in proper order. Accordingly a new Act was passed in 1784 which virtually put the control of British India into the hands of one of the Cabinet Ministers at Westminster.

Warren Hastings did not approve of this new measure, which was the reason for his resigning his post and coming home. He was replaced as Governor-General not by an employee of the Company, but by a distinguished English statesman, Lord Cornwallis. Cornwallis had never been to India and at first refused the appointment; but eventually he took up his duties in 1786 and, despite his inexperience, he was—from the British point of view—a great success. He was the first of a long line of Governors and Viceroys, hardly any of whom had any prior knowledge of India, but all of whom ruled large tracts of that country with great dignity and in the name of the King of England.

The character of British rule in India

Only thirty-two years elapsed between the appointment of Dupleix in 1741 and the Regulating Act of 1773. But in that brief time the face of India had been changed beyond recognition and an entirely new type of bond forged between Asia and Europe. In 1741 the foreign merchants were groups of aliens, tolerated so long as they behaved, confining themselves to trade, and possessing small armed bands merely for their own defence. It was Dupleix who first tampered with this state of affairs, and the British who took over his schemes and reaped a vast harvest, which took even themselves by surprise.

For the British suddenly found themselves ruling in India an empire for which there was no precedent. The Spanish had acquired an even larger empire in America, but that had consisted of colonies where thousands of Spaniards made their homes. Nothing of that sort happened in India, which attracted few British people apart from those who went either to trade or to govern. Nor could a parallel be found in the Spanish rule of the Philippines, for there the imperial power had made a deliberate effort to impose its own culture on its subjects—a task which the British never had any intention of attempting in India. The Portuguese empire of Albuquerque was still more different, for that had been a purely oceanic dominion, based on the control of commercial shipping and of a few sea-ports. Britain, on the other hand, was eventually to rule some two-thirds of the Indian sub-continent. The European people who came nearest to equalling the British achievement were the Dutch, who by the middle of the eighteenth century had imposed economic control over several of the islands of Indonesia. But in the Dutch possessions it was the trading company which continued to be in control; not until 1900 did the government in Holland take over responsibility for the administration. The Dutch Empire was an example of crude economic exploitation. The British were not of course quite innocent of exploiting India; but at least the British Government now recognised that they had a serious responsibility for her people's well-being.

130

The expansion of British rule during the nineteenth century

Cornwallis had been instructed by the British government to put an end to the military expansion which the East India Company had been carrying out in India. But before long he found himself engaged in fighting, merely with a view to putting down some of the disorders which were still ravaging the country. As their troops were superior, the British invariably won the wars that they waged for this purpose, and so their empire grew. Lord Wellesley, who was Governor-General from 1798-1805, and the Marquis of Hastings who held office from 1813-1823, both added considerably to the territories ruled by Britain.

These men were not conscious of themselves as aggressors. On the contrary Hastings claimed to have 'bestowed blessings on millions'. He went on to say: 'Multitudes of people have even in this short interval come from the hills and fastnesses in which they have sought refuge for years, and have reoccupied their deserted villages.' Bearing in mind the chaos that had succeeded the decay of the Mogul Empire, this claim was no doubt justified. Any form of government is better than chaos, and the Indian peasants were at that time much more concerned with law and order than with nationalism, about which they knew nothing and cared less. Moreover the British, in the early days of their rule, were careful to study the customs and traditions of their new subjects.

The Indian Mutiny

In 1848, however, Lord Dalhousie was appointed Governor-General. He was as anxious as his predecessors to give the Indians good and wise rule, but he made the mistake of introducing reforms of a type that were being carried out in the Britain of his day, but which seemed strange and unacceptable to a people whose history and customs were totally different. For example he built a number of excellent roads, laid the foundations of a national railway system and also established a telegraph system. Dalhousie never doubted that the Indians would welcome these innovations. But the telegraph was too novel and seemed to many Indians to savour of evil magic; so did the railway engines, and even the roads were resented by some, simply because they disturbed a way of life that had existed virtually unchanged for thousands of years. Many Indians genuinely felt that the familiar social fabric was being cut away under their feet. Consequently there was a good deal of discontent among both Muslims and Hindus. The Muslims had by now recovered from the lethargy into which the collapse of the Mogul Empire had thrown them. At first they had refused on religious as well as political grounds to co-operate with the British. Consequently all the most attractive posts were taken by Hindus. In the 1850's, however, they awoke to what was happening, and many of them gave their support to a revolt which broke out in 1857.

Because this revolt started in the army the British regarded it purely as a military matter, but in fact large numbers of civilians took part. After first suffering some serious reverses, the British eventually quelled the rising, but it nevertheless had a profound effect on the government of India. For it was now decided that the East India Company, after its two hundred and fifty years of existence, should be disbanded. British possessions in India had become so extensive that it was no longer appropriate that a trading concern should exercise even a limited control over them. So the company was dissolved, the Queen of England became the Head of the Indian state, and the Governors-General became Viceroys.

The world in 1700

Once again we must retrace our steps and take another glimpse at the state of the world, this time in 1700.

THE MIDDLE EAST

The Turkish Empire was still the dominating political power in the region, despite the fact that in 1699 a war against Europe had ended in defeat. The weaknesses arising from the indifference of the rulers to the social welfare of their subjects were still present, but in all other respects the government at Constantinople was firmly established, and the Sultan's word was law throughout the greater part of the region. In recent years the Russians had made a great effort to expand towards the Black Sea at the expense of Turkey. Their armies had however been driven back.

The Sultan continued to be on bad terms with the Shah of Persia, and the two powers were still bitter rivals. In 1638 the Turks had captured the key city of Baghdad from Persia, but the struggle was still indecisive, neither power being able to overcome the other.

INDIA

The seventeenth century had been for India the great century of the Mogul Empire: Akbar had still been on the throne in 1600, while in 1700 Aurangzeb's long reign was drawing towards its close. During recent decades the boundaries of the Empire had been pushed further and further south, until nearly the whole of India acknowledged Mogul rule. Aurangzeb, although an old man, was still formidable, but his dominions were suffering from considerable internal decay. The Hindu tribe of the Marathas was in a state of open rebellion, and it was only the continued existence of the old Emperor which kept the rest of the country in order.

Meanwhile the British East India Company had two years previously been given permission to establish a factory at Calcutta in addition to their existing bases at Bombay and Madras. By now, as a result of Colbert's policy, the French had also acquired factories in India.

THE REST OF SOUTHERN ASIA

The Dutch still had a stranglehold on the commerce of the region, though they had not yet—except in the Moluccas and the Bandas—made any attempt to control the internal life of the various islands and sultanates. One of the principal features of the seventeenth century in this region had been a great Islamic religious revival. This had led to a good deal of missionary activity, and had tended to unite the Muslims in a stronger hostility against the Europeans than they had previously felt.

CHINA

In China the century had seen the collapse of the Ming Dynasty, which in 1645 had been replaced by that of the Manchus. This family had originated in Manchuria just beyond the north-east border of China. Before long they annexed Korea, and in the following decades expanded their dominions westwards as well. The Manchus were at this stage vigorous and powerful, and China was as great as ever.

JAPAN

Early in the seventeenth century Ieyasu Tokugawa had made himself Shogun, and his family were now firmly established in that hereditary office. Under their influence Japan had gained steadily in strength, and in 1637 had adopted a policy of excluding foreigners. A few Dutch, English and Portuguese merchants were allowed to carry on their business in one port, but the trade was rigidly controlled. The Shogun, however, had insisted that in return a certain quantity of western-style cannon should be delivered regularly to his government. Japan therefore had not shut out foreign influences quite so completely as China had done.

SIBERIA

The infiltration of Russians into Siberia had continued and at an increased speed. In 1632 they had reached Lake Baikal, and fifty years later had advanced so far that they came into conflict with the Chinese. China was too powerful to be defied, and in 1689 a treaty was signed by which Russia agreed to withdraw from the region of the Amur Valley.

RUSSIA

Russia was at this time under the rule of Czar Peter the Great, who had made it his policy to establish as many contacts as possible with the west. To this end he was busy waging war against Sweden, some of whose territory he coveted. An attempt had also been made to reach the Black Sea; but owing to the effective resistance of Turkey, Russia was still without a coastline in the south.

EUROPE

During the seventeenth century Europe had not maintained the great burst of activity that had characterised the preceding period, although steady progress had been made in scientific research. In the field of politics nationalism had continued to develop, and in general it was a period of absolute monarchy. In England the authority of the sovereign had been considerably curbed, but Louis XIV had created in France the most autocratic régime that Europe had ever seen. Under his rule France had become a standing menace to the security of the other powers, who were constantly forming themselves into military alliances in an attempt to preserve the balance of power. In 1700 one major war had ended only three years earlier, while another was already brewing.

Meanwhile European interest in other continents continued unabated. The Spanish-American empire was as strong as ever, and a series of English colonies had been founded on the Atlantic seaboard of North America. In Asia the Dutch were the most successful imperial power, but the Portuguese still held a few ports, and both England and France maintained a few trading-stations. The Philippines were still under Spanish control.

AFRICA

A change had come over the relations between Africa and Europe, for although the slave-trade was still operating exactly as it had been in 1600, and although most of the remainder of the continent was as impenetrable as ever, a new foreign contact had been made in the extreme south. In 1652 the Dutch had landed on the Cape of Good Hope and founded a colony. Originally this had been intended to serve a purpose similar to the various Dutch coastal stations in Asia. The settlers, called Boers, soon developed a deep attachment to their new homeland, however, and had already begun to regard themselves as different in many ways from their former compatriots in Holland.

LATIN AMERICA

The Spanish colonies as well as Brazil now had all the stability that attaches to communities that are well over a hundred years old. Many of the Spanish inhabitants came out to America only to make money, and then went home to enjoy a wealthy old age. There were on the other hand families that had been in America for generations and had a strong patriotism towards their own colony. The original Indian inhabitants had settled quite contentedly under Spanish rule, and the numerous African slaves, though hardly in a happy situation, were nevertheless by now a stable element in the population.

NORTH AMERICA

Profound changes had occurred in North America since 1600, when practically the whole continent had been at the disposal of the native Red Indians. Now there were no less than twelve English colonies scattered along the east coast between the St Lawrence and Florida. The colonists were firmly rooted in their new homes and few of them had any desire to return to England. Further north, however, the French had penetrated to the St Lawrence and had discovered the Great Lakes. They did not found many colonies, but devoted most of their time to cutting timber and trapping animals for fur. These activities contributed to the prosperity of the French motherland but did not attract to Canada a settled population of any size. Some exploration had been carried out in the great Mississippi valley, but most of the continent was still unknown to the Europeans.

AUSTRALIA AND NEW ZEALAND

The long isolation of Australasia had now been broken. In 1642 a Dutch sea captain, Abel Tasman (1603-1659), had been sent by the Governor of the Dutch East Indies on one of the many voyages of exploration that he made in his career. On this occasion he came upon the island south of Australia which was called Tasmania in his honour. A few weeks later he reached New Zealand. On another voyage in 1644 he discovered the north-west coast of Australia. As yet no Europeans had taken any strong interest in these discoveries, and there had been no thought of colonisation.

7 New ideas: the Age of Reason

During the great European Renaissance the study of the natural sciences, which had for centuries been smothered and imprisoned within walls of prejudice and indifference, was released by men such as Kepler, Copernicus and Galileo. These men had been inspired to look at old books of learning with new eyes, but even they—revolutionaries though they were—found it hard to break away from the past. Copernicus reached the correct conclusion that the sun, not the earth, was the centre of our part of the universe; but he felt the conclusion to be so peculiar that he was terrified of publishing it in case he should be laughed at. Kepler also failed fully to grasp the truth which he had accidentally touched on, namely that the planets revolve in an ellipse. Both these men helped to break down old barriers and open the way for a new kind of scientific study, but they did not pursue that new road themselves. Tycho de Brahe advanced some way upon it and provided a pointer to the future by compiling a great storehouse of observed facts about the stars. Then during the seventeenth and eighteenth centuries there was a tremendous surge forward by a number of original thinkers all over Europe who devoted their lives to studying and developing all the sciences then known.

The scientific method

One of the greatest of these new thinkers was a Frenchman, René Descartes, who was born in 1596. He was a star student at a Jesuit college and had all the wealth of Renaissance learning at his disposal, but he found it unsatisfying and suddenly decided to abandon books in order to study life itself. With this end in view, he became a soldier and travelled all round Europe. Later he left the army but continued to wander until he reached the age of thirty-three. Then he went into retirement and began to absorb and evaluate the observations he had made and the impressions he had received. He ruthlessly overthrew all tradition, resolving that he would believe nothing until he had proved it. He rated the human power of reasoning so high that he regarded it as the proof that humans exist at all. '*Cogito ergo sum*', he declared, 'The fact that I think shows that I exist.'

Descartes applied his treatment of doubt (as a preliminary to understanding) to the question of God's existence. And after deep reflection he came to the reasoned conclusion that God does exist, and is perfect; for man could not have in his mind the idea of perfection unless it existed; therefore perfection does exist, and perfection is God.

Descartes's writings made a great impression on his contemporaries, and he was summoned by Queen Christina of Sweden to come and live at her court so that he could discuss philosophic matters with her. Unfortunately the Queen was an unusually energetic woman who liked to rise at five in the morning to get in a philosophy session before breakfast. The early hours, combined with the bitterly cold climate, were too much for Descartes, who was taken ill and died in 1650 at the age of fifty-four.

A considerable part of his life overlapped with that of the Englishman Francis Bacon (1561-1626), though the latter spent more than half his life in the sixteenth century and was in many ways more typical of the Renaissance than of the seventeenth-century thinkers. The breadth and variety of Bacon's interests were characteristic of the Renaissance, for he was a lawyer, an essayist and a statesman as well as being a scientist. But he had this in common with Descartes, that he refused to accept any conclusion unless he believed it to be backed by adequate evidence. Also he had a passion for practical experiment. In fact it was in pursuit of scientific truth that he contracted his death illness. He wanted to discover just how far a low temperature would delay the process of decomposition, and he caught cold while stuffing snow into a dead chicken.

Isaac Newton (1642-1727)

When the Frenchman Descartes died in Sweden in 1650, there was in England a little boy aged eight living on a small estate in Lincolnshire, called Woolsthorpe, in the care of his grandmother. This was Isaac Newton, one of the greatest geniuses of all time. In due course he went as a student to Cambridge, but when the plague broke out in that town he was forced to come home to Woolsthorpe for several months, where he pondered many things, including what it is that causes apples (or any other objects) to fall to the ground.

It was while he was still quite a young man that a whole series of great truths dawned upon him. Perhaps the greatest of all his achievements was in the field of astronomy. Kepler had found that planets move in an ellipse, though he had not understood why. Galileo had studied and reported upon the behaviour of projectiles fired from the earth. Newton perceived that the law of gravity which draws objects towards

138

ISAAC NEWTON

DESCARTES

each other, combined with the momentum which forces a projectile away from its starting point, would have the effect of directing the planets into an ellipse. But Newton was a mathematician as well as an astronomer, and he did not publish his theory until he had worked it out very exactly in mathematical terms. His work in physics was equally remarkable. He studied the nature of light, and discovered the existence of the spectrum in which all colour is contained.

Newton did not however spend all his time in a laboratory—or even in an orchard. He was an extremely busy man who was constantly called upon to undertake public services. He served for a time as a Member of Parliament; he was also a craftsman, devoting much effort to the construction of concave mirrors for use in telescopes. In 1702 he was made President of the Royal Society. This association, which was typical of the great interest which men of the seventeenth century took in science, had actually originated in the middle of the English Civil War. In 1645 a group of scholars living in London had formed the habit of meeting weekly to discuss 'experimental philosophy', by which they meant the sciences. The meetings lapsed during the period of the republic, though some of the original members continued to meet in Oxford. When the monarchy was restored under Charles II they returned to the capital, and in 1662 were granted a royal charter; but it was not until Newton became president that the Royal Society achieved the great reputation which it has ever since retained.

Newton's genius was unequalled even in a talented generation, but important work was being done in other countries in the fields of mathematics and astronomy. In particular we may mention a Frenchman, Jean Picard (1620-1682), who calculated with almost complete accuracy the radius of the earth, and also made considerable progress in determining its distance from the sun.

Medical science

Meanwhile man's intense interest in stars, planets and infinity had not blinded him to the desirability of learning more about his own body, and the study of medicine had made huge strides. In England William Harvey (1578-1657), a doctor and lecturer in anatomy, after years of painstaking research, had triumphantly proved his theory that the blood circulates through the body and that the heart is in effect a pump. Similar work was being carried out in other parts of Europe, and these theoretical advances paved the way for the unprecedented success in saving and prolonging human life which was such a feature of the late eighteenth century in Europe. It was at that period that the average expectation of life was enormously increased. By the middle of the twentieth century this achievement had been passed to other continents, so that one of the great problems we face today is the prospect of the population of the world becoming too large.

An important contribution to these advances was made by Edward Jenner (1740-1823), whose name will be always associated with vaccination. Jenner was not the first man to infect a patient deliberately with a small dose of a disease in the hope that he would thus be preserved from a serious attack; but it was he who realised the significance of the fact that people (milkmaids chiefly) who had suffered from cow-pox, never contracted smallpox. He carried out some very bold experiments of exposing vaccinated children to a serious infection of smallpox. The experiments were successful—so successful indeed that henceforward Jenner had hardly any time to himself. Requests came from far and wide, and he complained that he was 'a vaccine clerk to the whole world'.

His interests were not however confined to medical science. As a younger man, he devoted a lot of time to the physiology of birds. He was also an ardent botanist and did some work on the plant specimens which Captain Cook brought back from his first voyage, about which more will be said later.

Chemistry

Another figure of the eighteenth century who pursued a wide variety of interests was Antoine Lavoisier (1743-1794). Born in Paris, he had an excellent education and determined to secure a regular income in order that he might pursue his studies. He therefore sought and obtained an appointment as Assistant Farmer-General of taxes. The system of taxation in France at that time was grossly unfair as well as being extremely inefficient. It was not in Lavoisier's power to remedy the injustice, but he corrected what inefficiencies he could. This in no way exhausted his energies, however. As early as 1766, when he was only twenty-three, he had won a public competition for the best method of providing street-lighting in a town. For this he received a medal from the King, and as a result secured further employment with the government. He applied his chemical talents to the improvement of gunpowder, and also experimented with the application of science to farming methods.

In addition to all these practical tasks Lavoisier found time in his laboratory to conduct many theoretical experiments. He discovered the composition of water, and in 1790 drew up the first table of chemical elements ever to be compiled. In this he was carrying on the work of the English chemist Boyle (a founder-member of the Royal Society) who had first defined the elements.

Meanwhile Lavoisier had been overtaken by political events. In 1789 the French Revolution began, and during the next few years many Frenchmen indulged in an orgy of throwing away the traditions of the past. Along with everything else, it was decided that the old system of weights and measures should be abolished, and Lavoisier was concerned in evolving the new metric system, destined later to be adopted in many parts of the world. The metre (a little less than forty inches) was chosen as a unit of measurement because it was thought to be an exact fraction of the circumference of the earth.

But although Lavoisier served the new revolutionary government as loyally as he had served the monarchy, the fact of his having been a tax collector stood against him. During the Reign of Terror he was accused of treason and sentenced to the guillotine. A reprieve was refused on the grounds that the 'Republic had no need of scientists'. This was a tragic waste of a useful life, and a surprising event to happen in the eighteenth century, which prided itself on being the Age of Reason. Generally speaking scientists were respected even when they had been born into a humble station in life.

	Noms nouveaux.	Noms anciens correspondans.
Substances simples qui appartiennent aux trois règnes & qu'on peut regarder comme les élémens des corps.	Lumière..........	Lumière.
	Calorique.......	Chaleur. Principe de la chaleur. Fluide igné. Fèu. Matière du feu & de la chaleur.
	Oxygène........	Air déphlogistiqué. Air empiréal. Air vital. Base de l'air vital.
	Azote	Gaz phlogistiqué. Mofete. Base de la mofete.
	Hydrogène......	Gaz inflammable. Base du gaz inflammable.
Substances simples non métalliques oxidables & acidifiables.	Soufre..........	Soufre.
	Phosphore......	Phosphore.
	Carboné........	Charbon pur.
	Radical muriatiq.	Inconnu.
	Radical fluorique.	Inconnu.
	Radical boracique.	Inconnu.
Substances simples métalliques oxidables & acidifiables.	Antimoine	Antimoine.
	Argent..........	Argent.
	Arsenic.........	Arsenic.
	Bismuth.........	Bismuth.
	Cobolt..........	Cobolt.
	Cuivre.	Cuivre.
	Etain...........	Etain.
	Fer	Fer.
	Manganèse......	Manganèse.
	Mercure.	Mercure.
	Molybdène......	Molybdène.
	Nickel..........	Nickel.
	Or.............	Or.
	Platine.........	Platine.
	Plomb..........	Plomb.
	Tungstène......	Tungstène.
	Zinc.	Zinc.
Substances simples salifiables terreuses.	Chaux..........	Terre calcaire, chaux.
	Magnésie.......	Magnésie, base du sel d'epsom.
	Baryte..........	Barote, terre pesante.
	Alumine........	Argile, terre de l'alun, base de l'alun.
	Silice...	Terre siliceu e, terre vitrifiable.

Lavoisier's Table of Elements

Captain Cook (1728-1779)

Such a man was James Cook, the son of a labourer who contrived to give the boy some slight education, but was obliged to apprentice him to a grocer at the age of thirteen. James succeeded a few years later, however, in entering a more congenial apprenticeship, this time to a ship-owner. He took to the sea at once, and spent some years voyaging around the coast of Britain and across to the Baltic Sea. Then in 1755 his career really began when he joined the Royal Navy and saw service in Canada during the war of 1756-63 that was fought against France. In the intervals of military action Cook spent his time surveying, and made charts of the St Lawrence River and the coast of Newfoundland. His experience of navigation had given him an interest in astronomy in addition to his love of geography, and notes of the observation he had made of an eclipse of the sun were actually printed in the publication of the Royal Society.

By this time James Cook was not only progressing satisfactorily up the ladder of promotion in the Navy, he was also becoming known as a man of science. In 1768 he was put in command of a ship that was to carry a party of scientists to Tahiti to observe the transit of Venus across the sun's disc. Cook was also charged with the task of trying to locate the 'southern continent'. Geographers believed that there was a continent somewhere south of Africa or South America, but nobody knew its shape or how large it might be.

After leaving Tahiti the good ship *Endeavour*, with her cargo of scientists, cruised about the southern seas and visited New Zealand. This land had already been discovered by a Dutch explorer but as yet little was known about it. Cook circumnavigated both islands (giving his name to the strait that lies between them), made charts of the coasts, and then sailed westward to Australia. Australia had also been discovered earlier, but as the previous explorers had chanced upon the arid desert of the west, they had not been favourably impressed. The *Endeavour* on the other hand landed on the attractive east coast, and as many interesting plants were discovered and taken back to England, their landing place was given the name of Botany Bay. Cook then sailed along the north coast of Australia, establishing the fact, which had hitherto been in doubt, that this huge island was separated from New Guinea.

In 1771 Cook returned to England in triumph, was fêted and promoted and despatched on a second voyage a year later. The object this time was to make a serious search for the southern continent. He sailed to a latitude of between 60 and 70 degrees south and then went round the world at that level, thus proving once and for all that the supposed continent did not exist. On the other hand, he did discover many groups of islands in the Pacific.

After this trip Cook was promoted to the rank of captain. Plans were immediately put in hand for yet a third voyage, which set out in 1776 with the object of finding a north-west passage from the Pacific to the Atlantic. In this venture Captain Cook, like so many explorers before him, was doomed to disappointment. Ice prevented his ships from making the passage. He withdrew to warmer waters and began the voyage home. But on the way he became involved in a fight with the natives of an island in the Pacific and was hacked to death.

Starting from obscure beginnings, James Cook had by talents, hard work and courage won his way into the affection and admiration of his countrymen, and had made an important contribution to man's knowledge. He had travelled to many parts of the world about which little was known, had made careful observations and recorded what he saw on map or chart.

The development of physics

Meanwhile scientists of another kind were exploring a more abstract field of knowledge. The study of physics had made rapid strides since the time of Newton, and in the eighteenth century some particularly bold and interesting experiments were made in an endeavour to find out more about the elusive but dangerous power of electricity. The way was led by an American, Benjamin Franklin (1706-1790), who was born in Boston in the colony of Massachusetts.

Franklin began as a printer and journalist but his interests all his life were legion. He went to live in Philadelphia, where he founded a debating society for the discussion of topics of general interest, and also an academy which later grew into Philadelphia University. Then for eight years from 1746 to 1754 he devoted himself to the study of electricity, and established the fact that lightning was an electrical force. Some of his experiments were extremely dangerous to himself, but his researches had the practical result of making other people safer, for he discovered enough to invent lightning conductors. He also discovered the difference between positive and negative electricity. He had too many irons in the fire, however, to keep permanently to his research work and soon became immersed in politics; but the study of electricity was

144

Top left—VOLTAIRE
Top right—EDWARD JENNER

Right—BENJAMIN FRANKLIN

carried on by others, notably by two Italian physicists, Luigi Galvani (1737-1798) and Alessandro Volta (1745-1798).

Galvani was primarily interested in medicine and the allied sciences of physiology and anatomy, on which subjects he lectured at Bologna University. He found that if he attached a silver wire to the leg of a frog and another of copper to one of the animal's nerves, he could produce violent twitchings in the leg. He recognised this as an electric current, but believed the source of the current was to be found in the nerve and muscle. Volta however stormily disagreed with him, and maintained that the source of the current lay in the wires. Volta also made the immensely important discovery that electric power can be stored: he constructed a pile of discs made of copper, zinc and flannel and soaked them in brine, thus inventing the first electric battery. He further succeeded in measuring the force of electricity, giving his name (volt) to one of the units of measurement.

Volta enjoyed a successful career, and was able to pursue his work as a professor undisturbed. Galvani on the other hand became painfully involved in politics, though not so disastrously as Lavoisier. When revolution came to his part of Italy he did not lose his life, but his principles caused him to resign his position. Indeed we cannot get a true picture of the kind of world in which the scientists of the late eighteenth century were working unless we bear in mind that political upheavals were going on all around them.

The development of political thought

Obviously the precise and clean-cut 'scientific method' could not be applied to politics, for they do not lend themselves to controlled experiment. On the other hand it was impossible for political thinking to remain untouched by the new spirit of scepticism. Inevitably traditions, however venerable, would now be challenged; and political institutions would be required by their critics to prove their worth. Among the theories which came under fire during the eighteenth century was of course the Divine Right of Kings. Most ordinary people still accepted the absolute authority of monarchs without thinking—it seemed to them as natural as the air they breathed; but the more advanced thinkers openly stated their doubt of the rulers being vice-regents of God. Some of them went further and expressed doubts as to whether God in fact existed. The humanism that had been born in the Renaissance was becoming more arrogant, and the sense of sin and of human weakness was growing steadily thinner.

146

The first effect which this tendency had on political theory can be seen in the writings of Thomas Hobbes (1588-1679). Hobbes had lived through the disorders of the English Civil War, and this bred in him a passionate desire for strong authority. His most famous book, *Leviathan*, published in 1651, described a man in his natural state as a complete savage. Left to himself such a creature's existence would be 'nasty, poor, brutish and short'. It would in fact be intolerable, and Hobbes argued that men had therefore joined together in their own interests and had agreed to accept the authority of a sovereign power as the only protection against disorder. The preservation of that power is of such importance to the whole community that rebellion must be condemned, not because it is blasphemous (as in the theory of Divine Right), but because it is anti-social.

The next outstanding political theorist was John Locke (1632-1704) who was a young man of nineteen when *Leviathan* appeared. Just as Hobbes's views had been largely shaped by the civil war, so were Locke's by the Revolution of 1688, of which he wholeheartedly approved. In 1690 he wrote a treatise on *Civil Government* in which he agreed with Hobbes so far as to admit that the state exists for man's advantage, since he cannot hope to live in peace without it. But Locke had greater faith in human nature than had the author of *Leviathan*. He did not feel that rebellion might immediately result in chaos. On the contrary he maintained that since men had accepted the state for their own good, they had a perfect right to change its nature if they were no longer satisfied with it. He was not prepared to say that any individual had the right to rebel, but asserted that the citizens as a whole had a right to replace a bad government by one more to their liking.

Locke was a cautious man whose views were formed by a revolution that was almost unique for its lack of violence. But in the next century his idea of revolt being in certain cases justified was taken up, embroidered, and inflated beyond recognition by a French writer, Jean-Jacques Rousseau (1712-1778).

Rousseau was a writer of genius but singularly lacking in any kind of mental discipline. He believed in the simple life, and reacted sharply against the complexity of the society into which he had been born. His political theories were idealistic but wholly impracticable. His most famous book was *The Social Contract*, which appeared in 1762. As the title suggests, Rousseau followed Hobbes and Locke in explaining the existence of the state as being in essence the result of an agreement or contract entered into by men because it is to their advantage to have law and order. But his view of man's nature was extraordinarily naive. He maintained that in each man there is an element of idealism that desires the good of all above his own selfish advantage. In a society these ideal impulses all unite to form a general will, which is quite different from a mere majority vote, first because it is common to *all* (not just to a majority), and secondly because it is in its very essence

ADAM
SMITH

good. Rousseau believed that this general will could only reveal itself if all the members of the state were present together at one time—which meant that the only satisfactory form of society could be the kind of small city-state that existed in ancient Greece.

Obviously such a remote ideal could have no relevance to French society in the eighteenth century; but vague though most of the book is, it begins with the ringing sentence, 'Man is born free, but everywhere he is in chains!' This statement really did hit the nail on the head: the majority of Frenchmen were galled by an unjust social system and an inefficient government. Those who suffered most could not read and write, but there were also plenty of educated men who chafed at the way of life imposed on them. To these people, filled with a strong but as yet unorganised discontent, Rousseau's words acted as a clarion call.

148

Another man of letters was Voltaire (1694-1778) who as well as being a dramatist, was a poet, an historian and a wit. He hated tyranny and cruelty, and believed in liberty and toleration; but he was no democrat, for he distrusted the foolishness of the man in the street. He lived in great comfort himself and was the friend of many aristocrats. Kings invited him to their palaces, and indeed counted themselves fortunate if they could secure such an amusing guest. But though possessed of a brilliant wit, warm sympathies and a great deal of common sense, Voltaire was not a constructive thinker. It was easier for him to satirize what he thought wrong than to say what should be put in its place.

Like Rousseau, Voltaire wielded enormous influence over his compatriots, and helped to precipitate the French Revolution. It was a feature of that movement that it was destructive of the past but failed to produce any stable government other than an autocracy.

The new science of economics

The bright flame of curiosity that had shed its light on every branch of natural science, as well as leading men to a new view of politics, also inspired certain thinkers to take a fresh look at the processes of buying, selling and producing. These activities formed a large part of their lives, and they wanted to understand the forces which controlled them. A group of men calling themselves the Physiocrats did some work on the subject in France; but the outstanding contribution came from a Scotsman called Adam Smith (1712-1790). In the course of a single work, *The Wealth of Nations*, published in 1776, he virtually founded the science of Economics.

Smith exposed the fallacy of the mercantilist belief that gold is wealth, demonstrating that real wealth consists only of what is useful and necessary to human life and comfort. Once convinced of this truth, his readers were at once aware that economic processes must be studied with great care, since they were complicated and much harder to understand than the operations of gold. Smith then went on to assert that the kind of government control over trade, which had been a feature of European economic life for more than two hundred years, was pernicious and must defeat its own ends. For economic processes will not conform to the laws of any land; on the contrary they follow laws of their own, which it behoves men to discover. His teaching called for the repeal of most commercial and industrial regulations.

Adam Smith did not claim complete freedom for manufacturers and merchants to pursue their own interests, because he believed firmly in man's overriding duty to God and the need for sympathy and kindness to others. But his general call for freedom was taken up by others, while the exceptions he had laid down were often ignored. Consequently there was wide public support for the policy of *laissez-faire*, or 'let alone', which was misinterpreted as a justification for any kind of exploitation of the workers. Nevertheless, despite misinterpretation, *The Wealth of Nations* had a profound influence on economic thinkers in the nineteenth century, and the ideas it contained inspired a greater fluidity in the pattern of world trade.

The separation of science from religion

Throughout the Feudal Ages the Christian Church had been the storehouse of knowledge in Europe. It is true that during that period education was nearly always at a low ebb, and that hardly any scientific thought worthy of the name was going on. Nevertheless such knowledge as had been preserved from earlier times was in the hands of priests and monks, who made it their business to maintain schools and found universities, and regarded this as part of their duty to God. During the Renaissance, too, scientists such as Kepler never doubted that their search for a greater understanding of the universe was merely one facet of their desire to know more about God. They realised that since God made the world, every additional piece of information we gain about its working, tells us just so much more about God Himself. The churchmen of the sixteenth century also appreciated this truth. Scientists and mathematicians received a measure of help and encouragement from the leaders both of the Roman and of the Reformed Churches, and the Jesuit Order, which made teaching one of its special functions, carried the new learning into the New World and even into farthest Asia.

During the seventeenth century, however, the sense of religion and science being two facets of the same truth began to weaken. One cause of this was the religious quarrels that were raging all over Europe. Different groups of Christians found themselves bitterly attacking other people's opinions and violently defending their own. All this intolerance bred an attitude of mind which regarded as a humiliating defeat any admission that one might be mistaken. Consequently Christians of all persuasions were deliberately putting on mental blinkers just at the very time when physicists were discarding all their preconceived notions in a passionate search for new truths. Most of the scientists came to regard the churchmen as unenlightened, determined to cling to traditional beliefs and opposed to any advances in knowledge.

150

8 New ideas applied to machinery

The European Intellectual Revolution of the seventeenth and eighteenth centuries, which we were studying in the last chapter, was not unprecedented in man's history. For example, in the sixth century B.C. the thinkers and scientists of ancient Greece had also taken a sudden leap into new knowledge and understanding of the world about them. But the 'scientific method' evolved by Descartes and his contemporaries, led to one development which was entirely unprecedented—namely the large-scale invention of machinery. Both the Greeks and Romans would have been capable of inventing quite complicated machines in ancient times, if they had felt the need of them. But as both these civilisations depended on an abundant supply of slave labour for their manufactures, there was no motive for such a development. In the eighteenth century, however, a shortage of labour happened to coincide with the great advances in scientific knowledge. The scientific knowledge was common to all western Europe: the shortage of manpower, on the other hand, was most strongly felt in Britain. So it was in Britain that the Industrial Revolution began.

In one sense this revolution is still going on, as man is even now devising more and more machinery to save him more and more trouble. But the term Industrial Revolution is used here to describe the rapid series of inventions, as the result of which it became normal in Europe for articles to be made by machine instead of by hand, and for transport to depend on something faster than human or horses' legs. These changes, which of course spread in due time to all the other continents, produced fundamental changes in human life, and displaced a mode of working that had continued almost unchanged for several thousands of years. Yet most of these inventions were packed into a short period of some eighty years.

As late as 1760 most manufactures were still made by hand, either in the living quarters behind a town shop, or in a country cottage. In the cottages the householder and all his family took part in the spinning or weaving (for it was mostly the textile industries that used rural labour). Even the children took a hand in the work from the age of about seven. This may seem shocking, but it must be remembered that there were no schools for the children to go to. They also helped on the land, for each family in the village was entitled to a share of farm-land, as well as having the right to pasture their animals on the common. The life was rough, but it was varied; and the family had the satisfaction of living and working as a unit. But by 1840 all this had changed. By then it was normal for industrial goods to be turned out in large quantities from

A model of Newcomen's pump, from which James Watt
developed his steam engine

factories situated in smoky towns where the workers spent their whole lives, separated during working hours from the other members of their family, rarely seeing the country, and never working on the land.

Changes in the iron industry

Although most of these changes were compressed into the eighty years from 1760 to 1840, some of the inventions belong to an earlier date. As early as 1712 a Cornishman called Thomas Newcomen was struck by the clumsy inefficiency of the horse-drawn pumps used for extracting water from the tin-mines of that region. He applied himself to the problem for ten years, and at last succeeded in making an entirely new

152

type of pump which was driven by steam. This invention scored a huge success in Cornwall, but did not spread elsewhere for many years, for the very good reason that the pumping of water had not as yet presented any difficulty in other types of mining.

There was, however, an acute problem of another kind facing the iron industry, namely the severe shortage of fuel for smelting. Coal cannot be used for this purpose because it contains chemicals which make the iron brittle. Consequently from time immemorial wood charcoal had been used. But by the eighteenth century England's forests had been nearly stripped bare and the country had been reduced to importing a lot of iron from Sweden, where the forests were too numerous for wood ever to be lacking. This was not of course a satisfactory arrangement for the British government, which was perpetually engaging in wars and therefore wanted its supply of iron for armaments to be independent of foreign markets.

In 1710 an ironmaster called Abraham Darby (1677-1717), who had a family business in Coalbrookdale, discovered that if coal were first partially burned, or 'coked', it could then be safely used for smelting. This new process rapidly spread and the iron industry took on a new lease of life. More of the mineral began to be taken out of the ground, and by the second half of the century Newcomen's steam pump was adopted in several iron mines. The industry began to enjoy a boom, and the second Abraham Darby (1711-1763) followed up his father's good work by devising further improvements in the processing of iron.

The development of the steam engine

Despite the years of hard work that its inventor had put into it, however, Newcomen's pump was by no means perfect, and was also extremely expensive. Its deficiencies were noticed by an engineer called James Watt (1736-1819) who was employed by Glasgow University as an instrument-maker. He was deeply interested in the harnessing of steam to work machinery, and by 1776 he had improved the steam-pump and was producing it at a quarter of its former cost. But Watt, one of the great inventive geniuses of all time, was still not satisfied. Steam was being used to drive a piston up and down; but he believed that it might be used to turn a wheel. After five years of hard work he achieved this crucial advance in 1781. Since the turning of wheels is a vital principle in practically every type of machinery, the process of invention now received a colossal impetus.

The cotton industry

Although machinery depends on the careful arrangement of revolving wheels, the inventors of machines had not waited for Watt's steam engine before getting to work. Where there is an obvious need, resourceful men will endeavour to fill it; and in the cotton industry in the middle of the eighteenth century there had been an overwhelming need to increase the output of spun thread. Plenty of raw cotton was available because it was coming in large quantities from the new colonies in the West Indies, as well as from India. Moreover cotton was becoming popular with the wealthier classes. India produced a very fine cotton cloth known as muslin, which could be made up into attractive dresses for women, and as the standard of living in Britain was rising steadily, the wives and daughters of country gentlemen were as anxious as great ladies to buy soft and pretty materials. Weavers were in good supply, but there were not enough cotton spinners to keep them occupied. Yet the number could not be increased for there was no pool of unemployed on which to draw. The only way would be to find a means to increase the output of each worker.

A sudden realisation of how this could be done came to James Hargreaves in 1765. He and his family were cotton spinners, and one day his wife Jenny overturned her spinning wheel, which continued to whirl round as it lay on its side. Watching it idly, Hargreaves suddenly perceived how a new kind of spinning wheel could be made which, by a system of interlocking wheels, would spin eight or ten threads simultaneously. He got to work at once, and his invention made an enormous sensation. The cotton merchants were delighted, but Hargreaves's fellow workers were frightened and furious. In 1767 they mobbed his house, because they believed that many of them would soon be thrown out of work. In this they were mistaken for they did not realise the extent of the demand for cotton thread, which would keep them busy even if they were given the new Spinning Jennies to work with. Nevertheless in a way they were right to fear the arrival of machinery, for it was destined to alter the workers' way of life completely, and to condemn them for many years to terrible suffering. There would still be plenty of employment, but the wages and conditions would be appalling.

In the first place it soon became impossible for the spinners to work in their own cottages as they had always done before. The Jennies were improved and enlarged until they were capable of spinning a hundred threads at a time. Such large machines could not be housed in a cottage,

154

Hargreaves's Spinning Jenny

so the employer had to build a special workshop, and the spinners were obliged to leave home each day and go out to work. But though the Jennies were now so large, they were still hardly machines in the real meaning of the word, since they depended on human muscles to keep them going. Inventors were already at work, however, trying to harness another form of power, and in 1769 Richard Arkwright (1732-1792) invented a Water Frame which was turned by falling water. This caused an even greater upheaval in the lives of the workers. The larger Jennies needed a special workshop, but the workshop could be built in or near any village. The Frames, on the other hand, had to be erected near a waterfall. There were plenty of waterfalls in Lancashire, the region where the cotton industry was located, but often the new manufactory (or factory) was perforce situated in a remote spot too far from the workers' homes for them to walk to and fro each day. When this was so, the employer had to build them new houses near the factory. These building projects, however, were rarely adequate to accommodate the great influx of workers that before long poured into the towns. Conditions of appalling overcrowding prevailed, with serious consequences to public health.

Arkwright's Frame was superior to the Jenny in some ways; it made a much stronger thread. On the other hand it could not produce the fine yarn that was needed for the more expensive types of cloth. However in 1779 Samuel Crompton (1753-1827) invented a spinning machine which combined the best features of the Jenny with those of the Water Frame. It was worked by water-power, but was capable of producing yarn as fine as the Jenny could make. This cross-breed machine was nicknamed the Mule.

The Mule was a great success, but the spinning section of the cotton industry had overreached itself. The supply of raw cotton, which had seemed a few years before to be inexhaustible, had now become inadequate, for the new machinery could use only the long-fibred cotton which grew in India but was not obtainable from America. Also there was a terrible bottle-neck in the weaving section of the industry. Both of these problems, however, were eventually solved.

The shortage of long-fibred cotton was remedied by an American, Eli Whitney, who was living in Georgia shortly after the United States had been formed. Although he was not a cotton-planter but a law student, Whitney was an observant man and took an interest in the cotton fields with which Georgia was now covered. Noticing that the process of separating the cotton boll from the rest of the plant was clumsy and inefficient, he abandoned his law studies for the time being, in order to devise a machine. He was a quick worker and within a few months had invented a machine he called a Gin, which treated even the short-fibred cotton in such a way that it could be spun on Crompton's Mule. The Gin was patented in 1794.

The problem of speeding up the weaving process, on the other hand, took longer to solve. Not that mechanisation was entirely unknown in that section of the industry. On the contrary the first weaving machine had been invented in 1733, more than thirty years before the Jenny. It was a device for propelling the shuttle from one side of the loom to the other. This modest invention roused the fury of the workers just as the Jenny was to do; and the inventor John Kay was so hounded by the mob that he left the country and went to live in France. When first invented, the Flying Shuttle had done much to speed up the weaving process, and had in fact contributed to the critical shortage of spinners in the 1760's; but by the time that spinning had been fully mechanised, further improvements were urgently required in the weaving process. Cotton firms offered rewards and inventors racked their brains. Then the solution came from an unexpected quarter. A clergyman called

156

Edmund Cartwright (1743-1822) happened to learn, in a chance conversation, about the desperate need for a power-loom. He immediately put aside all his other pursuits and thereafter interested himself in engineering and invention. He produced a power-loom of a kind quite quickly, but these machines did not become really efficient until about 1813.

Wool textiles

Once the cotton industry had been mechanised, wool manufacturers began in their turn to consider the possibility of introducing machines into their mills. One difficulty here was the tendency of wool to break

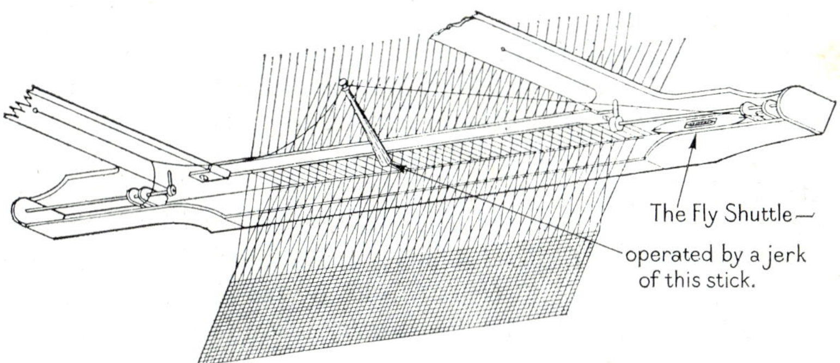

Kay's Flying Shuttle

as soon as any pull is exerted upon it. Cotton is much stronger. Eventually this problem was overcome, and satisfactory machines for both spinning and weaving wool were contrived. But even when this stage was reached employers were reluctant to invest in the machines, as they were expensive and the world-supply of wool was strictly limited.

Unexpectedly, the answer to this final problem came from the other side of the world. At the time when Cartwright was working on his first power-loom, the British government was making up its mind to use the newly discovered Australia as a dumping-ground for convicts. The first of these men arrived in Botany Bay in 1788, and from this unpromising beginning a flourishing colony developed. When it was found that Australia was suited to sheep-breeding, the prosperity of the settlers was assured. Huge fortunes were made by the graziers in the colony, while in Europe the wool factories could in future depend on steady and adequate supplies of raw materials.

Developments in coal mining

The machinery used in the textile trades had developed steadily from dependence on human muscle (the Jenny) through dependence on water power (Arkwright's Frame) to the use of steam. Once Watt had invented his 'rotative' steam engine, its advantages were so obvious that it was only a matter of time until all machines were run on this new power. But first there had to be a revolutionary increase in the output of coal, since this was the only fuel available for heating water to produce steam.

At the beginning of the eighteenth century coal mining had been a very minor industry, and most of the coal-fields in which Britain is so rich, were still lying unworked. There were two reasons for this. In the first place there could be no deep mines until a means had been found of pumping water out of the pits; consequently only those seams which lay near the surface and could be approached horizontally were of any use. Secondly, it was impossible for such a bulky commodity as coal to be carried on pack mules, which were at that time the only available method of transporting goods. Consequently the mines that were near to the sea were the only ones in use. London got its coal from Newcastle by means of coastal shipping. It was known as sea-coal, and was not regarded as a satisfactory fuel.* By the eighteenth century, when coal was being used in almost every house in London, the resulting smoke was a danger to health as well as comfort. Nevertheless the steady dwindling of England's forests obliged town dwellers to make more and more use of coal, and the output rose steadily if slowly. It was not until industry began to need coal, however, that the mines had to be developed on a really large scale.

Darby's system of coking coal caused a minor boom, but the invention of the steam engine multiplied the demand practically overnight. Fortunately the problem of draining the deeper seams had already been solved by Newcomen's invention of 1712, and steam pumps soon came into general use. Deep mines were excavated, and the men sent underground to hack the coal out of the seam. The next problem was to convey it to the pit-head. No machinery was available for that purpose, so the employers used child labour. Rails were laid in the low narrow passages of the mine, along which trucks could be hauled, and children (cheaper to employ than adults) were forced to strap round their hips a harness attached to the truck, and then crawl on hands and knees to the

* In Shakespeare's *Much Ado About Nothing* (about 1599) one of the silly, ineffectual watchmen is called Seacoal.

158

shaft. Up the shaft ladders were fixed and women (cheaper than men though a little dearer than children) had baskets tied to their backs. The baskets were filled with coal, and they spent their long working day climbing up the ladders with one load, and coming down for the next.

The women could not refuse to do this work nor could they refuse to send their children to the mines and factories; if they had done so, both they and their children would have starved, for wages paid to men were not meant to be sufficient to keep a whole family, and the changes already brought about by the Industrial Revolution had deprived the working class of the small holdings of land on which they had formerly grown much of their food.

Very few people were shocked by this appalling state of affairs, and it was not until 1833 that an Act of Parliament was passed to protect workers from the inhuman exploitation which most employers took for granted.

The canal mania

Although women and children might be employed to convey coal from the seam-face to the surface, they could not transport it overland. Where the sea or a river was handy, trucks could be used to take it to a barge or ship. All too often, however, nature had not provided a waterway where it was wanted. The first to tackle this difficulty was the Duke of Bridgewater, who owned some very rich coal mines which were capable of producing far more coal than could possibly be bought and used in the immediate neighbourhood. The Duke realised that if only he could find some means of sending his goods to the growing town of Manchester, centre of the rapidly expanding cotton industry, he would make a great deal of money. He therefore decided to make his own waterway, and engaged a famous engineer, James Brindley (1716-1772), to construct a canal. This was likely to be expensive as the terrain to be covered was hilly, and the Duke assumed that a large number of locks would have to be made in order to raise and lower the barges as they passed along the canal. Brindley however had different ideas. He was a man of singular talent who had been born into a poor family and had never learned to read and write. But he could put his ideas on paper in the form of drawings, and could tackle the most complicated engineering problems in his head. This was his first canal, and he boldly determined to dispense with locks wherever possible by digging cuttings or raising embankments in order to correct the natural rise and fall of the land. He even carried his canal right across a river on an aqueduct raised thirty-nine feet above the banks. All this of course was expensive, but once the canal was in use the barges could move along it far more rapidly than if they had been obliged to pass through a large number of locks. The whole canal took only two years to build. It was opened in 1761 and made a fortune for its owner and a brilliant reputation for its engineer.

Brindley was at once offered commissions by other enterprising canal-builders. He constructed more than 300 miles of canal in all, for there was a sudden craze for making these waterways. Among many other enterprises, he was concerned in the making of the Caledonian Canal. The idea of cutting a waterway between Loch Ness and the Moray Firth was of course irresistible; but as comparatively few ships have any need to follow that route, the canal was never a great success. On the other hand the network of waterways that were constructed in England between 1760 and 1795 proved a wonderful help to trade and industry by linking the ports of London, Bristol, Liverpool and Hull with one another and with the industrial towns of the Midlands. By means of these waterways the coal and the iron-ore, with both of which Britain abounds, were brought together, and this enabled the country to lead the world, both industrially and commercially, throughout the nineteenth century. The new and increased output of iron was used not only for making the ever-growing number of steam engines, but also for constructing the bridges which formed such a vital part of the new forms of transport that were being developed. It is interesting to find the third Abraham Darby (1750-1791), who was still operating the family business, helping to build the first iron bridge in England. It crossed the Severn not far from Coalbrookdale.

Another advantage of the canals was that they provided safe transport for fragile goods—a fact that proved invaluable to the potteries which were now developing in the Midlands and turning out products of the finest quality, which achieved international fame. Each waterway had its towpath along which plodded the draft horses, probably very pleased to be employed in this way rather than on the dangerous, uneven roads.

Roads

At the time when the canal mania began, the roads of Britain were in a shocking state. Most of the people living in country districts had to give up visiting their friends in the winter, and a man who travelled extensively through Britain might write a book about his adventures as though he were an explorer. The trouble was that no one was really responsible for road-mending, with the result that even the main highways became scarred with deep ruts and pitted with potholes. In wet weather a road became a morass, and in dry weather the hard, mud-caked ridges were so uncomfortable to both carts and carriages that drivers often made a détour along the verge in search of a smoother surface. But drivers who did this inevitably sank their own wheels into the new land, and no lasting benefit resulted. It was not an infrequent occurrence for a coach to fall into such a deep rut that it overturned and spilled out its occupants.

At the end of the seventeenth century a movement to improve the roads was started. A group of people would form themselves into a trust and make themselves responsible for the upkeep of a particular stretch of highway. To reimburse themselves, they levied a toll on all the users of the road, who were stopped by a turnpike erected across the road at either end of the trust territory and forced to pay—often very much against their will. The Turnpike Trusts, despite their unpopularity with the public, did a useful job, but they did not account for more than a portion of all the roads in the country, and their repair work was not very effective simply because no satisfactory technique of surfacing roads was then known.

The first man to tackle the problems of road construction was— surprisingly enough—blind from childhood. John Metcalf (1717-1810), nicknamed Blind Jack, had always been interested in roads and used to study them as he walked, feeling with his hands and visualising the geography to himself. When he was already middle-aged he entered a competition for the best method of laying a road, won it, and was thereafter employed on many road-building projects in the north of England, constructing more than 180 miles in all between 1765 and 1792.

About ten years before Metcalf embarked on his career, two men were born whose lives almost coincided and who each made an out-standing contribution to the roads of Britain. They were J. L. Macadam (1756-1838) and Thomas Telford (1757-1836). Telford was a general engineer, who spent much of his life in the planning of docks, harbours, canals and other public works. But he was also responsible for engineering no less than 1,000 miles of roadway, carrying his highways over bridges and through cuttings in order to lessen the gradients. Macadam is remembered less for his engineering than for his solution of the old problem of how to provide a durable surface for a road. His system of laying small stones and binding them with tar proved a lasting success, and introduced a new word—'macadamising'—into the English language.

On these new roads there travelled newer and faster stage coaches, rushing along at what seemed then the breathtaking speed of eight to ten miles an hour. Rival coach-owners competed for custom, and the brisk competition between them kept the horse-drawn traffic operating at the greatest speed of which it was capable.*

Railways

Even while Telford and Macadam were doing their best work, however, a rival and more rapid form of transport was developing in the form of railways. To trace the inventions in this field we must return to the story of the coal mines. The coal was taken from the pithead to the nearest river or canal by trucks. These trucks were normally drawn by horses, but to eliminate unevenness in the road, which would have reduced their speed, they usually ran along wooden rails, upon the tops of which plates of iron were laid. As the iron industry developed, it became normal for the rails to be made of this stronger material. But as soon as Watt had harnessed steam to turn a wheel, it was obvious to engineers that it was not beyond the bounds of possibility to produce a locomotive which would turn wheels in such a way as to project itself forward. This was clearly just what the coal mines needed, and inventors got to work accordingly. In 1802 Robert Trevithick made a locomotive of this sort which was used in South Wales. Twelve years later George Stephenson (1781-1845) followed this up with an improved model which actually ran over a nine-mile track. The idea spread and in 1821 he was commissioned to construct a longer railway linking two important industrial towns, Stockton and Darlington. This railway brought another innovation, as it was the first ever to carry passengers. Hitherto it had been assumed that the new form of transport would be suitable only for goods, and there was some reason for this view because the early locomotives were dreadfully dirty. Nevertheless the idea of passenger trains had come to stay.

Stephenson's next undertaking was a railway linking Manchester with Liverpool, a project which taxed even his resourceful genius. In order to take his line out of Liverpool he had to force a cutting through a thick ridge of red sandstone, and—worse still—further down the route

---

* A vivid description of what it was like to travel in a stage coach and of the rivalry between different coaches can be read in Thomas Hughes's book *Tom Brown's Schooldays*.

Stephenson's *Rocket*

A model of a coach used on the Stockton to Darlington railway,
the first line to carry passengers

he was faced with the appalling problem of a large boggy marsh, the Chat Moss. Stephenson had innumerable bundles of heather brought and forced down into the Moss. For a long time the bog continued to swallow up the heather without it making any noticeable difference, but at last a sound surface was achieved and the rails were laid. When the track was completed a competition was held for the best locomotive. Stephneson, whose energies had not been entirely absorbed by laying the line, entered his famous steam-engine the *Rocket* and won the prize by attaining a speed of fifteen miles an hour. This started a railway mania, similar to the canal mania, and by the end of the nineteenth century Britain had been covered by a close network of lines.

The development of steamships

The invention of the steam locomotive revolutionised transport all over the world. By the end of the century railways had been laid across North America, a line had crossed Siberia, and the continent of Africa was being opened up for the first time. Britain was never able to keep her new industrial knowledge to herself, nor did she try, except early in the Industrial Revolution when skilled workmen were forbidden (though unsuccessfully) to go abroad. But the start which the British had gained gave them a political as well as a commercial superiority in the world. Almost every invention we have examined so far had, for reasons already explained, emanated from Britain. The only exception was the cotton Gin which had originated in America. Now another American contributed a much more vital invention than the Gin, useful though that had been.

While the British engineers were concentrating all their energies on how to harness steam to land transport, Robert Fulton (1765-1815), a citizen of the United States, was trying to harness it to water transport. Fulton began life as an artist, but while on a visit to England he met James Watt, and as a result developed an interest in engineering that was to last throughout his life. He began work on a steamboat, and took his idea to France when Napoleon, in an effort to catch up with Britain, offered rewards to inventors. Fulton launched his first steamer on the River Seine, but the French did not seem particularly interested. He therefore returned to his own country, and built a better steamship on the Hudson River in 1807. This met with immediate success because America was badly in need of an invention of this kind. Railways were still in their infancy—indeed they had hardly been born—and all the products of the middle states in the U.S.A. had to be exported by water

164

A Mississippi steamboat

down the Mississippi. But though this river will bear boats swiftly *down* its stream, the return journey was extremely slow until steamers became available. The Americans therefore quickly grasped the importance of Fulton's invention, and before many years had passed, steamers were plying busily on the great rivers of America, carrying an ever-increasing share of the country's commerce.

Then a further step was taken. In 1819 a steam engine was fitted into an ocean-going vessel. Steam was in this case only to be used in case of the ship getting becalmed, for the quantities of fuel required per mile were too great for sails to be abandoned altogether. The engines were soon improved, however, fuel-consumption was reduced, and from 1838 onwards there were some ships at sea that relied entirely on steam. The opening of the Suez Canal in 1869 dealt the final blow at the old sailing ships, for they were not allowed to use the canal. So within three-quarters of a century of Fulton's earliest steamboat, the new form of power had conquered not only inland waters, rivers and canals, but also the oceans of the world.

The results of the Industrial Revolution

The wind of change that swept through Britain in the century following

1760 was a veritable hurricane; and it was inevitable not only that the age of machinery should spread rapidly all over Europe and to the United States, but also that it should have a profound effect on world politics.

Perhaps the chief result was the new mobility of people. In Europe up to the nineteenth century, as elsewhere in the world except in the nomad areas, it was normal for a man to live, work and die in the place where he was born. But the Industrial Revolution changed all that, for the machines meant factories, and factories had to be manned. The workers were obliged to leave their old homes and come to live near their place of work. When one employer had found a good location for an industry, others would follow him and set up shop close-by. So there grew huge sprawling, mainly hideous, industrial towns. The country villages dwindled and the focus of national life moved to the towns. Before this new economic necessity, the Feudal System (which had in any case died much earlier in Britain) could stand no longer, and quietly withered away.

But the new mobility was even more widespread. The invention of steamships made voyages across the world more tolerable than they had ever been before. All over Europe enterprising families, glad to take advantage of their freedom from feudal ties and reluctant to endure the bitterly hard life in the new industrial towns, decided to emigrate. Thousands of them crossed the Atlantic to try their fortune in the United States. The British, of course, had a lead in the movement, and they flocked in large numbers to Canada, Australia and New Zealand. Moreover a sprinkling of people from nearly every European nation went to Africa—a continent so dangerous to shipping trying to penetrate inland, that until railways were invented it had remained virtually unknown.

A new and intricate system of world economics developed. Ever since very early times the division of labour has been an important part of man's economic life. Each man engaged in one occupation—farming, making pots, weaving, tailoring, working a smithy, or whatever it may be—and relied on exchanging most of the goods he made for the many other goods that he required. But after the Industrial Revolution this division of labour operated on a world-wide scale. Some regions, such as Europe or the eastern part of the United States, were highly industrialised; while others such as Canada, Australia, New Zealand, and the middle west of America, concentrated on growing food to maintain the industrial populations. Few countries were now self-sufficient.

166

This imparted a new danger to international war, for any country might now find itself cut off from essential supplies; at the same time it was a cause of war since governments were often anxious to gain control of regions which were rich in raw materials. Consequently the nineteenth century saw the climax of western imperialism. In the closing years of the century the leading European powers met in conference and carved up Africa between them. Not only were they seeking raw materials; they were also looking for new customers. For as machines became more and more efficient, the output of the factories tended to exceed the home demand. This could lead to unemployment and a trade slump; but if a government could only stake its claim to a part of Africa or Asia, then its new subjects might well be educated into feeling a need for the industrial goods the mother country was anxious to dispose of. Another facet of nineteenth-century imperialism was the need for coaling stations. The new steamships, even though their fuel-consumption was greatly reduced as time went on, still needed to be able to call at well-spaced ports in order to replenish their supplies of coal. There was therefore something of a rush, especially on the part of Britain and the United States, to gain control of islands dotted across the Pacific and Atlantic Oceans.

In all these enterprises there was a close understanding between the governments and the business-men who put up the necessary capital. The capitalist economy, which had developed during the sixteenth century, expanded enormously as a result of the Industrial Revolution. In the days of the old domestic system, when, for example, a cotton merchant needed only enough money to buy up raw cotton and distribute it to the cottages who were on his pay-roll, a man did not need to be very rich to go into business as an employer. But when expensive machines had to be bought and maintained, when a factory had to be built, and probably workers' houses to go with it, when it was not worthwhile employing workers at all unless a large number were employed, then men could only venture into business if they had access to a large sum of money. They did not need to own it themselves, but they had to be able to persuade others to lend it to them at interest. So every large concern soon came to depend on the money of a number of people who knew nothing of the work being done, and had probably never even seen the factories. All that the investors knew was that they had lent money, and all they cared about was the prompt payment of their dividends.

There was thus an inevitable tendency for the employer to feel more akin to the shareholders than to his own workers. In the early days of the factory system, the owner was often a friend of his workers, moving about the workshop and lending a hand if necessary. As businesses expanded, the owners grew more remote; they made more money and preferred to live away from their factories. They also employed many grades of supervisor and rarely saw the workers on the floor. Class distinctions became wider and wider, and the gap between the 'bosses' and the 'workers' widened into a great gulf.

In the early days of the Industrial Revolution the working class—men, women and children—suffered unspeakably. Children as young as five or seven years old were forced to work as long as ten hours a day, and they were beaten if they were thought idle or fell asleep. Extraordinary though it may seem, this system of slavery was defended on the grounds of freedom. In 1775, Adam Smith's book *The Wealth of Nations* had debunked the old mercantilist theories. Smith very rightly pointed out to his readers the fallacy of the old belief that gold was wealth. Since true wealth consisted of commodities, industry—instead of being as formerly under rigid government control—must be free to operate according to its own nature. Every time a bargain is struck each party to the deal endeavours to do as well for himself as he can. Consequently, it was argued, the decision reached will represent the greatest possible benefit to both parties. Freedom to get the best terms you could was believed by Adam Smith to be essential to a healthy economy, and he declared that it was fatal for the government to interfere in such matters. It followed therefore that employers must be free to bargain with their workers. To lay down a minimum wage would be interference. The economists tried to make themselves believe—apparently with great success—that the workers were free to refuse a wage offer if they found it unsatisfactory. This of course was nonsense. They were forced to accept what they were given or else to starve. So for many years the workers were shamefully exploited; they had no vote and no prospect of doing anything for themselves.

Fortunately, by the 1820's the conscience of a small number of men and women was aroused. In particular Lord Shaftesbury (1801-1885) visited factories and mines and was appalled by what he saw. In the early part of his career he was a Member of Parliament, and he made speech after speech in the House of Commons describing the unfortunate child-workers as a 'crooked alphabet' and demanding that legislation should be passed to protect them. The influence of Adam Smith was still strong and public opinion was hard to move, but at last Parliament was willing to concede that women and children were really not in a position to bargain for themselves. So in 1833 the first effective Factory Act was passed, which forbade children under nine years of age to be employed in either a factory or a mine. Another Act passed in 1844 limited the working hours for women and young children. The men were still left to fight their own battles, which they did by forming trade unions. The employers were deeply alarmed by this development, and every effort was made to prevent the men uniting. Membership of a union was even punished at one time by transportation to Australia. But gradually public opinion thawed, the trade union movement developed, and more and more social legislation was passed to protect the working class from the type of liberty advocated by the economists.

The final effect of the Industrial Revolution was to raise enormously the standard of living of working people in all countries affected by it. For the goods that were being produced in such profusion eventually found their way into the possession of the workers. Comfortable furniture, varied food, labour-saving gadgets and television sets would never have come within the experience of working people had it not been for the invention of machinery and the development of the factory system.

The Agricultural Revolution

Inevitably the Industrial Revolution was accompanied by a corresponding series of changes in agriculture. It has already been mentioned that when machines grew large and had to be housed in factories, the workers were obliged, if they wished to be employed in them, to leave their former village homes. Actually the pressure being exerted on the workers was twofold. They were being lured into the towns in search of work, and they were also being pushed out of the villages whether they had work to go to or not.

Throughout the Feudal Ages nearly everybody living in a village had the right to a holding of land sufficient for him to raise food for his family and himself. The total arable land of the village was divided into strips and each family held an appropriate number of these strips. The purpose of dividing it into such small allotments was to ensure that a few families did not secure all the best land, while others were left with the worst. Each man also enjoyed the right to graze his animals on the common pasturage. The output from his farming would not satisfy all his needs, but in the agricultural off-seasons he and his family would probably do some kind of industrial work, such as spinning or weaving, for which they were paid on a piece rate.

In the second half of the eighteenth century this system still survived in about half of England. It had much to recommend it, but there was one serious disadvantage—it did not allow for any large-scale improvement in agricultural methods. And since at this time so many scientific discoveries had been made, a number of the landed gentry had come to realise that their land could be made to yield much more food if only the farming were organised more scientifically. For example, it was known that a different rotation of crops would make possible the production of root crops which could be used to feed animals in the winter. Normally these were nearly all killed off in the autumn and salted for meat, only a few being left for breeding purposes to keep the flocks and herds going; this was done because—in the absence of root crops— there was no means of feeding the stock in winter. But the rotation of crops could not be altered without the consent of the whole village. Moreover it was of little use for one man to improve his methods unless the land he was working could be enclosed with a hedge. For in the open-farming system that prevailed, every strip was exposed to weeds from the land of a negligent neighbour. Similarly, though it was now known that sheep and cattle could be greatly improved by careful breeding, so long as the animals were all herded together, there could be no control of breeding. Would-be reformers in the areas where the open-field system was still in operation felt all the more frustrated because small enclosed farms existed in other parts of the country.

There was a way out of this difficulty, however. An Act of Parliament could be applied for, authorising a man to have all his strips in one place and to enclose them. He might also persuade some of the villagers to part with their holdings to him, in return for a payment of money. Enclosure Acts became extremely common in the second half of the eighteenth century; and often advantage was taken of the ignorance of the villagers to persuade them to part with their rights for a quite inadequate price. Never having handled a large sum before, they might well be dazzled into accepting an offer, only to find that when the money had run out they were faced with starvation. When they found themselves in this situation, they had no option but to drift into the new industrial towns in search of work or become labourers on an enlarged farm.

However, although some of the newly enclosed and large farms owed their origin to sharp practice, excellent progress was made in methods of farming. One of the earliest pioneers in this field was Jethro Tull (1674-1741), who began life as a lawyer but gave up the law in favour of farming. He travelled abroad for some years and made a very careful

170

study of foreign agricultural methods, as he wished to lose no opportunity of learning anything that might be of use to him. Circumstances took Tull from one farm to another during his lifetime, and sometimes his health compelled him to give up his researches for a period; but whenever he was able to settle on an estate he worked extremely hard, testing his own theories and improving output by new types of cultivation.

A generation after Tull's death, a famous landowner known as Coke of Norfolk inherited in 1772 the large estate of Holkham, which was graced with a magnificent house. Coke, who was later made Earl of Leicester, was an ardent agriculturist and turned his land into a model farm. It is interesting to note that at a time when the nobles of France could find nothing better to do than fritter their time away in Versailles, some of their English counterparts were taking an intelligent interest in the land and its products. Britain undoubtedly benefited greatly from this fact.

The result of the Agricultural Revolution was that the nation became in the end a great deal better fed. The yield of crops per acre was multiplied, while sheep, pigs and cattle increased enormously in size. At first the changes consisted mainly in the adoption of new farming principles, but during the latter part of the nineteenth century machines were introduced into farms in Britain. In other countries the mechanisation of farming was much more rapid and complete, especially in the 'new' countries, where the fields were very large and therefore suited to machinery.

The immediate result was unfortunate for the country-dwellers. Only the well-to-do could afford to operate the large enclosed farms, and capitalism entered into the farm as it had into industry. Most of the former holders of strips went to the towns; the remainder sank to the condition of farm workers.

9 New ideas applied to politics

The philosophers and political theorists of the eighteenth century had seriously undermined the old theory of the Divine Right of Kings. To be sure, all over Europe kings were still sitting on their thrones, and, except in Britain, they continued to wield power which appeared, on the surface, to be unlimited. But nobody any longer claimed that men had a religious duty to obey their sovereign even though he ruled badly. Rousseau's *Social Contract*, published in 1762, fitted in with a spirit that was already abroad. It was very shortly afterwards that bitter quarrels broke out between the British colonists in America and their king, George III. The colonists clearly found thoroughly distasteful whatever contract it was that bound them to their king, and they successfully broke the bond and set up a republic. Moreover they had many sympathisers in Europe. France became their ally simply in the hope of avenging herself on Britain for previous defeats; but many of the French soldiers and officers who were sent to America came back imbued with a great admiration for the colonists, and an increased resentment against their own woefully inefficient government. Voltaire's deadly ridicule and inspired pen added to the criticism which was beginning to burn against the King of France.

The Enlightened Despots

Voltaire, however, was popular with kings. They laughed at his wit and invited him to their courts; and several of them took his words to heart. They realised that they had no right to exact obedience from their subjects unless they gave them something of value in return. These sovereigns made it their declared business to rule in accordance with the best ideals of the Age of Reason. They earned for themselves the description of the Enlightened Despots.

Chief among them were King Frederick II of Prussia, known as Frederick the Great (1740-1788), Joseph II of Austria (1766-1790), and the Empress Catherine II of Russia (1763-1796). Catherine summed up the attitude each took to their duties when she said, 'The nation is not made for the sovereign, but the sovereign for the nation', a remark which was in pointed contrast to the arrogant claim of Louis XIV of France that he was himself the state.

All the Enlightened Despots worked extremely hard at their desks,

172

and also contrived to keep themselves abreast of the thought of their time. They encouraged education and often endowed colleges and schools. Moreover they appreciated the significance of the scientific discoveries that were being made all over Europe. They established new industries and encouraged inventors. They also interested themselves in agriculture. Frederick in particular, by studying the new farming methods, succeeded in having large tracts of his kingdom, which had

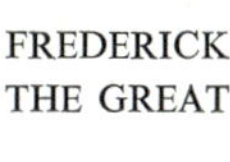

formerly been quite unproductive, brought under cultivation. And he, like the other sovereigns, was touched by the new spirit of humane compassion. All the Enlightened Despots disapproved of torture, and with varying degrees of thoroughness limited its use in their domains. Joseph of Austria even went so far as to issue a decree abolishing serfdom throughout his empire, but the other two were not prepared to go as far as that. And as Joseph's efforts proved entirely fruitless because the landowners refused to implement the decree, Europe remained in the grip of the Feudal System, with every peasant bound to the place where he was born. It was Britain's good fortune that the system had died out earlier on her shores than elsewhere, and that was one of the reasons why the Industrial Revolution could begin there.

Although the Feudal System was still too strong to be swept away, the legal system which went with it was modernised. Frederick, Catherine and Joseph all introduced extensive legal reforms. The nature of the law was changed as well. They no longer wished, as their predecessors had done, to claim the right to decide their subjects' religion. The religious intolerance which had led to so many wars and to so much persecution in the sixteenth and seventeenth centuries, had declined. It became fashionable in the Age of Reason to deride any form of fanaticism. This tendency went so far that there was a serious decline in genuine religious feeling of any kind; but at least Europeans no longer believed that it was God's will that they should fight and burn each other, and the despots granted their subjects religious freedom.

It was a fortunate accident that in the second half of the eighteenth century so much of Europe should have come under the rule of these genuinely progressive sovereigns, but their work did not last. This was partly due to the inherent weakness of absolute monarchy—the fact that there is no guarantee that a clever monarch will have a clever heir. Joseph, Catherine and Frederick were all succeeded by sons possessed of very inferior talents, and their work was rapidly undone. But the ensuing collapse cannot be blamed wholly on chance, for the seeds of failure were sown in their own actions.

The enlightenment of the Despots was limited to their home policy. At home they were prepared to be guided by the dictates of reason, but in foreign affairs they were the slaves of their own greed. And while they were laboriously building up wealth and sound finances, they were simultaneously throwing away their money on futile and endless wars. They held similar opinions on many subjects, and might therefore be expected to be friends and allies; but in fact they were ready on the slightest provocation to fight each other in a general scramble for territory. Austria, Russia and Prussia all increased greatly in size during this period. They robbed their weaker brethren without scruple, most of their advances being made at the expense of Poland, which in 1763 was a large independent state, but by 1795 had completely disappeared off the map of Europe. These successes—such as they were—had been bought at too high a price, for the domestic reforms of the Enlightened Despots were largely undermined by the way in which their kingdoms were bled white, both of men and money, in the incessant campaigns.

The growth of Prussia

It should be noted that while Russia and Austria were leading powers of some long standing, Prussia had only recently expanded from very

174

small beginnings. In the early Feudal Ages Europe had consisted almost entirely of quite little states. Sometimes the rulers claimed the title of king; sometimes they were known only as dukes or counts. As the centuries passed, much larger kingdoms were formed. France, Spain,

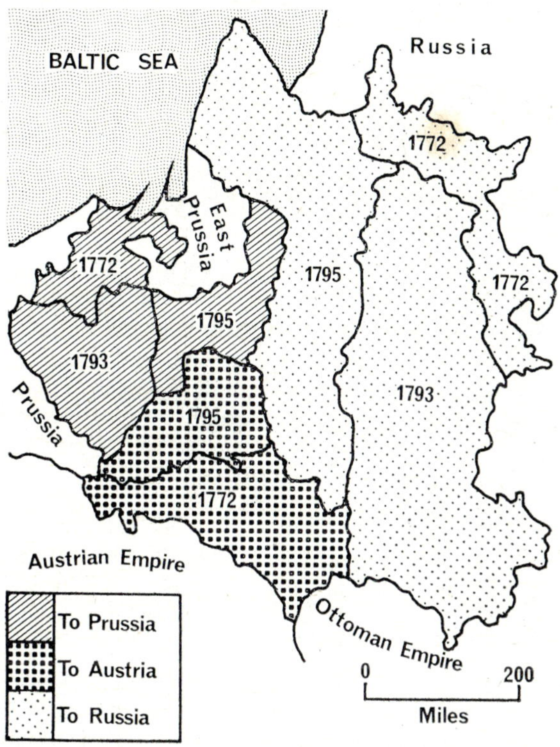

Map 7—The partitions of Poland

England—and later Britain—began to expand to the boundaries they enjoy today. The Dukes of Austria, also, gained more and more territory and became emperors. Only in Germany a vast cluster of little states remained. But one of these states, Brandenburg, began in the seventeenth century to outstrip all its neighbours.

The ruling family of Brandenburg were called Hohenzollern, and they had a marked talent for making advantageous marriages with heiresses to other territories. Moreover a cousin of the family was ruler of Prussia, which was some distance from Brandenburg—right outside

Germany, in eastern Europe. In due course Prussia came under the rule of the Elector of Brandenburg, who found it more valuable than any of his other lands; for in Germany he was obliged to acknowledge the Holy Roman Emperor (in practice always the Emperor of Austria) as his overlord, while in so far as he was ruler of Prussia, he was independent. In 1713 therefore, when Europe was being re-arranged after the last of Louis XIV's wars, the then Elector, Frederick III, persuaded his fellow-sovereigns to recognise him as King Frederick I of Prussia. His son Frederick William I made a hobby of building up a huge army. He never used it, as he disliked the idea of the soldier's uniforms being messed up in battle; but at the time of his death his son Frederick the Great inherited this instrument of war, which he immediately put to constant use.

Many of Frederick the Great's wars had no useful result but he won some notable victories, and, as we have seen, considerably enlarged his kingdom. He and his father between them laid the foundations of the militarism which was the chief characteristic of Prussia for the next hundred years, and which was passed on to the rest of Germany in the late nineteenth and the twentieth centuries.

The outbreak of the French Revolution

It is not surprising that while the Enlightened Despots all admired Voltaire, they detested Rousseau. For Voltaire, though ready to level his sarcasm at tyranny, had too high a respect for law and order to advocate outright revolution. In fact he demanded reforms in order that the danger of revolution might be averted. Rousseau on the other hand believed that no worthwhile change was possible before a basic upheaval of the existing system had been carried out. Nor was his a lone voice. No other political writers had the talent of Rousseau or Voltaire, but political pamphlets were streaming from the presses and were being widely read. Everywhere there was a tendency to denounce tyrants. In Britain this wave of feeling had little practical effect, because the powers of the monarchy had already been clipped, and in Prussia, Austria and Russia the rulers had the prudence to adapt themselves to public opinion. In France, however, there was hopeless misgovernment, and it was there that revolution broke out.

Louis XIV had attached so much authority to the Crown that there was no other symbol against which popular fury could direct itself. And as the century wore on, and Frenchmen experienced none of the reforms that were bettering the lot of Austrians and Prussians, resent-

176

ment grew. The Feudal System was particularly oppressive in France because the nobles were residing at Versailles instead of living on their estates. Moreover the peasants were subject not only to heavy taxes, but also to a complicated series of regulations that bound their lives at every turn.

One great grievance of the peasants was that they were liable to forced labour on public works; while another was the obligation—even less justified—to buy a huge quantity of salt each year, not because they wanted or could use it, but because the government wanted the tax that was levied on every pound sold. Agriculture, the main occupation of France, was at a dangerously low ebb on account of the landlords' neglect; while the trade of the country had also fallen on bad times because internal customs barriers were raised all over the country. Sometimes a cartload of goods, travelling only a few miles, would be taxed several times over. The lot of the peasants was indeed wretched. They were always ill-housed and badly clothed, and frequently they were hungry. They knew little or nothing of Rousseau for they could not read or write; but if ever they should be driven by extreme famine, it was clear that they might break out, and if that happened there was no force in France strong enough to control them.

Of more immediate danger to the government was the educated middle class, who could and did read both Rousseau and Voltaire. Politically France was divided into three classes or estates—the nobility, the clergy and the rest. The great majority of the nation were lumped together into the nameless mass of the Third Estate. The first two estates enjoyed many privileges, the chief of which was that they paid no taxes, despite the fact that between them they owned nine-tenths of the nation's wealth. Furthermore the nobles had a monopoly of commissions in the army and navy, as well as of appointments in the diplomatic service. Even ministerial posts were rarely available to members of the Third Estate, no matter how talented they might be. Louis XIV had made a point of choosing his ministers from the middle classes, but by the second half of the eighteenth century the impoverished French monarchy tended to sell government posts for money; and the purchaser, if he had been born in the middle class, often at the same time bought entry into the nobility. Generally speaking a member of the Third Estate, however brilliant, could not hope to be allowed to serve his country in any important capacity. This fact was particularly galling to them in view of the useless and frivolous lives led by the nobility at Versailles.

Not only were the middle-class people prevented from serving their country: they could not even express their opinions. There had once been in France a kind of parliament, known as the Estates-General, but this had not been summoned since 1614. Consequently the middle class, deprived of a share in the government and even of a voice, simmered with discontent. The majority of them had no desire for violence; they had no wish to destroy authority, whatever Rousseau might say. What they did want was an opportunity for balanced sensible action, the chance to rescue their society from the slough of muddle and injustice into which it had sunk.

In 1774 Louis XVI came to the throne at the age of twenty. He was quite unable to deal with the dangerous situation which he had inherited from his predecessors, for the immunity of the nobility from taxation was as great a danger to the government as it was an injustice to the Third Estate. However much the peasants might be ground down, they still could not supply the King with enough money to carry on the work of government. One finance minister after another tried desperately to save France from bankruptcy, but the country's solvency had been finally undermined by the participation in the North American War of Independence. It might be sweet for France to be revenged on her old enemy Britain, but it was a luxury that she could not afford.

The summoning of the Estates-General

The financial breaking-point was reached in the spring of 1789. The government went bankrupt, and it was clear that some entirely new expedient must be tried. Since the Estates-General had not met for a hundred and seventy-five years, to summon it now seemed revolutionary enough; and Louis was persuaded not only to call for an election but also to invite the people to submit lists of grievances. These soon came pouring in, and in due course the elected representatives of the three Estates arrived at the meeting places chosen for them at Versailles.

Meanwhile, however, the winter of 1788-1789 had been abnormally cold, and famine had been added to the miseries already endured by the poor of France. Unemployment was rife, and a crowd of idle, hungry, desperate people drifted into Paris in search of work and food. Neither of these was to be found in the capital, any more than in the provinces; but having once arrived, the mob stayed on because there was really nothing else for them to do. Versailles is only a few miles from Paris, and during the next few months the Paris mob lurked in the background and at intervals broke out into positive action. Whenever this occurred, the trend of events was diverted along some new line.

The delegates arriving at Versailles were, however, neither hungry nor a mob. Most of them were peaceful, respectable lawyers, and they had no intention of overturning the monarchy. All they wanted was to draw up a constitution which would limit the power of the King and open up reasonable opportunities to the Third Estate. But there was one point on which they were determined from the first to take a firm stand. It had been the custom in former times for the three Estates to meet separately. In that case each Estate reached its own decision on any subject of discussion, and no resolution could be passed unless it received the support of two Estates. It was obvious that although some of the nobles and some of the clergy sympathised with the reformers, there would be no hope of effecting any important changes if they had to depend on a majority vote of one of the upper Estates. If on the other hand all the Estates sat and voted together, reforms would be passed without difficulty, since the Third Estate had as many members as both the other two taken together.

The character of Louis XVI and Marie-Antoinette

It was typical of King Louis that, having once agreed to call the Estates-General, he should then take fright and insist on the Estates meeting separately. He was a well-meaning man but he was timid by nature, and his upbringing and experience of life had fostered his timidity. Life at Versailles, which had been prescribed by Louis XIV over a century before, went on unchanged. Although the King had absolute power, he, too, was the slave of the elaborate ritual that the Sun King had evolved.

Having all his life proceeded along these rigid lines, Louis found it extremely difficult to imagine what the consequences of any novel action would be. Consequently, once the Revolution had begun, he was often driven by circumstances into some course of action, but later was invariably overtaken by panic and would try to reverse what he had already done. Even his own relations found him alarmingly inconsistent. One of the royal family in a moment of exasperation said, 'When you can keep together a number of oiled ivory balls, you may do something with the King.' Sometimes he was persuaded of the imperative need for reform; sometimes he was even mildly enthusiastic about it; but these moods never lasted long enough to do any good. Always he would suffer a reaction and draw back at the critical moment.

Louis was also unfortunate in not having any firm and sensible adviser, and he fell entirely under the influence of his queen, the Austrian Marie-Antoinette. One of the nobles, the Comte de Mirabeau, who was

THE TENNIS COURT OATH

a reformer and preferred to be a delegate of the Third Estate rather than to sit with his fellow-nobles, tried hard to make Louis see sense; but Mirabeau's influence was always countered by that of the Queen, and he remarked bitterly that the King had only one man about him and that was his wife.

Marie-Antoinette had come to Versailles as a child, and lacked the intelligence and the education ever to look beyond the palace walls to the France that lay beyond. She took luxury so much for granted that she was incapable of economising, even when she was making serious efforts to do so. When told that the people had no bread, she asked why, in that case, they did not eat cake; and she continued to give extravagant and ostentatious banquets even when famine was at its height. The people hated her, though they felt some respect and a kind of liking for the King.

The Tennis Court Oath, June 1789

Once summoned, however, the members of the Third Estate were absolutely resolved not to disperse until they had carried out the necessary reforms. Led by Mirabeau, they called themselves not the Third Estate but the National Assembly, and invited the other Estates to join them. In a panic at this development, Louis tried to suppress them by the silly ruse of locking them out of their meeting-hall one day. But they promptly moved into a nearby covered tennis court, and thereupon took an oath that nothing would make them depart until they had provided France with a constitution. This show of firmness won the day, the King gave in, and the clergy and nobles joined forces with them. Then this united and genuinely national assembly settled down to the sober task of drawing up a constitution, a task which took them just two and a quarter years.

The storming of the Bastille, July 1789

Meanwhile, however, the hungry mob in Paris, whose hopes of immediate prosperity had been roused by the summoning of the Estates, felt that nothing much was happening after all. On July 14th they suddenly broke out into unreasoning violence and attacked the Bastille, an old fortress which had once been a prison for political offenders, though it was now mainly occupied by lunatics. They succeeded in gaining admission, and in a state of great excitement rushed on to the Hôtel de Ville (the equivalent of a town hall), where they established an entirely new type of local government for the city of Paris, which they called the *Commune*. Louis was forced to say that he approved of these arrangements, and the extremists felt that the revolution had now really started.

The abolition of feudalism

A similar feeling of exaltation inspired the National Assembly, which on the night of August 4th indulged in a perfect orgy of liberation. Moved by an unexampled sense of camaraderie with the common people, one noble after another rose to offer the willing surrender of his privileges. In one long and emotional sitting a whole host of decrees were passed abolishing all feudal rights and dues, and giving the peasants all the reforms they had ever desired. This was revolution on a grand scale, and as far as the peasants were concerned, nothing more needed to be done. They took no interest in constitutions, and were henceforth prepared to accept happily any sort of government, provided only that their new rights and liberties were guaranteed.

The March of the Women, October 1789

The Assembly, still flushed with enthusiasm, then proceeded to draw up a Declaration of the Rights of Man as an introduction to the constitution which was their main task. Liberty of speech and liberty of person were very rightly proclaimed; but not content with that, the Declaration proclaimed that in accordance with Rousseau's notion of the General Will, all the citizens must participate in the making of laws—an ideal which was obviously entirely impracticable. It would have been better if the Assembly had tackled the problem of famine, which was still acute.

By October the Paris mob, finding that high-sounding declarations did nothing to fill their stomachs, once more erupted into politics. A march of women to Versailles was organised, though there were eye-witnesses who later declared that some of the so-called women concealed beards beneath their shawls. There seems little doubt that most of the demonstrators were hungry women whose cry for bread was perfectly genuine, but they were egged on and directed by agitators. They poured into the palace courtyard and could only be pacified by a promise that the King and his family would forthwith leave Versailles and come to live in Paris.

This move had more significance than the storming of the Bastille, for the royal departure from Versailles marked the end of the system of Louis XIV. His unfortunate descendant was not actually brought to his capital in shackles, but from now on the King and Queen were virtually prisoners, and they knew it. At any time the mob might start howling for their blood and force Louis into action of which in his heart he was afraid.

The flight to Varennes, June 1791

But for all his indecision Louis was a man of principle, and in July 1790 he found himself deeply disapproving of the policy of the National Assembly. It did not take the deputies very long to realise that they were still faced with the financial crisis that had caused them to be summoned. Money must be found from somewhere, and since the peasants had been freed from the unjust burden of taxation which they had borne before, the shortage of money was more acute than ever. There was only one source of wealth still untapped—the Church; so the Assembly passed the Civil Constitution of the Clergy which turned the clergy into civil servants, to be paid by the state. The same Act confiscated all the considerable church property in France.

Louis, virtually a prisoner, was forced to give his consent to this measure, but when later the Pope condemned it, he felt terrible remorse. He now came to the conclusion that he dared not stay in France lest he should be forced again to act against his conscience, so he planned to escape into the Austrian Netherlands, where he could throw himself on to the protection of his nephew, the Emperor of Austria. His wife, their two children, and his sister were to go with him. A king in distress is always appealing, and Marie Antoinette was beautiful; so they were not lacking friends and followers who were prepared to take considerable risks in order to help them. But unfortunately their folly and their ingrained habits of luxury were stronger than the sense of their own danger. Weeks of delay followed the decision to flee, while a suitably large coach was being specially built. Marie-Antoinette also insisted on taking a maidservant, when the sensible course would have been to have a competent man in the carriage with them.

The royal fugitives crept out of their palace prison safely enough and reached the coach, but after that a number of unforeseen delays occurred, and they fell behind their schedule. At one place where there was some delay, Louis stuck his head out of the carriage to investigate. This proved fatal, for though he was disguised as a valet, a bystander recognised his face from its likeness on the coins of the day. The alarm was raised and at the next town, Varennes, they found a barricade across the street. The royal family were pulled from the coach and shut up for the night in a room at the local inn, while a crowd outside the window yelled for vengeance. Then the next day they began an appalling journey back to Paris. A jeering mob went with them all the way, shouting insults, climbing into the carriage with them and even spitting in the face of the Queen, whose hair had turned quite white before they were once more led into the terrifying city from which they had escaped just a few days before. They were taken again to the palace, but there was now no doubt in anybody's mind that they were captives. The guards were doubled, and they were obliged to give up any hope of another flight.

The Varennes escapade had achieved nothing except to ruin the popularity which Louis had once enjoyed, and to persuade even moderate men that the monarchy must now be brought to an end.

The end of the National Assembly

It was while public opinion was in this unpromising state that the honest but tardy National Assembly proudly produced the constitution on which it had been working since 1789. They had limited the power of the King of course, but, having formed their ideas two years earlier, they still allowed him far more influence than was now acceptable. Moreover, being prudent men, they had at last perceived the danger of giving too loose a rein to the General Will and had limited the right to vote to those who possessed some property. This was a sensible provision designed to prevent power from falling into the hands of irresponsible extremists.

Unfortunately, however, the National Assembly spoiled what they had done by passing an admirably unselfish but ill-advised ordinance, which prevented any of their own number seeking election in the Legislative Assembly created under the new constitution. Thus with the King reduced to a figure-head, and all those who had political experience compulsorily retired, France was delivered into the hands of any fanatic or unscrupulous adventurer who had the talents to come to the fore.

During the ensuing months a number of political clubs were formed, the most powerful of which was the Jacobin Club, so called because its meetings were held in a building that had once been the convent of St Jacques. In its early days this club was the scene of lively discussion between all sorts of reformers; but as time went on control fell into the hands of violent extremists, the most extreme of all being Maximilien Robespierre, a lawyer who had been elected to the National Assembly in 1789.

The beginning of the Revolutionary Wars, April 1792

Throughout the winter of 1791-1792 France drifted on, governed according to a constitution which was out of date before it came into force, and with all the extremists in the country gathering into armed gangs. The nation was obviously in no condition to embark on an international war, but nevertheless in April 1792 war was declared against Austria, whose Emperor was the nephew of Marie-Antoinette, and to whose territory the royal family had been fleeing the previous summer. The Legislative Assembly took pains to declare that this was no ordinary war of the usual eighteenth-century pattern. Revolutionary France would not stoop to a mere scramble for territory: this was a struggle of ideals. 'Peace to the peoples! death to the tyrants!' was to be the new battle-cry.

In this mood of exaltation the French never doubted that they would win the victories which their cause deserved; but the first engagement resulted in a serious defeat. The mob suspected (with reason) that Louis had betrayed military secrets to the Austrians, and the resentment against him which this suspicion aroused was inflamed when the Austrian commander, the Duke of Brunswick, issued a manifesto threatening terrible penalties against the Parisians if they should touch the King. Paris was in no mood to be dictated to. The Cordeliers Club, which unlike some of the other clubs consisted entirely of Parisians, resolved to destroy the monarchy once and for all. On August 10th under their leader, Georges Danton, they launched a furious attack on the Tuileries palace where Louis was lodged. The terrified King fled with his family to the Legislative Assembly which held its meetings in an adjoining hall; but the deputies were as frightened as the King, and were forced to pass a decree suspending him from office.

Louis was removed with his wife and children to the Temple prison, and France became a republic. Yet another assembly was elected to draw up yet another constitution, while Paris ran with the blood of royalists and priests who were massacred in huge numbers.

The turn of the tide of war, September 1792

At this moment, just as the Republic had been established, the tide of the war turned almost by accident. The summer had been a disastrous one for France, for her territory had been invaded by Prussia. But Prussia, according to the custom of the day, depended on the services of hired soldiers. They had no personal interest in the war, and Danton had been lavish in distributing bribes to them. Partly because of this and partly for political reasons, after suffering a mild reverse at Valmy in September 1792, the Prussian army retired, giving the French the impression that they had won an important victory.

Nothing succeeds like success, and this encouragement had an extraordinary effect on the new republic. The whole nation became wildly enthusiastic for the cause of liberty against tyrants. Men flocked into the army; and though they were short of equipment, short of artillery, and even short of proper clothing, they won victory after victory. A contingent of volunteers from Marseilles marched into battle singing a rousing battle-song that became the national anthem of France. For the first time in European history a national army had come into existence, and for this resolute force the mercenary armies of the old monarchies were no match. Their victories were a defiance of all the laws of probability, but they continued to occur.

The Reign of Terror, 1793-1794

After the victory at Valmy, the Assembly issued a declaration that France would help any people seeking to overthrow its king, and then proceeded to bring Louis to trial. There was no attempt to administer genuine justice, for Robespierre openly told the judges that on this occasion it was their business to be statesmen. The verdict was therefore a foregone conclusion, and in January 1793 Louis was guillotined. Paris exulted in this public affront to tyranny, but the execution produced a profound shock all over Europe. The complete breakdown of all established law and order in France naturally worried the surrounding governments, and the offer of the Assembly to give military aid to rebels anywhere in Europe brought their anxieties to a head. Within a matter of days Britain and Spain had joined Austria and Prussia in war against the Republic.

Even in France itself a number of people had been shocked by the King's death, especially in the west, where a rebellion consequently broke out. Thus in 1793 France, despite her recent military successes, found herself in a perilous position. All her neighbours were at war with her; there was open rebellion inside her own borders; and then to make matters worse her chief general deserted to the enemy. In this dire emergency extreme measures were taken. Supreme authority was entrusted to a group of nine men, known as the Committee of Public Safety, of whom Robespierre was by far the most prominent and the most powerful. A special law court called the Revolutionary Tribunal

186

was set up to deal with cases of treason, and a great witch-hunt for supposed traitors was instituted.

A horrible blood-lust seized Frenchmen everywhere, and especially in Paris. To watch the execution of traitors became a daily entertainment for the mob. Every day the prisons were visited by officials who read out the names of those chosen for death that day. The victims were loaded onto carts and drawn through the street to the scene of execution, where one by one they were forced to mount the steps of the guillotine while the gloating mob counted the heads as they fell into the basket.

Inevitably the day came when the unhappy Marie-Antoinette mounted the scaffold. During the last months of her life she learned in a hard school the lessons which had never been taught her in the days of her royalty. When planning to escape in 1791, she declared that she could not be expected to look after her children herself; but in prison she had occupied herself caring for them as best she could, and mending the clothes of the whole family. She had brought many of her troubles on herself by the consistently bad advice which she had given to Louis on political matters, which she did not understand but was determined to influence. But many of the victims of 'Madame La Guillotine' had committed no treason and were guilty of nothing worse than belonging to an aristocratic family. Or they might have been denounced by some-one who had a private spite against them. Long before the Terror was over, all pretence at administering justice had been abandoned and people were being executed on the mere suspicion of a bad moral character.

A madness had seized on France which brought with it a determination to break away from the past in every particular. A new calendar was introduced* and new weights and measures—even a new religion. It was indeed with some sense of fitness that the Committee of Public Safety abolished Christianity. In its place they set up the worship of the Supreme Being. A huge public ceremony inaugurated this new religion, and Robespierre was its high priest.

This position suited him exactly. His was the master mind behind the Reign of Terror. He deliberately drove France along this road of violence because he believed that virtue and terror must go hand in

* The new months, which corresponded roughly but not exactly to the months of the old calendar, were called Nivose, Pluviose, Ventose, Germinal, Floreal, Prairial, Messidor, Thermidor, Fructidor, Vendemiaire, Brumaire and Frimaire, meaning respectively snowy month, rainy month, windy month, seed month, flower month, meadow month, harvest month, hot month, fruit month, wine month, mist month and cold month.

hand. In his way he was a virtuous man. He was scrupulously honest and avoided every sort of self-indulgence. He had an unbounded faith in Rousseau, and kept a copy of the *Social Contract* always on his desk. He was also extremely hard-working; but he loved no one and in his fanatical pursuit of a just society ignored all the misery and injustice that were going on around him and for which he was responsible.

Naturally his sinister rule of France did not go unchallenged. One group of deputies after another tried in the Assembly to put a stop to the Terror. But Robespierre could always accuse them of treason, and he could always bank on the backing of other terrified groups who felt that blind support of the leader was their own best insurance against being denounced and condemned. Thus Danton and his followers, once the most extreme leaders of the Revolution, were brought to the guillotine in April 1794. As he passed Robespierre's house on his way to the scaffold, Danton called out 'Infamous Robespierre, you will follow me!' He was right. Three months later on Thermidor 9th (July 27th) a group of deputies, terrified that they would be the next victims, rose and shouted down Robespierre in the Assembly. During the ensuing struggle he was shot in the jaw, and the next day his execution brought the Terror to an end.

The Directory, 1794-1799

During a period of five years France had tried a number of different constitutions and none of them had proved satisfactory. Now after eighteen months of terror, the people desired only peace and quiet. So the new constitution of 1794 was carefully designed never to allow power to fall into the hands of any individual or any small group. There were two assemblies, an upper and a lower house, which were designed to check each other, while the executive authority was entrusted to five Directors. All the outstanding personalities had been swept from the political stage, and under the Directory France settled down to a period of undistinguished inactivity which was at first welcome to the weary people, but which after two or three years began to seem rather dull.

There was one subject, however, which the French could discuss with interest and one compatriot whom they could regard with pride. This was Napoleon Bonaparte, a Corsican by birth, who in 1789 had been a young army officer, so poor that he could afford only one meal a day. He was an admirer of Rousseau and approved of the Revolution, being even a follower of Robespierre. This revolutionary flavour to his youth proved useful to him later in life; but in fact his love of order was

188

ROBESPIERRE

NAPOLEON BONAPARTE

much stronger than his love of liberty, and he soon became disgusted with the events of the Terror. Not that bloodshed as such ever caused him to flinch, for his first political success was gained when he suppressed a rising against the newly formed Directory by firing on a Paris crowd. In recognition of this service he was put in command of an army that was sent to invade Italy in 1796, and he conducted the campaign so brilliantly that France was soon ringing with his name.

This did not altogether please the Directors, who feared with reason that their own meagre reputations might be outshone. So in 1798 they agreed readily to Bonaparte's suggestion that he should carry out an invasion of Egypt. Egypt was officially under the rule of the Sultan of Turkey, an ally of France; but a temporary rebellion against Turkish rule gave the French a good excuse, while the government's real reason (apart from getting rid of Napoleon) was to strike an indirect blow at Britain by threatening her control of the Mediterranean and her trade with India. Napoleon himself, however, had another motive—overwhelming personal ambition. 'My glory is already threadbare', he declared, 'This little Europe is too small a field. Great celebrity can be won only in the East.' It was no wonder that the Directors hoped that life would be more comfortable if he were out of Europe; but they soon felt the effect of his absence. He had defeated one by one all France's former enemies except the British, and it was in an attempt to subdue them that he had gone to Egypt. But as soon as he was out of the way, the defeated powers began to plan a second coalition. Austria and Russia renewed their alliance with Britain. Turkey—offended by the invasion of Egypt—also became a member of the coalition.

Meanwhile Napoleon had been meeting with less than his usual success. As always he could gain victories on land, and in 1798 he had decisively won the Battle of the Pyramids; but shortly afterwards Nelson, with a British fleet, had destroyed the French ships as they lay in harbour. Bonaparte was thus cut off from supplies and could not put his victory to account, beyond marching into Syria. While there, he learned from some English newspapers that came into his hands that the coalition powers in Europe were making excellent headway in their war against France, and that in consequence the Directory had become unpopular.

Napoleon as First Consul, 1799-1804

Here was his opportunity, and he determined to seize it. Deserting his unfortunate army, he took two small ships across the Mediterranean, landed in France, and shortly afterwards carried out a lightning *coup d'état* which overturned the Directory.

Napoleon had a lively imagination of his own, and a knack of appealing to the imaginative qualities of the French people. The new constitution was given a flavour of ancient Rome, for the country was to be governed by Consuls. There were to be three of these officials, of whom he was to be the first. Three years later in 1802 he made himself First Consul for life, and then in 1804 declared himself Emperor. On each of these occasions he held a plebiscite, giving the French people the opportunity to give or withhold their approval of his actions; and in every plebiscite he received overwhelming support.

Thus in the space of fifteen years France had come full circle from an absolute king to an absolute emperor.

Napoleon's home policy

In spite of the restoration of one-man rule, however, the most important social and economic changes brought about by the Revolution were carefully preserved. Napoleon realised that the majority of Frenchmen were peasants, and that his popularity depended on his endorsement of the privileges and liberties which had been given to them in August 1789. Furthermore he sensed that although they had allowed the Terror to go on in Paris and other cities without any strong protest, they deeply disapproved of the break that had been made with the Roman Catholic Church. The worship of Reason, or the Supreme Being, had never appealed widely to France, and shortly after he gained power, Napoleon fully restored the liberty of Frenchmen to worship God according to the practices of the Roman Church, while also allowing them the right to follow other religions if they chose. He then proceeded in 1801 to sign a concordat with the Pope, in which he struck a hard bargain, for he firmly refused to restore to the Church the property which had been seized from it under the Civil Constitution in 1790. This meant that the French Government must continue to pay the salaries of the clergy, and Napoleon also claimed for the state the right to appoint bishops. Naturally this arrangement was far from being wholly acceptable to the Pope, but at least it marked an improvement on what had preceded it.

The Emperor was determined to court the support of the middle classes as well as of the peasantry, and with this end in view he founded the Legion of Honour, thus establishing a new type of nobility based not on birth but on talent. Any outstandingly clever man, whatever his origins, was eligible for the highest awards that the Legion had to offer. Napoleon took a further step in the same direction when he carried out a number of educational reforms. He did little or nothing for elementary education, but he established a number of secondary schools for middle-class boys, many of them run on semi-military lines. Moreover, although the Industrial Revolution—now in full swing in Britain—had hardly started in France, he realised that technical advance would be a pro-minent feature of the coming years, and insisted that science and mathematics should be taught in these schools.

Napoleon also offered rewards to inventors, and it was a result of this policy that Robert Fulton came to France and launched his first steam boat in Paris. Industry was fostered, and several new types of manufacture were started during the Napoleonic Wars in order to make up for the imports that would have come from Britain if they had not been prevented by blockade. The Emperor was also an imaginative builder and town-planner. Being always intensely interested in his own victories, he planned the erection of the Arc de Triomphe in Paris and designed the network of roads radiating from it that still stand today. He was also a patron of art. During his European campaigns he stole huge quantities of art treasures, especially from Italy, and these were placed in the Louvre, formerly a royal palace but now converted into a museum. At the same time roads, bridges and canals were being built all over France. These public works, together with the unending demands of the army, banished any fear of unemployment.

But the most outstanding of Bonaparte's peaceful achievements was his codification of the laws of France. Before the Revolution they had been a mixture of a variety of old traditions, and had grown up without any logic or system. Even before Napoleon came to power in 1799, a start had been made on the work of reducing this chaos to order. Most of the work was naturally done by professional lawyers, but the First Consul took a close personal interest in it, and the 'Code Napoleon' was not only applied most successfully to France but also copied by many other European nations.

Napoleon's wars

All these reforms won for Napoleon the love and admiration of his subjects, but his military exploits, though they had little lasting effect, occupied the greater part of his time and energy.

The execution of Louis XVI had shocked France's neighbours into forming a coalition against her. From the very beginning the revolutionary armies won astonishing victories, and once Napoleon had been given an important command, the coalition swiftly collapsed—except for Britain which he could not reach by land. This pattern of events was to be repeated over and over again. England, enjoying the immunity given to her by the Channel, remained invincible. Every time she held on in the struggle; and every time her former allies, as soon as they had recovered from the drubbings Napoleon had given them, rallied round to join her in yet another coalition. Only for eighteen months or so, between 1802 and 1803, was there a treaty between the two principal enemies; and even then neither country had any serious intention of keeping the peace.

With the help of his generals, Napoleon won remarkable victories on land, but though he might contemptuously describe the English Channel as 'a ditch which it needs but a little courage to cross', the fact remained that he never enjoyed command of the sea. Consequently his military career is marked by his successive attempts to find some means of defeating his island foe.

His Italian campaign of 1796-1797, which has already been mentioned, finally disposed of Austria, the last remaining continental member of the First Coalition of 1793. And, as we have seen, Napoleon followed it up by his first attempt to get to grips with Britain, who supplied large sums of money to her allies but did not put an army in the field.

Her trade with India meant a great deal to Britain, and had Napoleon succeeded in his plan for controlling the Mediterranean and the Middle East, she would have suffered considerably. But the British had a stronger navy than the French; they also had Nelson; and Bonaparte soon found that his land victories were useless without adequate naval backing. He was not a man to cry over spilt milk. He cut his losses, abandoned his army, returned to France and never again tried to carry out operations outside Europe.

He returned not only to seize power in France, but also to face the Second Coalition, which had been formed in 1799 during his absence. A few swift campaigns were sufficient to bring every member of the alliance to terms—again except Britain. It was then that a temporary peace was made, and Napoleon used this breathing-space to plan his next attack. This time he resolved on an invasion of Britain, and for the purpose he collected 100,000 men around Boulogne and built hundreds of flat-bottomed barges for their transport. England took the threat of invasion very seriously indeed. Small fortifications known as martello towers were built along the Channel coast, and the inhabitants went in nightly fear of the arrival of 'Old Boney'. But they need not have worried. Napoleon was powerless to move his army across the Channel unless he could gain naval control; and this he failed to get even for a few days. At last in the summer of 1805 he abruptly abandoned the attempt, having learned of the formation of the Third Coalition. Marching his hundred thousand soldiers at his usual incredible pace across Europe, he won a crushing victory over the Austrians and Russians at Austerlitz. A year later in 1806 he inflicted on Prussia the worst military disaster she had ever suffered, and in 1807 he broke the Russian resistance at Friedland. Once again he had polished off his continental enemies; but still Britain remained.

Ever resourceful, Napoleon now tried a different and quite original mode of attack. His interest in trade and industry made him well aware how much England depended on European trade as an outlet for the spate of manufactured articles that were pouring out of her new factories. The whole economic process would be halted if this trade were cut off, and the British, now unable to return to their old pre-machine way of life, would be faced with starvation and ruin. Napoleon therefore determined on a boycott of British goods all over Europe. To succeed, the ban had to be complete, but he felt himself to be master of Europe now and had little doubt of making his orders effective. He began with Russia and met the Czar on a raft in the middle of a river so that the negotiations might be completely secret. The Treaty of Tilsit followed, in which the two emperors carved up Europe between them, arranged for the partition of Turkey at some future date, and agreed that no goods were to be bought from English merchants in any port under their control.

This 'Continental System' was a shrewd idea and might well have reduced England to submission. But the British navy was still a factor to be reckoned with, and the British government replied to Napoleon's ban by imposing a blockade on every European port which became a party to it. This meant in effect that any port refusing to admit British ships, found that the ships of all other nations were being kept away too. The Continental System did indeed cause great suffering to the British people, but it also brought poverty and hardship to the continent, and before long the subject nations began to ask themselves why they should endure all this in the cause of a quarrel which was not theirs. A good deal of surreptitious smuggling went on, and then Portugal, openly defying the Emperor, declared her intention of trading with Britain as and when she chose.

Napoleon of course moved in his massive war-machine to punish the Portuguese for their insubordination, but in this campaign he met with severe reverses. This encouraged the resilient Austrians to try one more action against their hated and inveterate enemy. Napoleon quickly disposed of them at the Battle of Wagram in 1810, but the next year Russia also revolted against the Continental System, and it was in Russia that the downfall of the French Emperor first began.

The question obviously arises why Portugal and Spain, neither of which had enjoyed any military renown for centuries, should have succeeded in resisting Bonaparte when so many more practised nations had dismally failed. The fact was that in the Peninsular War the conditions were lacking which had formerly ensured French success. In his early days Napoleon derived great strength from the fact that many of the common people of Europe had regarded the French revolutionary armies as heralds of liberty and were prepared to accord the same welcome to Napoleon. They welcomed him with open arms, and expressed great enthusiasm when he deposed their former rulers (often foreigners) and replaced them by members of his own family. Pursuing this policy in Spain, which he needed to control before he could fight Portugal, he disposed of the legal Spanish king and put his own brother Joseph on the throne at Madrid. But the Spanish people refused to show any enthusiasm for their new monarch. Strongly Roman Catholic, they

194

already execrated Napoleon, who had invaded the Papal States and had even kidnapped the Holy Father himself. Thus for the first time Bonaparte found himself campaigning among a bitterly hostile population. This made more difficult his usual practice of feeding his army by buying or otherwise obtaining possession of the local food supplies. Even if the Spanish had been friendly the requisition of supplies would still have been extremely difficult, as the country was more poverty-stricken than any land in which Napoleon had so far conducted a campaign.

Napoleon was further hampered by the mountainous terrain. One of his chief talents was his capacity for marching his armies so quickly from one point to another that he was always taking his enemies by surprise. It was thus that he had come into contact with the Austrian troops in 1805 almost before the Austrian high command knew that he had left Boulogne. But feats of that sort could not be accomplished in the Spanish mountains. Nor could he put into effect his other outstanding talent, which was for manoeuvring his enemies into such a position that their forces were divided into two halves which could then be dealt with separately. For in this campaign the British had landed an army in Portugal under the command of the future Duke of Wellington, who built himself a series of extremely strong earthworks, known as the Lines of Torres Vedras. Securely entrenched within these fortifications, the British were able to defy the French marshals, even the bravest of whom hesitated to launch a direct attack on them.

Yet another cause of the French failure in the peninsula was that Napoleon himself was rarely there, and the troops missed the unique encouragement which he had been in the habit of giving them. Napoleon had a wonderful knack of saying the right things to an army. He combined realism with romance, and appealed simultaneously to their imagination and their greed. Thus at the outset of his Italian campaign he had told his troops frankly, 'You are badly fed and nearly naked,' but added, 'I am going to lead you to the most fertile plains in the world. You will find there great cities and rich provinces. You will find there honour, glory and wealth.' And when he was addressing his army before the Battle of the Pyramids, he inspired them with the reminder, 'Forty centuries look down on you!' But by 1808 when the Peninsular War broke out, Napoleon had many civil duties to attend to; he could no longer be primarily a general, and inevitably his generalship lost something of its old magic.

Despite these reverses in Spain, however, Napoleon in 1810 seemed to be at the height of his power, for after the victory at Wagram he had

Napoleon watching the burning of Moscow from the Palace of the Kremlin actually demanded and obtained the hand of an Austrian princess in marriage. But the British were still defying him in Portugal; he himself described the Peninsular War as a 'running sore'; and the patience of Czar Alexander of Russia was wearing very thin. When Alexander finally refused to support the Continental System any longer, Napoleon made the fatal decision to invade Russia. Secure in his own military genius, he did not stop to consider that very few invasions of that vast country have ever met with success.

This was Russia's finest hour. For over two centuries her rulers had been working steadily to establish the country as one of the leading powers of Europe. During the eighteenth century, under Catherine II, great progress had been made. Now Alexander I and his generals planned a campaign which was to give Russia the principal credit for defeating the terrible Napoleon, and to carry her afterwards right into the innermost councils of Europe.

The plan was simple, though it called for great self-denial. The Russians knew that they could not hope to defeat the French Emperor in a pitched battle, so they decided not to fight such an engagement unless forced to do so. They therefore retreated before the French, luring them on, but destroying every particle of food as they went. This was not what Napoleon was used to. He usually decided both the line and the speed of march and he invariably lived on the country through which he was passing. His troops began to suffer from hunger, but they could console themselves with the reflection that they were advancing towards Moscow much faster than had been expected.

Just before they reached the capital, the Russians at last made a stand at Borodino, and then all Napoleon's old powers of leadership came to the fore. Hungry though his soldiers were, he led them brilliantly and secured a resounding victory. Greatly cheered and believing all their troubles to be now over, the French came to Moscow. Here at last they would find food and shelter. But the 'scorched earth' policy of the Russians did not stop even at their own capital. The population had fled, after first firing the city, and Napoleon's soldiers found only smouldering fires and blackened ruins. Without any easing of their now frantic hunger, they were forced to retreat back to France. And now the Russian armies appeared, barring every route except the ravaged road by which the French had come. Fighting minor skirmishes every day, dying like flies, broken and unbelieving, the remnant of the vast army stumbled home. Out of more than 600,000 who had left France, scarcely a thousand lived to fight again.

This fatal campaign destroyed Napoleon's reputation for invincibility. Not only the kings, but the peoples of Europe took heart. The old claim that the French armies brought liberty in their train had been finally exploded. In 1813 the Fourth and final coalition was formed, and at the Battle of Leipzig, known as the Battle of the Nations, Napoleon was defeated in the open field. After that his fall was only a matter of time. In due course the allies invaded France and forced him to abdicate, but allowed him to retain a tiny token kingdom in the island of Elba, off Italy. He was kept under guard there, and the statesmen of Europe believed that they could now safely settle down to re-arrange the continent which the French had been so rudely disturbing for more than twenty years. But Napoleon had got his second wind. He escaped from Elba and returned to France. Once again his compelling personality worked its charm on his countrymen, who flocked to his standard and followed behind him to try conclusions with the allies for the last time. The engagement took place at Waterloo in June 1815. Napoleon suffered his final defeat, and this time he was shut up on a rock in the middle of the Atlantic where he could do no further harm.

Estimate of Napoleon's work

Napoleon had done unspeakable harm, ravaging Europe year after year and bleeding France white of her young men. Nevertheless his home policy had given the country certain solid gains, which crystallised some of the best elements of the Revolution. He had also, incidentally and almost in spite of himself (since he was actuated always by personal ambition), carried throughout Europe the seeds of liberty and democracy. He did no more than flourish them in order to win over the population and establish his own power; but the seeds were scattered and took root, and were destined to come to flower and shape the history of Europe throughout the nineteenth century.

10 The growth of European imperialism in Asia

We have already followed the Portuguese, the Dutch and the Spanish in their penetration of Asia; and we have seen how Spain imposed her direct rule over the Philippines, while the other powers contented themselves with commercial empires based on the control of key ports and shipping routes. We have also seen how the British, a couple of centuries later, acquired almost accidentally a land empire covering a large portion of the sub-continent of India. Now we must examine the other changes imprinted upon Asia by the European impact. Our general aim will be to trace the course of events up to 1800, but inevitably in several areas we shall be carried well into the nineteenth century.

China and Japan were still refusing to admit foreigners into their territories, except in very small numbers and on strict conditions; and the Russian advance across Siberia, halted in 1689, was still at a standstill; it is therefore to southern Asia that we turn.

Indonesia

The great Indonesian chain of islands known to the Europeans as the East Indies, had always been an object of great interest to foreigners because of their large output of spices. It was for this reason that the first Portuguese viceroy, Albuquerque, waited only until his control of the Arabian Sea was secure before advancing through the Straits of Malacca towards Indonesia. He then sent out various parties to explore the islands and established a chain of bases. A few years later the remnant of Magellan's expedition cruised through the area from the opposite direction, having crossed the Pacific in the course of their voyage round the world. Spain was just as interested as Portugal in spices, and for some years the two European powers were rivals for the control of Indonesian trade. Eventually, however, they were both driven out by the Dutch. The Spanish, who by now had an empire in the Philippines anyway, did not suffer greatly by this; but the once invincible Portugal was humbled to the dust. Encouraged by her obvious weakness, both French and English merchants also tried to secure a portion of her former possessions in Asia; but throughout the seventeenth century it was the Dutch who were the strongest power in the East Indies. This was due in part to the unfailing support which they received from their home government. England and France gave their merchants their blessing but not much else. Holland, on the other hand, regarded the activities of the Dutch East India Company as part of the country's foreign policy, and backed them to the hilt. As the Company also had very large capital sums at their disposal, their position was unassailable.

The East Indies therefore became a Dutch preserve, but not—in the modern sense—a Dutch empire. For though they built themselves a powerful base at Batavia (now called Djakarta) and made it the seat of a Governor-General, they were extremely chary of incurring the heavy expenses of imperial rule, which would soon have swallowed up their profits. So they spread their net wide but did not sink it deep. They acquired coastal stations not only all over the East Indies, but also in Malacca itself, in Ceylon, India and even the Cape of Good Hope. All this territory they thought of as a single dominion; but in the event it was in the Indonesian islands that their control was finally transformed into something more like direct imperial rule.

At first, however, they merely advised and influenced the local sultans; and it is worth noticing that the sultans themselves often made it easy for the Dutch to get a foothold in a new area. The sultans were constantly at war with one another, and on more than one occasion, in order to score off a rival, they invited the help of the Europeans, who of course, being once in, never moved out. The Dutch bought up all the products that they knew would sell well in Europe, drove out other merchants, and exercised a near-monopoly of the spice trade. Later, as we have seen, they went a stage further by compelling the farmers on some of the islands to grow the kind of crops the Dutch wanted to buy instead of the kind of crops the Indonesians needed to eat.

In many ways this economic stranglehold was much worse from the point of view of the natives than direct rule would have been. The peasants of Asia had been accustomed from time immemorial to new rulers taking control of their homelands, imposing new taxes and laying down new laws, none of which made much difference to them. Now, however, the Dutch were interfering in almost every aspect of economic and social life.

But whatever other changes they brought in their wake, the Dutch did not convert the Indonesians to Christianity; indeed they had little wish to Europeanise them in any way at all. So they did nothing to stop the wave of Muslim missionary activity that swept over the islands in the seventeenth century. This was a period of great prestige for Islam. The Sultans of Turkey, who claimed to be Caliphs of all Islam, were at the height of their power; while nearer home Aurangzeb, the great champion of the Muslim faith, was ruling India. A large number of conversions took place in Indonesia, and this development reinforced the hatred already felt for the Dutch, since Muslim resentment of Christians was added to the dislike of the Asians for their European masters.

The Dutch fort at Djakarta

In 1743 the Dutch appointed as Governor-General a man by the name of Van Imhof, who introduced an entirely new element into the policy of his company, for he was a firm believer in direct rule. He was a contemporary of Dupleix, the French Governor in India, and he adopted tactics similar to Dupleix's. There was never a shortage of warring sultans in Indonesia, and Van Imhof started systematically supporting one contestant in a struggle of this kind in order to gain influence over him when he had been helped to power. This policy was carried on even after Van Imhof's term of office was over, and by these and other means Dutch rule had by 1760 been extended over the whole island of Java. At the same time a similar expansion was going on in some of the other islands as well.

In the eighteenth century the world was a much larger place than it is in the twentieth century, in that communications were slow and events in different continents were not so closely connected as they are today. Nevertheless the history of Indonesia was sharply impinged upon by the French Revolution. In 1793 the French revolutionary army, intoxicated with its own enthusiasm, marched into Holland and raised the great cry of 'Liberty, equality and fraternity'. The Dutch people were so infected with this enthusiasm that they carried out a small revolution of their own. They even went so far as to realise that, logically, they ought also to give the Indonesians liberty. As a step in this direction they abolished the political powers of the East India Company in 1798, and made the government of the mother country responsible for administering the islands. This might have been a great improvement, for undoubtedly the people of India benefited when the India Acts of 1773 and 1784 put a brake on the authority that the British East India Company had been exercising in Bengal; and from then on until the final dissolution of the Company, the governors of the Indian provinces constantly opposed the officials of the Company in the interests of the people they ruled. Unfortunately, however, events in Indonesia did not follow this course. The government officials were usually hand-in-glove with the traders, and nothing was done to remedy the abuses of the plantation system.

Once again, however, events in Europe caused changes in Asia. During the Napoleonic Wars Holland was an ally of France and was therefore at war with the British, who in 1811 sent a fleet to Java, which defeated the Dutch and took possession of their empire. The originator of this scheme was Thomas Stamford Raffles, who had proposed it to the British Governor-General in India. He was now appointed Lieutenant-Governor of Java, and during the short period when he was in control, he carried out many excellent reforms, especially on the plantations. But though concerned for the welfare of the Asians under his care, he was a firm believer in European imperialism and did much to extend the area of direct rule in Indonesia.

After Napoleon had been defeated and the peace treaties were drawn up, the British government (much to Raffles's disgust) returned Indonesia to the Dutch. On their return the Dutch did nothing to carry further the work of reform, but neither did they attempt to put the clock back by undoing the changes introduced by the British. They founded no schools and did nothing to introduce European culture into the islands. From the strictly imperialistic point of view they were wise in this; for experience has since shown that familiarity with the political ideas of their rulers has usually tended to fill subject peoples with a determination to enjoy the same privileges. So throughout the nineteenth century the Indonesian people continued under European rule, but with little or no knowledge of what Europe was like.

Malaya

Very close to the Indonesian island of Sumatra lies Malaya, just across the Straits of Malacca. When the Europeans first came to Asia in the sixteenth century, the Malay peninsula consisted of a large number of small sultanates. Most of the sultans were Muslims, and they therefore hated the Christian intruders and bitterly resented their conquest of Malacca in 1511. They were however divided among themselves and never succeeded in dislodging the Portuguese, who only left Malacca when the Dutch, after a long siege, drove them out in 1641.

The Asian resistance to European imperialism had not at this period gathered any real strength; and even as late as the eighteenth century Asian rulers could still be found who would invite the help of the foreigners against a fellow-Asian. Thus in 1786 the Sultan of Kedah in Malaya offered the valuable island of Penang to the British East India Company if they would give him military aid against a neighbour with whom he was at war. At first the offer was accepted, but later the Company was compelled to return the island, as the British government had been opposed, ever since the passage of Pitt's India Act, to the English merchants acquiring any further political power. Later however they were persuaded to a change of policy by Raffles.

This remarkable man began his career in 1795 at the age of fourteen when he obtained a post as a clerk in India House in London. Able young men who began in this way were often given the opportunity of going out east, and in 1805 Raffles was given a very highly paid post at Penang, where the East India Company had a trading-station, although it had been obliged to refuse political power. Raffles took a deep interest in the people among whom he worked, and quickly learned to speak Malay. He was also an enthusiastic naturalist and collected specimens of tropical plant and animal life. But he did not allow these hobbies to prevent him from keeping a careful eye on British interests in southern Asia. He was perpetually full of plans for weakening the Dutch and the French, although he could not always win the authorities to his view. He scored a great success over the invasion of Java, but was bitterly disappointed when, after all his good work there, Britain decided to return Indonesia to Holland. Nevertheless he still went ahead with his schemes. He left Java in 1818, and then, at the request of the East India Company, began to search for a suitable site for a new trading post in Malaya. He hit upon Singapore, an island just off the southern tip of the Malay Peninsula, the value of which—strangely enough—had not yet been perceived by any of the trading companies. The Dutch were furious when they discovered that Raffles had secured the island but they could do nothing to stop the deal, and in 1824 with the consent of

SIR STAMFORD
RAFFLES

its local ruler it was made a British possession. The harbour was developed and Singapore became an extremely busy port open to the shipping of all nations, and also of course a valuable naval base for Britain.

In 1826 Singapore was joined with the sultanates of Penang and Malacca into the Straits Settlement, which was for many years under the general supervision of the British Governor-General in India. Then in 1867 it was put under the control of the Colonial Office. A few years later Britain acquired suzerainty over the rest of Malaya. The peninsula had long been in a state of continual violence and unrest, and in 1873 the British suggested to the sultans that they (the British) should put a Resident into every state and in return for this privilege guarantee the preservation of order. The offer was accepted.

It is interesting to note that Raffles was knighted, that he left Asia soon after he had concluded the Singapore deal, and that he was founder and first president of the London Zoo.

Burma

Burma was a flourishing commercial centre long before the Portuguese arrived in Asia. Indeed a great part of the king's revenue came from customs duties. Cotton, wool and velvet were bought from India and Arabia, while gold, silver, lead, rice and sugar were among the regular exports. Pepper was also produced, but not in large quantities. For this reason the foreign merchants felt less interest in Burma than in Indonesia or India. There were from time to time some military clashes, but the main line of European advance lay to the south of Burma. Moreover, early in the sixteenth century a number of free-lance Portuguese soldiers entered the Burmese service, and were able to provide their new master with a well-equipped navy capable of meeting the Europeans on something approaching equal terms.

But despite her immunity from foreign interference, Burma was far from peaceful during the seventeenth century. There was constant political violence and unrest within the country, and she was also frequently engaged in wars with her neighbours, especially Siam. But her trade continued to prosper, and by the middle of the eighteenth century both France and Britain had founded trading stations on the Burmese coast. At this time these two powers were bitter rivals in India, which explains why they were also competing to establish their influence in Burma, which would have proved a useful military base in the struggle. They were both inclined to be touchy and arrogant, however, and this led to frequent quarrels with the very people they were trying to win as allies. The French actually resorted to arms and fought a battle against the Burmese who, repeating their clever performance of the sixteenth century, managed to capture a French ship and take over the artillery in it, which they put at the disposal of their own army. This enabled them once again to meet the Europeans with confidence, though after Clive had defeated the French, the British remained as their sole antagonists.

During the nineteenth century the British Indian Empire grew to its fullest size, and it became a cardinal point of British policy to create a ring of buffer states all round India. The idea was that these need not necessarily be under direct rule, but must at the very least be so influenced that they could be relied upon not to start hostilities. The diplomatic defensive ring so formed included at one time Iraq, Persia and Malaya, while overtures were even made to the intensely reserved

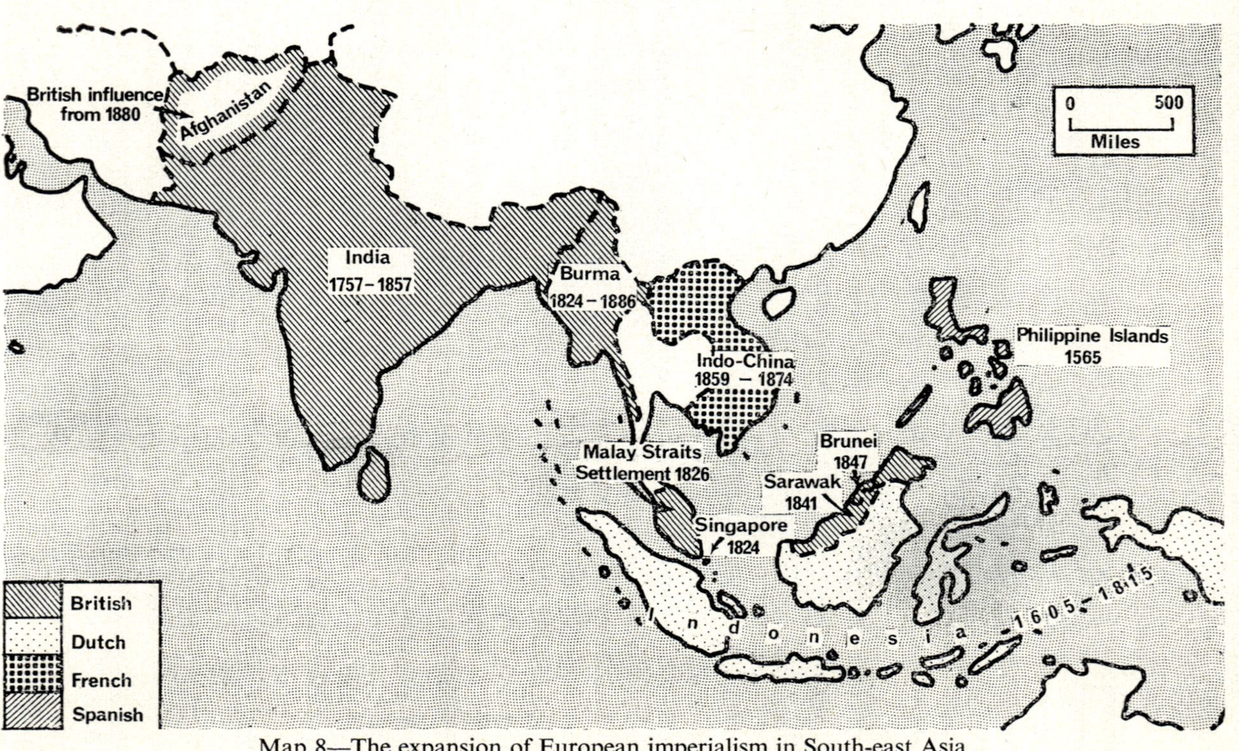

Map 8—The expansion of European imperialism in South-east Asia

country of Tibet. Obviously Burma was bound to figure in the scheme, and the British soon resolved to occupy the country. In a series of wars, beginning in 1824, 1852 and 1885, they gradually absorbed slice after slice of Burma until in 1886 the whole kingdom was made a part of the Indian Empire.

Indo-China

Europeans have given the single name of Indo-China to the south-eastern peninsula of Asia; but in fact the country falls into five natural divisions. In the east are the mountainous regions of Tongking in the north and Annam further south, both being inhabited by Annamites. Across the mountains to the west are Laos and—with a south coastal strip—Cambodia. Finally in the extreme south there is the coastal plain of Cochin-China.

In the sixteenth century the exploring Europeans passed Indo-China by, and the first contact of any note with the foreigners came in 1627 when a French missionary, Father de Rhodes, arrived to preach Christianity in Annam. Scholarly by nature, he made an intensive study of the language of Annam, compiled a dictionary and adapted its sounds to the Latin alphabet. He was much loved by the people among whom he worked, and this gave France an exaggerated idea of the readiness of the Annamites in general to accept the Christian faith. A new missionary society was founded, which was intended to effect the conversion of the whole of south-east Asia; and the French government even entertained some hopes that Indo-China might be used as a back door into the otherwise forbidden territory of China. Conversion did not proceed at the pace hoped for, but political relations between Annam and France became extremely cordial. In 1787 a formal treaty was signed at Versailles between Louis XVI and an Annamite prince called Nguyen Anh, who wanted France to help in modernising his army so that he could defeat his enemies in the peninsula. As the French Revolution broke out two years later, Louis had many other things to think about and the terms of the treaty were never honoured; but Nguyen Anh always remained friendly to his allies.

After his death, however, bad feeling developed, and the Annamites began to persecute Christians. This circumstance seemed to give the Emperor Napoleon III the opportunity he so much needed to indulge in some bold imperialistic gesture to remind his subjects of the greatness that had once attached to the name of Bonaparte. From 1859 onwards he therefore carried out a systematic occupation of Indo-China. First

Saigon was seized, then three years later the territory surrounding it. In 1863 Cambodia put herself voluntarily under French protection, and in 1867 most of Cochin-China was occupied, while in 1874 French rule was established in Tongking.

The peoples of the peninsula were not the only Asians to be concerned in this conquest, for the whole of Indo-China was officially under the suzerainty of China. The Emperor of China was pitifully weak at this period, however, and could do nothing to help his vassals. In 1885 he yielded to the inevitable, and the Treaty of Peking was signed by which the Chinese recognised French authority in Indo-China.

Siam (Thailand)

To the west of Indo-China lies a territory which is now called Thailand but was for many hundreds of years known as Siam. In the sixteenth century the political situation in this area was very fluid. There were a number of separate little states, one of which had however established some kind of authority over part of the Indo-Chinese peninsula and also over Malaya. This Siamese state came into rude contact with Europe when the Portuguese conquered Malacca in 1511. However, no further attack was made upon the kingdom, and five years later a Portuguese envoy arrived peacefully at the capital city of Ayudhya asking for trading relations to be established. A treaty was accordingly signed giving Portugal certain commercial privileges in Siam.

For the next few decades Siam was principally concerned not with the Europeans but with a lengthy war that she was waging against her Burmese neighbours. In 1568 Burma defeated Siam and carried the reigning king into captivity and exile. But a champion arose in the person of Marasuen, who was called by his followers the Black Prince. He overthrew his country's enemies and founded a new dynasty. This secured the kingdom a period of peace, during which commercial relations with the Europeans developed steadily. In 1612 an English ship arrived and obtained permission for an East India Company factory to be erected. The Dutch of course did not lag behind, and merchants came also from France and even from Denmark, while a brisk trade was carried on with Japan as well. Encouraged by all this, France in 1662 sent a religious mission, and this too was cordially received. But about twenty years later the French went too far: they started to put a garrison into the important fort of Bangkok. This made the Siamese immediately suspicious of all Europeans, and nearly all the foreign trade missions were forthwith expelled. Only the Dutch contrived somehow to maintain their position.

The eighteenth century saw another struggle with Burma. Once again the whole country was overrun, but once again it was saved by a champion of great military talent. This time it was a noble of Chinese descent called Pya Taksin. Having liberated Siam, he made himself king and then proceeded to add to his dominions by conquering a number of nearby provinces. But in 1782 he became insane and was succeeded by one of his generals, Chao Pya Chakkri, who proved to be a monarch of outstanding ability. Before he died in 1809 he had given the country much of the organisation it has today, removing the capital to Bangkok and successfully preventing any further Burmese invasions. Chakkri also established his suzerainty over Cambodia and Laos. Even after his death Siam continued to be strong and aggressive, and it was indeed from fear of the Siamese that Cambodia in 1863 sought the protection of France.

As soon as the French had carved out their empire in Indo-China, they began—as Britain had done—to desire buffer states between their own territory and the next important power. Siam benefited from this, as France and Britain agreed in regarding her as a suitable buffer between Indo-China and Malaya. Thus Siam—almost alone among Asian states in the nineteenth century—escaped any form of European domination.

The Philippine Islands

In the early sixteenth century, the group of islands lying to the east of Indo-China and Borneo were under the control of a number of different rulers. The islands in the north belonged to Japan, but those in the south were ruled by a number of Muslim sultans who had converted their subjects to their own faith. When Magellan arrived at the archipelago in 1520 he immediately became aware of the political divisions that existed, for the ruler with whom he stayed was even then at war with a neighbour. Always a man of action, Magellan offered to fight on his host's behalf, and lost his life in the battle. The rest of the party returned safely to Spain, taking with them the important information that these islands produced spice.

The Spanish then formed the design of conquering the islands, as a counter-stroke to Portugal's control of the Indian and Indonesian spice trade. For the time being their energies were absorbed in the conquest of America, but at last in 1565 an expedition under the command of Miguel de Legaspi arrived from Mexico. Legaspi succeeded in defeating all the islands, and gave to them the name of the Philippines, in honour of his own king. The Spanish had to fight hard to hold their conquest, for in addition to the jealousy of the Portuguese and the Dutch, their tenure was also challenged by Hideyoshi, the Shogun of Japan, who naturally resented this loss of his country's colonial possessions. But the Spanish were militarily very strong at that time, and they held on.

The Spanish also took very seriously their duty to bring Christianity to the Filipinos. A large number of friars moved in with the army, and this number was steadily maintained. They made little headway in the south where the people were Muslims, but in the north where they were challenging a religious faith of a much lower calibre, they made large numbers of converts.

The Spanish rule of these islands was in marked contrast to that of the Dutch in the East Indies, for in the Philippines everything was done to give the people a complete share in Spanish education and Spanish culture. The language of the conquerors was taught in all the schools and in every way possible the people were Europeanised.

During the Seven Years War which was fought in Europe between 1756 and 1763, the British attacked the Philippines and occupied most of the islands. But their occupation did not last more than a year or two and it left no mark on the history of the area.

The Spaniards returned to their old position, and in 1800 the colony appeared to be settled, happy and unlikely to change.

The world in 1800

THE MIDDLE EAST

The Turkish Empire was still the most prominent power in the Middle East, and it still presented an imposing facade to the world. Nevertheless the heart of the Empire was rotten. Already a few years earlier there had been a break-away movement in Egypt, and in 1800 a large French army was garrisoned there. It is true that they had achieved very little, even under Napoleon's generalship; but their failure to advance right across the Empire was due to the British navy and not to the Turks themselves, who had proved quite incapable of expelling the foreigners. They had also suffered severe defeats at the hands of the Russians, who, under Catherine the Great, had now advanced to the Black Sea.

The long struggle between Turkey and Persia had finally lapsed into inactivity. Persia had won a notable victory in India in 1739, when her armies sacked Delhi and stole the Peacock Throne; but on the western front she failed to recover Baghdad, though no further Turkish advances took place.

INDIA

The British Empire, though still limited in extent, was now definitely established. Many Indian states were prepared to resist any further European incursions, but the Indian armies were not a match for the British, and there seemed little reason to expect that these valiant efforts would prove to be anything more effective than rearguard actions.

THE REST OF SOUTHERN ASIA

Under the inspiration of Van Imhof, the Dutch had now greatly extended their area of direct rule in Indonesia. In this region there had been repercussions from the French Revolution, and in 1798 the rule of the Dutch East India Company had been officially replaced by that of the government in Holland. This should have led to many reforms being carried out, but, unfortunately for the Asian people, very few changes were actually made and the evils of the plantation system continued unchecked.

CHINA

Under the still vigorous Manchu dynasty, China continued—to outward appearances at least—a strong and healthy empire. All foreigners were still rigorously excluded.

JAPAN

There had been little change since 1700.

SIBERIA

As a result of the treaty signed with China in 1689, the Russian colonisation of Siberia had been brought to a standstill during the eighteenth century.

RUSSIA

The policy of westernisation which Peter the Great was already pursuing in 1700, had been carried much further by 1800. Catherine the Great, who reigned until 1796, had not only added a large slice of Poland to her territories, but had also taken her place as one of the leading monarchs of Europe. Moreover the wars she fought were not merely struggles to acquire more of the ice-free ports which Russia so desperately needed: often Catherine signed an alliance and engaged in a war simply in order to put her oar into the waters of western Europe. The wars were frequently trivial; but there was now no doubt that Russia was one of the great powers of Europe. Peter the Great had dreamed of such a state of affairs, but it had taken more than half a century of effort after his death for the dream to become a reality.

EUROPE

The focal point of Europe in 1800 was France. Since the Revolution that country had run through a bewildering succession of different constitutions. In 1800 she was ruled by a Consulate, with Napoleon Bonaparte as First Consul, which recalled the days of ancient Rome. This was a great improvement on the Committee of Public Safety which had shocked Europe to the core by its organisation of the Reign of Terror; but all the other powers were uneasily aware that violence had not yet died down in France. The French army was still exalted by its recent achievements, and the supreme generalship of Bonaparte had already been proved. Swift defeat was the probable fate of any state that challenged Napoleon; but the kings of Europe felt so strongly that law and order and established tradition should be maintained against the forces of revolution, that they were even now doggedly organising a fresh coalition against the French upstart.

212

The great writers of the Age of Reason were not as popular as they had been, for the French Revolution had provided a grim object-lesson of what unrestricted liberty could be like; but the scientific researches of the eighteenth century were being applied to the invention of machinery mainly in Britain, where the Industrial Revolution was now in full swing. In 1800 steam was being used as a motive power to turn stationary engines, but had not yet been applied to transport either on land or sea. The spinning of cotton was mechanised, but power weaving was only in its infancy, and the wool industry was still hand-operated. New and better roads were already being built, and central England was covered by a veritable network of canals; but railways still lay in the future.

The rest of Europe, as well as the United States, was aware of these extraordinary developments, and planned to adopt the new ideas as soon as possible.

AFRICA

The situation in Africa had not changed materially since 1700.

LATIN AMERICA

On the surface Latin America was also unchanged. None of the colonists had as yet challenged the authority of the motherland, but there was a good deal of suppressed discontent. A minority of colonists had been inspired by events in France and North America, as well as by the European writers of the eighteenth century, to dream of Latin American independence. This feeling was ready to flare into action if a suitable occasion should arise.

NORTH AMERICA

The eighteenth century had seen a number of important changes in North America. The French had been driven out of the continent altogether, and their position in Canada, where many French settlers remained, had been assumed by Britain. On the other hand the British government had itself been expelled from the thirteen British colonies, which had not only achieved their independence but had also united to form a new federal republic. In 1800 the United States of America was eleven years old and had fifteen members.

AUSTRALIA AND NEW ZEALAND

Australia had at last—more than a century after its discovery—been drawn into reasonably close contact with another continent. The English

213

explorer, Captain Cook, had paid a visit to the east coast in 1770, and had claimed the whole island on behalf of Britain. It was not at all certain at first that the British government would follow up the claim; but in the end they decided to use the new land as a base for transported criminals. The first batch of convicts had arrived in 1788, and a settlement had now been established. New Zealand, however, had so far been left alone.

INDEX

Abbas I (of Persia) 63, 64
absolutism in Europe 30, 34, 70-71, 72, 87, 88, 135, 190
Afghanistan 19, 123
Africa 1, 6, 9, 12, 19, 39, 52, 67, 135, 164, 166, 167, 213
Agricultural Revolution 169-71
agriculture 2, 5, 10-11, 51-52, 59, 61, 94, 169-71
Akbar, Emperor 64, 113-16, 117, 118, 120
Akbar, Prince 120
Albuquerque 38-40, 58, 59, 130, 199
America, Central 7, 14
America, North 17, 90, 91, 96-111, 136, 164, 172, 178, 213
America, South 16, 20, 135-6, 213
Americas, the 1, 7, 14, 15, 36, 50, 52-53, 67, 73, 96, 154, 156
Arabia 205
Arabian Sea 38, 39, 40, 58, 59
Arabs 1-2, 3, 9, 11, 12, 18, 37-38, 54, 56, 58, 59, 60
Arkwright, Richard 155, 156, 158
Asia 1, 2, 64-65, 112, 133-4, 211
   European settlement in 37-52, 90, 130, 199-210
   exploration of 9, 10, 11, 15
Atlantic Ocean 6, 9, 14, 50, 52, 53, 90, 98, 101, 166, 167, 198
Aurangzeb 117-21, 123, 133
Australia 7, 68, 136, 143, 157, 166, 169, 213-4
Austria 73, 174, 175
   and French Revolution 176, 183, 185, 186
   and Napoleon 190, 192, 193, 194, 195, 196
   and the Turks 56, 57-58

Bacon, Francis 138
Bacon, Roger 22
Banda Islands 51
Bastille, the 181
Belgium 72
Bible, the 5, 25, 27, 29, 33, 114
Black Sea, the 54, 62, 133, 135
Bonaparte, Joseph 194

Bonaparte, Napoleon, *see* Napoleon
Boston Tea Party 107
Boyle 141
Brahe, Tycho de 21, 23-24, 137
Brazil 67, 135-6
Bridgewater, Duke of 159
Brindley, James 159-60
Britain
   Agricultural Revolution 169-71
   and Louis XIV 91, 95
   and Napoleon 189, 192-4, 195
   Civil War 82
   English Revolution (1688) 84-85, 87, 147
   Industrial Revolution 151-69, 213
   limited monarchy 77-87, 135, 176
   Parliament 71, 78-87, 106-7, 108, 110, 127-8, 129, 168
   Reformation in England 34-35, 71-72
   Sovereigns:
      Anne 85
      Charles I 78-82, 96, 98
      Charles II 41n, 83, 84-85, 98, 99, 139
      Elizabeth I 16, 34, 72, 76, 78, 97, 116-17
      George I 85-86
      George II 85-86, 98
      George III 86, 87
      Henry VII 14, 71
      Henry VIII 34, 71-72, 78
      James I 78, 79, 81, 96, 99, 117
      James II 83-84, 98
      Mary I 34
      Mary II 84, 85
      Victoria 132
      William III 84, 85, 91, 104, 124
British, the
   colonial system 101, 105, 110
   East India Company 41-42, 107, 125-7, 129, 131, 132, 133, 202, 208
   in Australia 143-4, 214
   in India 42-43, 60, 104, 112, 123-32, 154, 156, 189, 193, 202, 205, 207, 211
   in Japan 48, 50, 134
   in N. America 96-111, 135, 136, 172
   in S.E. Asia 199-200, 202-5, 209
   voyages of discovery 16-17
Buddhists 3, 120
Burma 205-7, 208, 209

Historical Atlases

which can be used 'In Parallel' with Miss Bankart's books.

Intermediate Historical Atlas

Prepared under the direction of the Historical Association.

This atlas has been replanned to bring the story to 1963 and it now includes maps of the World at various dates from 1763, and others of regions outside Europe likely to be required in a modern study of history.
40 pages of coloured maps. 8 pages of index. 9 by $7\frac{1}{2}$ inches.   **4s. 6d.**

Atlas of Modern History

Prepared by the Atlas Sub-Committee of the Historical Association under the Chairmanship of Professor R. F. Treharne, M.A., Ph.D. Cartographic Editor: Harold Fullard, M.Sc.

Covering the 18th, 19th and 20th centuries up to 1962, spanning the world and treating Africa, America, Asia and Australasia as integral parts of 'One World' and not as mere appendages to Britain and Europe. The maps combine absolute clarity with exceptional beauty. 48 pages, preface, index. 11 by 9 inches.   **14s. 6d.**

GEORGE PHILIP & SON LTD.,
Victoria Road, London, N.W.10.